GUNS, DEMOCRACY, AND
THE INSURRECTIONIST IDEA

GUNS, DEMOCRACY, AND THE INSURRECTIONIST IDEA

Joshua Horwitz and Casey Anderson

THE UNIVERSITY OF MICHIGAN PRESS

ANN ARBOR

Copyright © by the University of Michigan 2009
All rights reserved
Published in the United States of America by
The University of Michigan Press
Manufactured in the United States of America
⊗ Printed on acid-free paper

2012   2011   2010   2009   4   3   2   1

No part of this publication may be reproduced, stored in a retrieval system,
or transmitted in any form or by any means, electronic, mechanical, or otherwise,
without the written permission of the publisher.

A CIP catalog record for this book is available from the British Library.

Library of Congress Cataloging-in-Publication Data

Horwitz, Joshua, 1963–
Guns, democracy, and the insurrectionist idea / Joshua Horwitz
and Casey Anderson.
p.   cm.
Includes bibliographical references and index.
ISBN-13: 978-0-472-11572-3 (cloth : alk. paper)
ISBN-10: 0-472-11572-3 (cloth : alk. paper)
ISBN-13: 978-0-472-03370-6 (pbk. : alk. paper)
ISBN-10: 0-472-03370-0 (pbk. : alk. paper)
1. Civil rights—United States.   2. Gun control—United States.
3. Firearms—Law and legislation—United States.   I. Anderson,
Casey, 1968–   II. Title.

JC599.U5H626   2009
323.4'3—dc22   2009014539

ISBN-13: 978-0-472-02199-4 (e-book)

To our fathers

Marshall S. Horwitz
(1937–2005)

David L. Anderson

ACKNOWLEDGMENTS

We want to express our appreciation to Colleen Ramsey Nguyen (for her hard work and attention to detail in assisting with research and copyediting); the board of directors, staff, and interns of the Coalition to Stop Gun Violence and the Educational Fund to Stop Gun Violence (for their patience and support with every aspect of our work); our friends and colleagues at the Johns Hopkins Bloomberg School of Public Health, including Steve Teret, Jon Vernick, Daniel Webster, Shannon Frattaroli, Sharon Wakefield, Lainie Rutkow, and especially Donna Hesson; our editors at the University of Michigan Press, including Melody Herr and James F. Reische; our family, friends, and colleagues who read drafts or excerpts at various stages, including Ladd Everitt, Sayre Weaver, Mike Beard, Saul Cornell, Carl Bogus, David Hemenway, Garen Wintemute, Jeri Bonavia, Gerald Linderman, Wayne Rohde, Sue LaLumia, Dennis Quinn, and Bruce Horwitz; and David Kairys (for leading us to the University of Michigan Press).

JMH and CBA

I extend a special thank you to my wife, Pam, for her loving support; to my daughter, Micayla, for always greeting me with great gusto and affection as I emerge from my basement writing den; and to my mother, Susan Horwitz, for her constant encouragement.

JMH

I am grateful to my parents, David and Linda Anderson, the best editors a boy could ever have. I also want to thank my wife, Mary, and my children, Kelly and Tyler, for their love and tolerance.

CBA

CONTENTS

INTRODUCTION

The National Rifle Association (NRA) sells everything from its political agenda to its merchandise with a simple equation: more guns equals more freedom. The NRA steadfastly maintains that thirty thousand gun-related deaths and three hundred thousand assaults with firearms in the United States every year are a small price to pay to guarantee freedom. As former NRA president Charlton Heston put it, "Freedom isn't free." When Heston told fellow NRA members that anyone who wanted to take his guns would have to pry them out of his "cold dead hands," he was advancing a theory of the relationship between freedom and firearms that has become a powerful political and social force in America.

When gun enthusiasts talk about the importance of an expansive reading of the Second Amendment to the defense of freedom, they are referring to freedom in a general sense, but they also have something more specific in mind—freedom from government oppression. In their view, unfettered access to firearms is the key ingredient in protecting individual rights from overreaching by government. They argue that the best way—in fact, the only way—to keep centralized authority in check is to ensure that individual citizens retain the capability to confront the government with force of arms.

This idea, which we call *Insurrectionism*, is part of a broader ideological perspective that opposes a strong, activist government in nearly all of its forms. For Insurrectionists, guns are both symbols and tools of freedom. The idea that individuals must be prepared for a violent confrontation with the state is only one tenet, albeit crucial, of a worldview that is hostile toward—or at least highly suspicious of—public education, immigration, international institutions, and almost any type of social program, especially when run by the federal government. Antigovernment sentiment is, of course, not confined to gun rights enthusiasts, but the Insurrectionist idea adds an emotionally charged element to the standard conservative critique: big government is not just inefficient or even corrupt but is an alien force that threatens to annihilate us if we fail to exercise constant vigilance against its natural tendency toward tyranny.

On occasion, the Insurrectionist idea spurs a lost soul or desperate tax delinquent or publicity-seeking paramilitarist to violent action. Timothy McVeigh was the poster child for the deadly consequences of taking the Insurrectionist idea to heart, but smaller armed confrontations between "citizen" and government are sufficiently common that they usually warrant only a brief mention in the local newspaper unless they escalate into full-scale shootouts. Rather than attempting to resolve their grievances through the courts or the political process, self-declared "patriots" challenge government authority through force of arms, often with bloody results. It is not surprising that Insurrectionist rhetoric eventually leads some people to take violent action, but the blithe acceptance of these outbursts of violence as a natural and perhaps inevitable reaction to government overreaching is remarkable.

After a disgruntled business owner who felt—apparently with some justification—that he was treated unfairly by municipal officials in the town of Kirkwood, Missouri, went on a shooting spree at a town council meeting in the spring of 2008 and killed five people, members of the public responded with outrage at the violence but not at the motives: some observers seem to see armed confrontation with the government as a prerogative of citizenship. Speaking at a community meeting a day after the massacre, one man said that the shooter was "a soldier who paid the price for liberty."[1]

And why shouldn't shooting public officials be a legitimate response by citizens who are aggrieved by the government? After all, at the time of the Missouri shooting, briefs were being filed and arguments being prepared for the Supreme Court arguing explicitly that our constitution guarantees every American the right to prepare for armed confrontation with the government. In *Heller v. D.C.*, a challenge to the District of Columbia's gun laws, the NRA, appearing as an amicus curiae, contended that one purpose of the Second Amendment is to protect an individual right to arm against the "depredations of a tyrannical government." The vice president of the United States and 305 members of Congress asked the Court to support that view. And in fact, in a landmark decision striking down parts of the District's gun laws, the Court found that the Second Amendment includes an individual right to insurrection. Justice Antonin Scalia wrote that citizens acting on their own are entitled to arm themselves and connect with others in a "citizens' militia" to counter government tyranny.[2]

This book asks readers to consider just how damaging this idea is to democratic values. When we began work on the book in 2004, we had no idea that the U.S. Supreme Court would endorse Insurrectionism, but it was already clear that the idea was gaining intellectual traction beyond the radical fringe. Right-wing populists are attracted to the idea that Insurrection through force of arms is a morally and legally legitimate instrument of political expression in a democracy largely because it fits neatly with their core ideological premises—that is, that the government should be kept in a condition of weakness because collective approaches to social problems are wasteful at best and more often constitute an insidious threat to individual liberty.

The NRA and its allies have been among the leading vehicles for popularizing the claim that a strong government is antithetical to freedom. The gun rights movement has become an integral part of the broader conservative coalition because the Insurrectionist idea advances the larger cause of demonizing government in virtually all of its forms. After all, if individual citizens have a right to decide when government taxation or regulation or infrastructure development amounts to tyranny, all government action is easily viewed as suspect.

This book argues that the Insurrectionist idea poses a serious threat to democratic values and institutions. In outlining how Insurrectionism made the transition from a radical set of claims about the centrality of firearms in the preservation of freedom to a mainstream legal theory that enjoys widespread political support (and why it poses such a danger to our democracy), we make three main arguments.

First, the Insurrectionist movement must be taken seriously because it has political and social consequences beyond firearms policy, and these consequences make it a major threat to much of the progressive agenda. The leading gun rights groups preach Insurrectionism as a core concept, teaching members and nonmembers alike that they should not trust the government and should be prepared to resist it with force. Recent public opinion research shows that many gun owners have accepted the Insurrectionist message and see resistance to government as at least one good reason for owning a gun.[3]

The core of the Insurrectionist dogma is its insistence that unrestricted access to guns of every kind is an essential element of freedom. Insurrectionists see the government as the enemy and condemn any and all gun regulation as a government plot to monitor gun ownership (presumably to lay the groundwork for confiscation of privately owned firearms in the event of a political crisis). By constantly hammering home the idea that the gun rights movement is essentially about the defense of liberty, advocates of the Insurrectionist myth have effectively turned *freedom* into a code word understood by the initiated to imply a quite remarkable conception of the role of private violence in our political system, eliminating the need to spell out the idea in detail or confront its logical implications.

The gun rights groups, with the NRA in the forefront, have created a communications network that reaches down into the grass roots and delivers messages, talking points, and voting advice to millions of Americans. Through various forms of mass media, such as television, radio, and billboards, they reach sympathetic fellow travelers who may not actually be group members or even gun owners. These efforts are usually invisible to anyone who lives in or near a large city, but every two years (and especially in presidential election years), the roads and airwaves of rural and small-town America are filled with pleas to "Vote Freedom First" by supporting candidates backed by gun rights groups.

The NRA's communications and grassroots capabilities allow it to swing a small but often critical group of voters in tightly contested campaigns. In an era when presidential elections are often decided by a handful of votes in a single state, this organizational capability is immensely valuable, even though most gun owners disagree with the NRA on many issues. By embracing the NRA, the right wing of the Republican Party gets access to a message machine that churns out antiprogressive propaganda not just during the election season but year in and year out. It is no wonder, then, that some of the leading lights of the "conservative" movement, such as Grover Norquist and David Keene, sit on the NRA's board of directors and embrace the Insurrectionist message.

More troubling from our perspective is this message's effect on the political prospects of progressive candidates. Pitifully few politicians have been confident enough to stand up to Insurrectionist rhetoric, and many have embraced it as a legitimate perspective on the role of guns in a democracy. Progressives (particularly those concerned about civil liberties) sometimes spout Insurrectionist rhetoric without thinking through what it means. Progressive political leaders should think carefully about the long-term costs and benefits of embracing an idea that is fundamentally antagonistic toward any form of government that is capable of undertaking ambitious efforts to solve difficult social problems.

Second, Insurrectionism derives from a view of the American experience and more generally of the modern history of the world that is wildly at odds with the historical record. The Insurrectionist myth that government is the enemy of freedom and that armed citizens have proven the best check on government power has been concocted from twisting the facts of historical events, with revisionist accounts of three episodes from the past playing an especially important part in the Insurrectionist delusion: the American Revolution and the founding of the American republic, the denial of civil rights to African Americans after the Civil War, and the rise of the Third Reich under Adolf Hitler. The touchstone of the Insurrectionist take on these events is that strong government is always the primary threat to human freedom and that private ownership of firearms is the only force that can keep this threat in check.

Insurrectionists teach that the lesson of the founding of the United States is that guns were so important to American freedom that the framers enshrined in our Constitution the right of every individual to own guns to ward off government tyranny.[4] From the Civil War, the Insurrectionists draw the conclusion that the government's disarming of the former slaves led to the subjugation of African Americans for one hundred years.[5] From the rise of the Nazis, Insurrectionists glean the insight that if the Weimar Republic had dispensed with gun control, Hitler would not have exterminated six million Jews and millions of other people.[6] In the Insurrectionist version of history, these three examples offer cautionary tales that illustrate the immense danger posed by gun control schemes.

This book offers a detailed examination of these arguments about the lessons of history. We show that the Constitution was specifically framed to prevent individuals from using mob power as a fourth branch of government and that protection for Insurrectionism, as advocated by a small group of radical Antifederalists, was the losing argument in the ratification debates. As for the Reconstruction and Nazi arguments, we show that the key factor in the horrors carried out by the Klan and its allies (and then eighty years later by the Nazis) was the disintegration of government power in the face of organized private violence. The problem with arming the oppressed to give them an opportunity to defend themselves is not that the freed slaves or the Jews of Europe did not have an adequate moral claim to use whatever means they could find to fight back. The victims of genocide are fully justified in taking up arms to defend themselves. The difficulty with the argument against gun control in World War II–era Germany or the Reconstruction South is that guns would not have helped to hold off the Nazis or the Klansmen for long. Without a commitment by legitimate democratic government to enforce the rule of law and its monopoly on force, a few more guns for former slaves would have provided little long-term help. In fact, a strong government that has the means and the will to enforce individual rights—the kind of government opposed by Insurrectionists—would have been a source of far greater protection. We argue, then, that historical experience counsels against the weak government favored by Insurrectionist thought and in support of democratic government empowered with the tools to protect itself and its citizens from the mob.

Third, the Insurrectionists cannot secure their substantive, procedural, or symbolic demands except at the expense of many other vital freedoms, most of which have no direct relationship at all to firearms. Despite their oft-expressed enthusiasm for the uncompromising defense of freedom, the Insurrectionists who lead the gun rights movement do not seem to mind trampling the democratic rights of others. The most obvious—but not the most important—example is the gun rights movement's willingness to compromise public safety. The insistence on gun rights absolutism ignores the practical impact of gun violence on the freedom of individuals to walk down the streets of their own neighborhoods. When crime data began to show that gun violence was increasing in the late 1980s and early 1990s, gun control groups developed proposals to address what they saw as a public health threat. The Insurrectionists, conversely, saw rising crime rates—and the political pressure to address them—as a threat to their ideological goals. While gun control advocates worked to marshal statistics in support of their legislative agenda, their counterparts in the gun rights movement moved to deflect any initiative that would allow the government to identify gun owners, even for purposes of investigating and prosecuting violent crimes committed with their guns.

The more fundamental danger, however, is not that the erosion of public safety imposes a cost on individual freedom. The more serious problem is that by inculcating gun owners with a paranoid, obsessively antigovernment political ideology, the Insurrectionist movement has helped to stoke hostility toward government power (e.g., international treaties and environmental regulation) and pluralism (e.g., by attacking immigration and affirmative action). By promoting the idea that no person can or should rely on anyone else for anything important, the Insurrectionists' warped worldview shapes negative attitudes about government, mutual obligation, and community.

Gun control advocates—and the progressive movement—have failed to appreciate the danger posed by this ideological blaze and the grassroots network fanning its flames. Without an organized and sustained effort to show how the NRA and other gun groups have become instruments of a broader reactionary movement, these groups will continue manipulating gun owners into joining a coalition of libertarians, right-wing populists, and religious "conservatives" who want to make war on public education, progressive taxation, civil rights, and virtually every other significant social and political advance of the past century.

In fact, the unchecked spread of Insurrectionism threatens the shared values and institutions that comprise our democratic system by undercutting support for a strong and effective government capable of protecting individual rights (including equal protection of the laws and the freedom to walk the streets in safety). The antidemocratic effects of Insurrectionism are more than simply an indirect consequence of the gun rights movement's alliance with the "conservative" movement. Antidemocratic values such as hostility to pluralism lie at the core of the Insurrectionist idea.

The authors are acutely aware of the strange illusion, so real and so compelling to some people, that the Insurrectionists are entitled to subsume their doctrines under the rubric of "conservative" political thought. So as a gentle reminder to readers, we have placed the term "conservative" and its derivatives in quotation marks wherever the text requires disavowal of a conceit suggesting that this misbegotten form of radicalism owes its ancestry to venerable traditions. More than a half century ago, conservative scholar Peter Viereck described the Insurrectionists of his day, the McCarthyites, as "rootless doctrinaires."[7] According to Viereck, "Conservatism is the art of listening to the way history grows," and he quoted August Heckscher as saying,

> Conservatism is rarely a program and certainly never a dogma. It is not an ideology. At its best conservatism is a way of thinking and acting in the midst of a social order which is too overlaid with history and too steeped in values, too complex and diverse, to lend itself to simple reforms. It is a way of thought which not only recognizes different classes, orders, and interests in the social order but actually values these differences and is not afraid to cultivate them.[8]

In short, Insurrectionism is a radical doctrine, and its use as a political tool is fraught with danger. Unlike the Insurrectionists, however, we do not favor undercutting other individual rights to check the growth of this noxious idea. No American can or should be punished by the government for expressing ideas, even when these ideas include the proposition that armed citizens should use force against the government as a form of political dissent. But what means are available to confront and discredit the Insurrectionist idea and the political organization that has been built around it? We have a few suggestions for ways to advance a progressive strategic alternative to the gun rights fantasy of Insurrectionism:

1. Recognize Insurrectionism as a threat to the entire progressive movement. Too many political progressives assume that the gun rights movement can be co-opted or simply ignored. Progressives fail to understand that the Insurrectionist idea is part and parcel of a broader reactionary worldview. Unless progressives recognize that the Insurrectionist premise of the modern gun rights movement is fundamentally hostile to the progressive project and its values, the "conservative" movement will use gun rights as a building block for organizing and propagandizing.

2. Isolate the Insurrectionists by embracing the self-defenders and the sporting gun owners. The fact remains that most gun owners are not Insurrectionists. The majority of gun owners keep guns primarily for self-protection or recreation, not to prepare for some future Armageddon. Insurrectionists do not deserve the cover provided them by self-defenders and sporting gun owners.

More than two hundred million firearms are in private hands in the United States, and almost 40 percent of homes contain at least one gun. Legislation to ban handguns has been extremely difficult to pass, and even if new handgun sales were outlawed—an unlikely scenario for the foreseeable future—the effect would be entirely prospective, albeit significant over time. Education about the dangers of guns in the home, coupled with rigorous regulatory and enforcement efforts to close the channels of illegal gun distribution, may now be the best way to convince Americans that their families and communities will be better off without unfettered access to firearms.

3. Reclaim the values and reframe the question. Gun control advocates have spent the past three decades trying to persuade the public that guns are dangerous, while gun rights groups have argued that guns are essential to our freedom. We need to challenge the idea that guns protect freedom and democracy. The most important threat posed by unfettered access to firearms comes from those who would use it as an Insurrectionist shibboleth. This ideology should have been completely discredited with the Civil War, and its ascendance represents a return to the days when our society was less free and less democratic. Progressives must be willing to stand up and say, "I believe in strong gun laws because I am a patriot, and I believe that accountability and personal responsibility are not only consistent with freedom and democracy but are essential to both."

The American debate over guns should be framed as a discussion about America's civic health. The questions should be, How can a commitment to democratic values be squared with the idea of violence against a democratic government? What role does respect for political equality and pluralism play in our system of government, and what is the relationship between the ideology of the gun rights movement and these values? Do we want to live in a society where people who want nothing more than to move about their communities without fear need to bring a firearm to protect themselves from violence? How have we allowed the debate over democratic values to become so cheapened and degraded? By answering these questions, we can begin a new debate about guns in America that can open the door to more effective approaches to violent crime as well as to a heightened respect for the values and institutions that make our country great.

PART ONE

THE INSURRECTIONISTS

CHAPTER ONE

WHAT IS THE

INSURRECTIONIST IDEA?

Insurrectionist is not a synonym for *gun owner*. Most gun owners do not belong to organizations that support—or whose leaders support—Insurrectionism. The 4.3 million members claimed by the National Rifle Association (NRA)[1] make it one of the nation's largest membership organizations, but the United States is home to an estimated 80 million gun owners. Even within the NRA, many members perceive it as a service provider—that is, they sign up to take advantage of discounted insurance or hunting gear and ignore its political views. Some other gun groups, such as Gun Owners of America (GOA), position themselves to the right of the NRA, claiming that they are more uncompromising in their opposition to regulation of firearms. The members of these groups join because of the politics. Gun Owners of America would never be confused with a member-services organization. In fact, GOA offers its members little beyond repeated exhortations to send in another check to beat back the threat of gun control.

Americans have different reasons for—and attach different meanings to—gun ownership. Some people use guns for hunting and other recreational activities such as target shooting or collecting. Others (who might best be called the "self-defenders") acquire guns to protect themselves or their families from crime. Nobody can say with certainty how many people own guns to protect themselves from the government. Of course, many if not most gun owners buy firearms for more than one purpose. The major gun groups preach Insurrectionism, teaching members and nonmembers alike that they should not trust the government and should get ready to resist it with guns. Recent public opinion research shows that many gun owners have accepted the Insurrectionist message and see resistance to government as at least one good reason for owning a gun.[2]

The core of the Insurrectionist idea is its shibboleth that unrestricted access to guns of every kind is an essential element of political freedom. Insurrectionists see the government as the enemy and condemn any and all gun regulation as a government plot to monitor gun ownership (and presumably to lay the groundwork for confiscation in the event of a political crisis). One of the leading Insurrectionist theorists, David Kopel, vividly sums up the Insurrectionist animus toward gun registration:

> It is improper to require that people possessing constitutionally protected objects register themselves with the government, especially when the benefits of registration are so trivial. The Supreme Court has ruled that the First Amendment prohibits the government from registering purchasers of newspapers and magazines, even of foreign Communist propaganda. The same principle should apply to the Second Amendment: *the tools of political dissent should be privately owned and unregistered.*[3]

Nelson Lund, one of the leading Insurrectionists in academia, posits that the Constitution establishes an individual right to bear arms to protect against federal tyranny: "An armed populace—even if it could not serve to deter tyranny as effectively as a legal prohibition against federal standing armies—would still constitute a highly significant obstacle to the most serious kinds of governmental oppression."[4] So Lund believes that the government, state or federal, is prohibited from limiting civilian access to almost any kind of weapons, including "grenades and bazookas," and that laws banning assault weapons or the carrying of concealed weapons are unconstitutional.[5]

The late Bill Bridgewater, former executive director of the Alliance of Stocking Gun Dealers, described in a widely circulated essay how American citizens could wage a guerrilla war against the U.S. government:

> One of these days a truly charismatic individual is going to walk out of the heartland of America and point out that the Declaration of Independence has never been repealed and that it "requires" all citizens to rise up against an oppressive government. With the current attitude toward our government and the people who populate it, a massive groundswell of support for throwing the current crop to the dogs and starting over again might not be so difficult.[6]

Bridgewater noted that the North Vietnamese, using as their model the tactics of America's war for independence, humbled the greatest military in the world. If the North Vietnamese could do it, the argument goes, American citizens—large numbers of whom already own sophisticated firearms—could succeed. Bridgewater did not live to see it, but the effort to pacify Iraq is a good reminder that even the most capable military forces face serious difficulties when confronted with the tactics of guerrilla warfare.

Bridgewater's essay, originally published in the *Bullet Trap* in 1994, is still making its way around the Internet. In 2006, it was posted on LizMichael.com, a site with the somewhat immodest motto "Political activism for the liberation of the world" that includes a series of articles citing Lund's work. By itself, the site is not particularly significant, but the ideas it promotes are staples of the strain of right-wing populism that has become a core element of contemporary "conservative" politics. It often marries antigovernment ideology to gun rights absolutism: Widespread private ownership of firearms is the ultimate guarantor of liberty. All gun control is an infringement of rights reserved for the people by virtue of our history. Government is the enemy. Our founding fathers believed that the individual's personal right to armaments as a check on overbearing government was essential to the protection of freedom and democracy. This idea was true then, and it is true today.

Unsurprisingly, the NRA and its ideological fellow travelers have tried to legitimize Insurrectionism to rationalize their opposition to even the most trivial gun regulations. Wayne LaPierre, the NRA's top executive, says, "The people have the right, must have the right, to take whatever measures necessary, including force, to abolish oppressive government."[7] In 1998, U.S. senator (and later attorney general) John Ashcroft somewhat awkwardly argued, "A citizenry armed with the right both to possess firearms and to speak freely is less likely to fall victim to a tyrannical central government than a citizenry that is disarmed from criticizing government or defending themselves."[8]

The Insurrectionist objection to the regulation of firearms may extend to state government, even though the reservation of authority to state-level officials in principle provides another check on overreaching centralized power. The Insurrectionist mind-set took on comic effect when one of the authors witnessed the spectacle of an aide to a Virginia state legislator objecting to restrictions on firearms on the grounds that he might need a gun to resist oppression by his employer. Asked by a lobbyist whether the aide's boss might vote for closing the loophole that allows people to buy guns without background checks at gun shows, the aide responded that he would not even pose the question to the legislator. The aide explained that because a background check would alert the government when a gun is purchased, he was uncomfortable with the process. "I need my gun to protect against the government," he said. The lobbyist reminded the aide that as a legislative assistant, he is an agent of the government he professed to fear. His response, relying perhaps on advice from his accountant, "I am not the government because I am a contractor." Leaving aside the absurdity of the objection that requiring background checks on firearm sales at gun shows would prevent law-abiding citizens from buying guns (when three of the five states with the largest number of gun shows require background checks and all sales at gun stores already require the checks), the notion that an employee of one of the oldest, most conservative legislative chambers in the world thinks that he personally needs a gun to protect himself from that legislature is a testament to how tightly some gun rights advocates have embraced Insurrectionist theory.

Until recently, few Americans not involved in private militias or other right-wing fringe groups that make up the "patriot" movement took seriously the Insurrectionist idea.[9] Despite some backpedaling in the wake of Timothy McVeigh's use of Insurrectionist justifications for the bombing of the Oklahoma City federal building, the major gun rights organizations have become more aggressive in advancing an Insurrectionist rationale for an expansive view of gun rights. The propaganda used by these outfits exploits the habitual American distrust of government, but the extent of uncritical acceptance of Insurrectionist interpretations of the Second Amendment is nevertheless striking. For example, Libertarian luminary Ron Paul, who raised $34.5 million in his bid for the 2008 Republican presidential nomination (which was more than fellow Republican Fred Thompson and only slightly less than Democrat John Edwards, both thought to be in the top tier of candidates at the outset of the race),[10] stated on his campaign Web site that a "gun in the hand of a law-abiding citizen serves as a very real, very important deterrent to an arrogant and aggressive government. Guns in the hands of the bureaucrats do the opposite. The founders of this country fully understood this fact, it's a shame our generation has ignored it."[11] Mike Huckabee, who won 257 delegates in the 2008 Republican primaries,[12] responded to a question at a town hall meeting in New Hampshire with the answer that the Second Amendment "gives me that last line of defense against tyranny, even the tyranny of my own government."[13]

Together with self-defense against violent crime, the imagined need to reserve the option to use force against the government is a central justification invoked by gun rights advocates in opposing legislation or regulation that would place any restriction, no matter how mild, on access to firearms. The philosophical, legal, and practical dimensions of the use of firearms for self-defense are beyond the scope of this book, but the political and policy agenda of gun rights groups goes well beyond protecting the right to self-defense against violent crime. Most kinds of gun control—such as requirements for background checks on gun purchasers—that are designed to prevent the direct or indirect sale of firearms to criminals do not diminish a law-abiding citizen's ability to keep and use a gun for self-defense. A gun that has been registered is no less effective than an unregistered firearm when aimed at a criminal. In fact, efforts to keep guns away from criminals (e.g., by applying the background-check requirement to all gun show sales or requiring owners to register their firearms) reduce the chances that the victim of a crime will be confronted by superior firepower when wielding a gun in self-defense. In addition, many firearms are ill suited for defensive use in the home or in a vehicle. A simple revolver is more useful and safer for home defense or personal protection than an AR-15, the semiautomatic version of the M-16 used by the U.S. military.[14]

Moreover, the claim that private ownership of firearms improves public safety is an empirical question. Academic analyses of private firearm ownership in terms of self-defense show that gun possession and availability actually increase the risk of death and injury.[15] Conversely, the claim that unfettered access to firearms can prevent government tyranny in the United States without fostering anarchy bears little scrutiny by serious thinkers and academics and cannot be tested by experimental methods. As a result, it is difficult to put the Insurrectionist idea to the test of real-world practice in the absence of a cataclysmic breakdown of the American system of government as we know it.

The Insurrectionist slant on history predicts that government unchecked by well-armed citizens will eventually murder its citizens, enslave them, or allow others to do so. Mistrusting even the strongest democratic institutions, Insurrectionists argue that the only safeguard that will prevent totalitarianism over the long run is a well-armed populace. But the Insurrectionist telling of history is a myth designed to perpetuate the needs of a gun rights industry (of which firearms makers and dealers are only a small part) headed by the NRA but comprised of an array of allied groups and entrepreneurs that flourish by bombarding gun owners with propaganda designed to convince them of an ever-present threat to their guns and their freedom in the form of a government run amok. Only by arming themselves to the teeth—while sending in their checks to the major gun rights groups and supporting the conservative movement's political goals—can gun owners head off this danger.

The myth that government is the enemy of freedom and that only armed citizens protect freedom, as we document repeatedly in this volume, has been concocted by twisting the facts of historical events and in particular by popularizing revisionist accounts of three episodes from the past that are frequently used to buttress support for the Insurrectionist delusion: the American Revolution and the founding of the

American republic, the denial of civil rights to African Americans after the Civil War, and the rise of the Third Reich under Adolf Hitler. The Insurrectionist interpretation of these events is that strong government is always the gravest threat to human freedom and that private ownership of firearms is the only hope of keeping this threat in check.

From the founding of the United States, the Insurrectionists draw the lesson that guns were so important to American freedom that the framers enshrined in our Constitution the right of every individual to own guns to ward off government tyranny.[16] From the Civil War and Reconstruction, the Insurrectionists conclude that the government's disarming of the former slaves guaranteed the continued subjugation of African Americans despite the introduction of formal legal equality for people of all races.[17] In examining the rise of the Nazis, the Insurrectionists argue that if the Weimar Republic had dispensed with gun control, Hitler would not have been able to exterminate 6 million Jews and millions of other people.[18] In the Insurrectionist account of history, these three examples offer cautionary tales that illustrate the immense danger posed by gun control schemes. For good measure, Insurrectionist ideologues have recently added to their list of historical illustrations of the folly of gun control, including the argument that in the twentieth century, governments caused the deaths of 114 million people through a combination of gun control and genocide[19] and the claim that the disarming of law-abiding citizens was in large measure responsible for the breakdown of order in New Orleans in the aftermath of Hurricane Katrina.

Insurrectionists see anonymous gun ownership as a check on government tyranny, but they are vague about who has the right to decide the moment when the government has become tyrannical and should be resisted with private armed force. Some Insurrectionist theorists, such as Kopel, have qualified their endorsement of revolution led by armed citizens by noting that a few folks sitting around their living room can't invoke the Second Amendment to justify taking up arms against the government. Yet even Kopel unequivocally states that a majority of citizens need not support the use of violence to legitimate armed resistance.[20] For some other Insurrectionists, taking up arms against the government is a personal decision.[21] Insurrectionists may disagree among themselves about exactly what triggers the right to take up arms against the U.S. government, but they share the view that armed resistance to tyrannical government is a legitimate response to a policy or action, even when that policy or action has been carried out by democratically elected representatives constrained by an independent judiciary with the power to vindicate individual rights against the state.

Insurrectionists confuse their antidemocratic sentiments with legitimate revolution, casting themselves as putative leaders of a modern-day revolt on behalf of "the people" to restore "true" democracy and freedom (with all of the self-righteousness and romanticism that are the imperishable companions of political violence). As we describe in detail later in this book, revolution is not sanctioned by the Constitution, does not enjoy legal protection as an individual right, and should be avoided unless there is a complete breakdown in democratic institutions of government. Our founders knew this, which is why they approached revolution cautiously, convened representative bodies to study it, acted through deliberative and democratic bodies (by the standards of the era), and immediately replaced the Crown with a more democratic government. The decision of an individual to take up arms against the government, when undertaken with like-minded friends or even with a "substantial minority" of the public, is at best extralegal and at worst represents an antidemocratic attempt to undermine representative government.

To the Insurrectionists, in their obsessive paranoia, no society can be free (at least in the long term) without more or less ubiquitous private ownership of firearms because no government can be trusted to respect individual rights if citizens do not retain a credible capability to confront an overreaching state with armed resistance. Kopel has written, "If Americans are to remain free—and to live as securely as freedom allows—then it must be recognized that guns play an important and necessary role in American society, and that Americans have inherited the right to arm themselves against those foreign or domestic enemies who would deprive them of life and liberty."[22] Or as LaPierre puts it, "The Second Amendment is the fulcrum of freedom in our nation, because freedom and the Second Amendment are mutually interdependent. They are the 'chicken and the egg'; neither can exist without the other."[23]

On its face, the "guns protect freedom" formulation sounds plausible, and anyone who would oppose the gun rights movement's superficially attractive goals may seem to be attacking freedom itself. Then-NRA president Charlton Heston, addressing the organization's annual convention in 2000, remarked, "I'm here because I love my country and I love this freedom. . . . It dawned on me that the doorway to all freedoms is framed by muskets." Referring to Vice President Al Gore, the Democratic candidate for president, Heston lifted a musket over his head and said, "So as we set out this year to defeat the divisive forces that would take freedom away, I want to say those words again for everyone within the sound of my voice to hear and to heed, and especially for you Mr. Gore: From my cold dead hands!"[24] At the 2007 NRA convention, LaPierre detailed that threats to freedom are everywhere and that the NRA membership, fully armed and ready for battle, is the last line of defense:

> So no matter what the animal rights terrorists throw at us, no matter what crime wave illegal immigrant gangs cause, no matter what deals are cut in the back rooms of the United Nations, no matter who is slamming gavels at the Supreme Court, no matter who is sitting in the White House, and no matter who wins what election or chairs what committee, if they are enemies of what's in that exhibit hall over there, if they threaten what that great hall preserves [guns], if they dare assault the one freedom that secures all freedoms, this National Rifle Association, millions and millions of members strong, you will rise and stand and we, together, will fight them all.[25]

Gun rights advocates have worked with a small stable of academics and think tanks over decades to churn out enormous volumes of "scholarship" intended to legitimize the link between guns and freedom. This work is not produced by the militia fringe but by mainstays of the conservative movement. Nelson Lund, for example, currently holds the Patrick Henry Professorship of Constitutional Law and the Second Amendment at George Mason University's Law School, a post funded by a million-dollar donation from the NRA.[26] Lund is not just some fringe renegade activist spewing Insurrectionist rhetoric on some low-budget radio station. He holds five academic degrees, including a law degree from the University of Chicago and a doctorate from Harvard University. He clerked for U.S. Court of Appeals judge Patrick E. Higginbotham and Supreme Court justice Sandra Day O'Connor. He has worked in the White House as associate counsel to President George H. W. Bush. Lund serves on the Board of Legal Advisors to the Heritage Foundation and has written a slew of articles on the Second Amendment, including "Have Gun, Can't Travel: The Right to Arms under the Privileges and Immunities Clause of Article IV." He also contributed the section on the Second Amendment to the *Heritage Guide to the Constitution.*[27]

Kopel is a prolific contributor to a variety of popular and quasi-scholarly publications and serves as the research director at the Independence Institute, an organization "established upon the eternal truths of the Declaration of Independence." The Independence Institute bills itself as a "free market think tank" and advocates tight limits on the role of state and federal government.[28] The Independence Institute is funded in part by a network of foundations such the Castle Rock Foundation, founded by the Coors family (also a major supporter of the Heritage Foundation), and the Southeastern Legal Foundation (which claims as one of its major accomplishments the successful effort to get former president Bill Clinton's Arkansas law license suspended).[29] Kopel is a frequent contributor to NRA publications and often appears as a featured speaker at NRA functions.

The NRA and its allies (including think tanks and foundations linked to the "conservative movement") have spent millions trying to camouflage as mainstream wisdom the highly dubious proposition that freedom is best protected from government by a well-armed and unregulated populace. In recent years, the NRA has made the connection between guns and the defense of liberty a central theme of almost all of its public communications. Then-NRA president Kayne Robinson's 2005 broadside against liberals, the media, and other bugaboos of the Right is representative of both the substance and tone of the contemporary gun rights lexicon: "Although the elite media and the snob left despise our freedom, we have right, history and liberty on our side," Robinson said. "We should never, never give in to the forces that would rob us of our freedom. Never, never surrender to the bigots who look down their noses at our freedoms."[30]

It would be difficult to exaggerate how thoroughly the "guns equal freedom" message has been incorporated into everything having anything to do with gun rights organizations and their cause. In the summer of 2006, for example, the NRA offered its members the opportunity to book passage on its "Freedom Cruise" with Wayne LaPierre, Oliver North, and Newt Gingrich, among other notables, on a Holland America ship. In addition, in the preface to his 2007 book, *The Essential Second Amendment Guide,* LaPierre writes, "In the Second Amendment, we have the purest and most precious form of freedom because it is the one freedom that gives common men and women uncommon power to defend all freedoms. . . . Thank you for keeping the flame of freedom burning brightly in American hearts. Yours in Freedom, Wayne LaPierre."[31]

By constantly hammering home the idea that the gun rights movement is essentially about the defense of liberty, advocates of the Insurrectionist myth have effectively turned *freedom* into a code word understood by the initiated to imply a quite remarkable conception of the role of private violence in our political system while communicating benign concern for civil rights to the uninitiated. Slogans such as "Vote Freedom First" allow the NRA to inculcate the idea that guns are the cornerstone of freedom without expressly spelling out the argument that citizens must prepare for violent conflict with the government or confronting the logical implications of that argument. In much the same way, "conservative" politicians use the phrase *culture of life* to remind "social conservatives" of their fealty without having to explicitly state a position on abortion or gay rights that might alienate moderate voters.

The NRA's 2006 national convention in Milwaukee was called "Freedom's Second Army," and its 2007 convention in St. Louis was advertised as the "Biggest Celebration of Freedom in NRA History!"[32] LaPierre refers to NRA members and their fellow travelers as the "pro-freedom voting bloc."[33] Building on this coded language, the NRA has introduced a new monthly magazine for its members called *America's First Freedom,* with features such as a "Freedom Index" that moves up and down in response to the victories and setbacks of the gun rights lobby. In the January 2007 issue, the index notes that freedom took a three-point hit (on a one-hundred-point scale) based on the election of a Democratic majority in Congress the preceding November; Mayor Michael Bloomberg's efforts to reduce the carrying of concealed handguns in the New York City; and Michigan voters' rejection of a ballot initiative that would have legalized the hunting of mourning doves.[34] Whenever any person, organization, or government entity does something the NRA doesn't like, freedom has suffered a defeat, even when the NRA's position favors limiting someone else's rights, as it has done in attempting to prevent private landowners from keeping firearms off their property.

The suggestion that the Constitution's core values are implicated in a debate about whether to allow residents of Michigan to shoot at mourning doves may seem tenuous at best, but the NRA is relentless in associating every aspect of the ownership and use of guns with the cause of protecting freedom. Each time the concept of freedom is invoked in connection with gun rights, the NRA reinforces the idea not only that the right to own a gun is an important freedom but that government is the enemy of all forms of individual liberty. The NRA's official communications consistently attribute just about every social problem to the heavy hand of government, even in situations where most observers would conclude that the source of the difficulty is the weakness of government action, not its excesses.

Perhaps the best example of the NRA's systematic attempts to interpret the breakdown of government as evidence that government is too powerful came with Hurricane Katrina. In *Freedom in Peril: Guarding the 2nd Amendment in the 21st Century,* the NRA rails against many of its perennial targets (e.g., Senator Hillary Clinton and filmmaker Michael Moore) but adds a new villain: the role of the military and local law enforcement agencies in responding to the hurricane.[35] While most Americans understood Katrina as a wake-up call for government to upgrade its disaster-response abilities, the NRA's communications apparatus now regularly releases videos, press releases, and direct-mail appeals arguing that efforts to disarm and evacuate residents of New Orleans as order broke down following the storm represented proof positive that government confiscation of firearms is a clear and present danger. *Freedom in Peril* notes that for a few terrifying days, New Orleans degenerated into anarchy but then goes on to make the curious claim that

> Katrina became the proving ground for what American gun owners have always predicted. The day came when government bureaucrats threw the Bill of Rights out the window and declared freedom to be whatever they say it is. A mayor and a police chief revoked the rights of law-abiding citizens. The Second Amendment was only as good as they said it was. And they had plenty of men in helmets and body armor with M-16s to prove it.[36]

The NRA and other gun rights groups now regularly point to the Katrina episode as a reason to pass state and federal legislation expressly forbidding law enforcement officials from taking guns away from residents of a disaster area. The NRA and its allies argue that chaos ensued in New Orleans because law enforcement disarmed law-abiding citizens.

Anyone who has reviewed the contemporaneous press coverage of the Katrina disaster knows that the NRA has its facts backward. The police and National Guard did not reach areas hit hardest by flooding until after order had already broken down, so it is hard to see how their efforts to limit access to firearms could have caused the disorder. Moreover, the police and military started disarming civilians they encountered in the area precisely because so many looters and other criminals were armed, and in a few cases they were keeping rescue personnel at bay by shooting at them. Some citizens were disarmed and forcibly evacuated because violence was impeding recovery operations. The Insurrectionist account of Katrina also ignores the role that easy access to guns—many stolen by criminals from residences and gun stores abandoned as the hurricane moved in—contributed to the problems faced by public authorities in restoring order and conducting rescue and recovery operations.

None of this has stopped Insurrectionist propagandists from moving aggressively to construct a Katrina mythology that portrays the denial of access to firearms as delaying the restoration of order. By reversing the chronology to put gun confiscation ahead of the chaos and violence in New Orleans, the gun rights movement has made the hurricane fit within its broader story line about how police—as part of the government—cannot be trusted to protect the innocent as armed criminals rape, rob, and murder but are quick to seize guns from these same innocent people who need firearms to protect themselves in the law enforcement vacuum after a natural disaster. According to the NRA, post-Katrina New Orleans was a criminals' playground with no police in sight, yet law enforcement officers were ruthlessly disarming residents who were then left with no way to defend their lives or property. In this retelling, the police represent the worst of both worlds, totally ineffective against the bad guys but highly efficient in disarming the good guys. The government is too weak to protect its citizens yet too strong to be trusted.

Guns did not play a decisive role in the catastrophic aftermath of Katrina one way or the other, but the disaster highlights the real-world consequences of weak and ineffective government. The losses of life and property resulting from Katrina were exacerbated by the government's failures to plan adequately and effectively for its response to a major hurricane in the area and to allocate the resources needed to deal with the problems created by the storm in a timely manner. These shortcomings point to the need for stronger and smarter government efforts to prepare for and respond to major emergencies. Viewed in this light, the insistence on portraying Katrina as a case study in the dangers of a government grown too powerful is counterproductive not only to improving disaster preparedness but also to a rational discussion of the role of firearms in a free society.

What makes the Insurrectionist propaganda so insidious is not just its effect on gun policy but also its role in advancing an antigovernment ideology that is hostile to progressive values and democratic institutions. The ideology behind the gun rights movement rejects community and consensus building in favor of a social compact that may be dissolved at any time, by anyone, based on narrow conceptions of self-interest. In this view, might (whether political or physical) makes right, and government can never make legitimate claims against individuals on behalf of the community, even when decisions are made by democratic means with strong guarantees for individual rights.

The Insurrectionist idea may not spur many gun owners to challenge the government to an armed showdown, although this idea guided Timothy McVeigh (who believed that destroying the Murrah Building was justified self-defense, because after the government action at Waco and Ruby Ridge it was clear to him that "there was an imminent threat to the lives of gun owners")[37] and continues to be used by white supremacists and other extremists to justify violence. Insurrectionist ideology is, however, regularly employed in service of organizing opposition to progressive political leaders and their ideas.

The gun rights movement has masterfully used its power to mobilize grassroots opposition to progressives as a way of building clout within the "conservative" coalition. We cannot say whether the leaders of the major gun rights organizations actually believe their own rhetoric, but they have shown they are not above using it in service to causes far removed from the fight to protect the constitutional rights they claim to hold dear. For example, the NRA has not hesitated to push for legislation forcing employers to allow employees to bring guns to work, an idea that requires the government to abrogate private property rights in favor of the interests of firearms enthusiasts who prefer never to go anywhere without a gun. It is also hard to believe that LaPierre, a political operative turned gun activist who makes eight hundred thousand dollars a year and lives in an elite suburban enclave just outside Washington, D.C., takes seriously the relentless attacks on the social, political, and economic elites he so closely resembles.

Some other figures within the gun rights movement cut their ideological teeth developing direct-mail campaigns aimed at senior citizens and religious fundamentalists, and gun rights advocacy sometimes seems to have more to do with frightening or angering gun owners into writing more checks than with any attempt to strip away restrictions on gun ownership through political action. In fact, the NRA's entire "Vote Freedom First" campaign to get gun owners to the polls in the 2000 elections was crafted by the Mercury Group, an inside-the-Beltway public relations firm, to frame candidates who supported the

NRA's position as "pro-freedom." The firm's Web site boasts, "We're masters at melding news with drama, politics with theatre and public affairs with popular buzz to make your message sing and your story sell."[38] Indeed, the gun rights leaders have effectively told a paranoid tale that the government is evil as a way of building a formidable financial and political force.

CHAPTER TWO

WHAT IS THE INSURRECTIONIST AGENDA?

Many on the left assume that support for an expansive view of gun rights is essentially just a manifestation of a muscular strand of libertarianism. Anyone who has studied the propaganda churned out by the leading gun rights groups, however, quickly comes to understand that gun rights advocacy has been harnessed to an ideological perspective that is better described as right-wing populism, which includes deep-seated resentment of the power and values of elites, xenophobia, and distrust of powerful institutions such as large corporations as well as activist government.

As an outgrowth of a set of political and cultural sentiments that extends far beyond gun rights, the Insurrectionist idea is often invoked in connection with issues that on the surface have little or nothing to do with the regulation of firearms. Not coincidentally, these issues largely mirror the priorities of the "movement conservatives" who emerged as a potent political force with the nomination of Barry Goldwater in the 1964 presidential election and have grown in influence within the Republican Party ever since. In other words, the Insurrectionist idea provides a theoretical framework that ties the interests of gun owners to the political priorities of movement conservatives by explaining gun rights in terms of a wider set of grievances.

Gun Owners of America, for example, is leading a coalition of right-wing groups opposed to federal influence on public school curricula,[1] and David Kopel, apparently energized rather than exhausted by his prolific writings urging Americans to prepare for armed rebellion against the government, also has found time to attack public education, arguing that compulsory education lies at the root of school violence. In an article advocating allowing children to drop out of school at earlier ages, Kopel asserts that "abolishing compulsory attendance beyond the fifth grade would almost certainly have an immediate, dramatic effect in reducing school violence in the United States." As a side benefit, Kopel suggests, larger numbers of dropouts will help justify reducing the amount of government spending on public schools, long a cherished goal of many conservatives: "There is . . . nothing unfair about reducing school funding when the number of students declines. If you have fewer customers, you need fewer resources."[2] If sixth-graders start dropping out, the schools will be safer and the taxpayers will save money—a winning proposition for antitax types and religious conservatives whose children do not attend public schools in the first place, but not so good for kids with a fifth-grade education.

Jews for the Preservation of Firearms Ownership (JPFO), a gun rights group that usually focuses on the need for ethnic, racial, and religious minorities to use firearms to protect their civil rights, has directly linked the destruction of gun rights with federal taxation and Social Security. JPFO's founder, Aaron Zelman, whose group believes that tax policies "destroy American rights," wrote in *Shotgun News* that this is because gun owners "pay increasingly outrageous taxes for guns and everything else, only to have our tax money spent to terrify and oppress us gun owners."[3] Zelman also has argued, in "Can the Second Amendment and Social Security Coexist? Terrified Politicians Believe One or the Other Has to Go," that the allegedly imminent collapse of the Social Security system will trigger a violent confrontation with the government that will, in turn, give "statists" their long-awaited excuse to confiscate all civilian firearms. Unfortunately, Zelman has no suggestions for shoring up the Social Security trust fund. Instead, he recommends that we "wean ourselves and our families from dependence on the all-pervasive nanny state. We should do the best we can to prepare ourselves financially for the future, independent of government handouts and Ponzi schemes. . . . We can't risk being dependent on a government that cheats us, then disarms us to avoid the consequences of its actions."[4]

For its part, the National Rifle Association (NRA) has campaigned to curb the influence of the United Nations[5] (attacking it as the "face of Global Socialism"),[6] built support for right-wing judicial nominations, and defended the George W. Bush administration's decision to allow road building to encourage logging on public lands (a policy that most hunters opposed).[7] The organization has also been busy warning America about "the unfolding Latino gang crime wave" at the same time its legislative allies have been trying to use the fear of illegal immigration as a campaign wedge issue. The NRA has gone beyond the usual tactic of complaining that illegal immigrants cost "real" Americans their jobs and has made the seemingly much more attenuated argument that illegal immigrants will be a major factor in the coming crime wave and that this will give cover to politicians who want to take away the gun rights of law-abiding citizens. As an NRA publication states, "The bottom line is that America, by its free and independent nature, is a breeding ground and safe haven for violent, illegal immigrant criminal gangs. American gun owners should not only draw even tighter rein on their rights, but also brace for a new and decades-long assault upon all their freedoms."[8] It is odd to think that our "free and independent nature"—the same nature that presumably makes us so enthusiastic about guns—also makes Americans tolerant of violent criminals from other countries, but no matter. The NRA asserts that the illegal immigrant lobby is so powerful that "most law enforcement officials won't acknowledge that an illegal alien crime wave exists."[9] (This might explain why so many Americans labor under the misimpression that most violent crimes are committed by the 290 million people who are legally within our borders.)[10]

Indeed, opposition to immigration—both legal and illegal—is a major focus of many gun rights propagandists. The Web site for the Liberty Belles, a minor gun rights group targeting women (slogan: "Putting the Second Amendment First"), makes some bizarre claims in "Open Borders Threaten Gun Rights." The Belles maintain that "we are importing Socialism. Organizations like the Communist Party USA and the New

Socialist [*sic*] are assisting the effort by attempting to fuel a revolution of underpaid workers who rise up against the evils of capitalism." In an effort to connect this contention to the cause of gun rights, they say,

> One can only assume that our newly imported Socialists are voting in American elections regardless of whether or not they have the legal right to do so. And without understanding the Bill of Rights or the cultural trademark of American individualism, we can expect illegal alien voters to elect Socialist politicians who promise "free" benefits to the poor. Regardless of party affiliation, these Socialist and Communist politcians [*sic*] will stamp out our gun rights with the same pen they use to grant aid to the misguided immigrants who voted for them.[11]

The Second Amendment Foundation (SAF) links a hard-line position on immigration with the fear of crime and has adopted the slogan "Border control, not gun control." Its widely read tabloid newspaper, *Gun Week*, often publishes articles arguing that the debate over public safety can be boiled down to a choice between regulating access to firearms and cracking down on illegal immigration. SAF founder Alan Gottlieb writes, "An overwhelming majority of American citizens think it is far more important to stop the flood of illegal aliens into this country than it is to restrict the rights of law-abiding gun owners."[12]

While immigration figures prominently among the grievances stoked by Insurrectionist organs, these outlets often highlight a wide range of other public policy controversies with only the most tenuous connection to guns. The NRA's flagship magazine, *American Rifleman*, frequently features complaints about the evils of judicial activism, international organizations, environmentalism, free trade, restrictions on prayer in schools, and even campaign finance reform.

Why do gun rights organizations go to such great lengths to tie the litany of right-wing grievances to firearms? Gun rights groups use their membership lists, communications infrastructure, and fund-raising capability on behalf of a wide range of causes dear to the hearts of "movement conservatives" because the Insurrectionist idea fits neatly into an ideology that preaches the evils of big government and the hated liberals who control it. The organizations seek to weaken government not simply by curbing its power over individuals but by defining as narrowly as possible the community whose interests the government may legitimately serve. Those who favor protection of the environment for the benefit of the public or who believe that the federal government should ensure that all children, including those born to illegal immigrants, receive an education or that senior citizens should have a minimum level of subsistence are condemned as "statists" who have no respect for the values of ordinary Americans. These "elites" are blamed for a host of evils, ranging from high taxes to sex and violence in the entertainment media—along with gun control and disrespect for gun owners.

These "elites" are, of course, the same people who offend right-wing populists. What Insurrectionism adds to the standard list of complaints about liberals who are "ruining the country for everyone else" is the claim that the elites who supposedly control the government are literally out to get ordinary people. Insurrectionists contend that if given a chance, the elites who control the levers of power in government, industry, and the media are likely to grab privately owned guns and enslave their owners as the condescending, paternalistic instincts that initially motivated their actions give way over time to totalitarian impulses. According to this line of reasoning, Americans have a patriotic duty to own guns because of the need to resist the oppression of elites.

The seeds of this debate (oversimplified here) are as old as the republic: Jeffersonians believed that freedom is preserved by limiting the role of the federal government, and Hamiltonians thought that a stronger federal government would be consistent with—and in some ways helpful to—the expansion of individual freedom. For many people, this debate was largely settled in favor of the Hamiltonians by events and perspectives that later reshaped the institutional structure and philosophical underpinnings of the American system—first the Civil War and later the New Deal. Both Abraham Lincoln and Franklin D. Roosevelt confronted crises that posed grave threats to our country. Both expanded the scope of the federal government's power in addressing these threats, invoking the founders and, in FDR's case, the ideas of John Maynard Keynes and others to assert that in some ways, a strong central government is essential to the defense of individual freedom. John F. Kennedy and Lyndon B. Johnson followed with the New Frontier and the Great Society, programs based on the premise that government intervention could defend and strengthen freedom for Americans.

The Insurrectionist dreamers share a fundamentally reactionary set of political sentiments that formed the basis of a backlash with roots in a complex collection of social and economic controversies. There is nothing inherently wrong with working to reduce the size of government and to limit the scope of its authority over individuals. Unfortunately for the rule of law, however, Insurrectionists take the "smaller government" rhetoric to a dangerous new place where gun owners, ready and eager to use violence to realize their desire for limited governance, emerge as an essential and legitimate counterbalance to a government they see as out of control.

As we will discuss in more detail later, the founders (an occasional intemperate remark by Jefferson notwithstanding) explicitly rejected the Insurrectionist theory of democratic government in the framing of the Constitution.[13] The Insurrectionist argument may seem wildly paranoid or simply absurd on its face, and most gun owners would not articulate their views about the importance of guns to the preservation of freedom in such stark terms. Even in watered-down form, however, the Insurrectionist vocabulary resonates powerfully among America's undersocialized, alienated, and disaffected. It helps carve out a place at the table of "movement conservatives" who need to welcome gun rights advocates into their tent to bind together a winning electoral coalition. As a small but vital part of that coalition, the Insurrectionists, bereft as they are of cosmopolitan sensibilities, conservative instincts, social skills, or even good humor, nevertheless prove themselves curiously capable, time after time, of using their organizational clout on behalf of the "conservative" movement.

CHAPTER THREE

WHO ARE
THE INSURRECTIONISTS?

Through the National Rifle Association (NRA) and its allied gun rights groups, the Insurrectionists have created an effective communications infrastructure that incorporates right-wing leaders, politicians at the highest levels of government, the bottom-feeders of the militia movement, and hate groups as well as a large grassroots network that can push Insurrectionist propaganda to millions of gun owners at a moment's notice. To be sure, most NRA members are not Insurrectionists, but the leaders of the NRA and allied groups have committed the Insurrectionist dogma to the service of the "conservative movement" and the Republican Party.

The NRA

Many political professionals believe that the NRA is the most powerful lobbying group in Washington. We and others have argued that the NRA's actual influence on elections is overrated. In politics, though, perception often trumps reality, and the NRA undoubtedly enjoys tremendous clout with legislators. This clout is based almost entirely on the NRA's ability to mobilize a grassroots network on behalf of its legislative and political goals.

The NRA's grassroots organizing and fund-raising efforts feature messages designed to appeal to gun owners as protectors of "America's First Freedom." To the uninitiated, these appeals to freedom sound innocuous, but to someone who is familiar with the political underpinnings of the gun rights movement, an appeal to freedom means only one thing: guns protect our freedom because the government cannot be trusted. The effectiveness of this message is self-evident: the NRA has millions of members, and it raises around $200 million a year, mostly from small donors.[1]

If the NRA limited its agenda to building a bipartisan consensus in favor of a limitless right to bear arms, it could be dismissed as no more than one of the peculiarities of American politics. Many progressives, assuming that the NRA is run by gun enthusiasts who want nothing more than to be left alone with their firearms, have concluded that it can be appeased by opposing gun control or simply by remaining silent on gun-policy issues. This understanding is overly simplistic. The NRA is an integral cog in the "conservative" movement's political machine, both because of its ability to deliver grassroots supporters and votes to Republican candidates and because of its willingness to engage in relentless propagandizing against liberals, government, and the Democratic Party.

The modern gun rights movement was born in 1977, when hard-liners took over the NRA at the group's national convention in Cincinnati. The most obvious immediate change came in the organization's attitude toward compromise. Where previous executives had been uncomfortable putting the NRA into direct public confrontations with elected officials, the new leadership adopted an unapologetically bellicose strategy in political and legislative matters.[2]

This change in approach produced some notable successes. In the early 1980s, the NRA nearly achieved its goal of abolishing the Bureau of Alcohol, Tobacco, and Firearms (ATF). Only when its leaders realized that the alternative was to transfer authority for enforcing federal gun laws to the Federal Bureau of Investigation (FBI) or another law enforcement agency that could not be so easily demonized did they decide to drop the effort and argue for reductions in ATF's budget. In 1986, the NRA won passage of the Firearm Owners' Protection Act, which rolled back key elements of the Gun Control Act of 1968 and drastically curtailed ATF's authority to bring criminal or administrative enforcement actions against rogue gun dealers who divert firearms to convicted felons and other prohibited purchasers.[3]

In the late 1980s, however, the NRA began to find that getting a reputation as a bully might prove useful in some cases but has serious shortcomings as a long-term political strategy. Wayne LaPierre's characterization of ATF agents as "jack-booted Government thugs" provoked President George H. W. Bush to resign his lifetime NRA membership,[4] and law enforcement leaders across the country were alienated by the NRA's strident opposition to legislation designed to prevent civilians from purchasing armor-piercing handgun shells. By 1994, the accumulation of bad publicity and ill will generated by the NRA's take-no-prisoners approach had seriously damaged the gun lobby's legislative agenda. Gun control advocates had built majority support in Congress for the Brady law, which requires background checks on all buyers who purchase firearms from licensed gun dealers. They followed up by winning passage of a federal ban on assault weapons. In addition to the first President Bush, Presidents Ronald Reagan, Gerald Ford, and Jimmy Carter publicly renounced their NRA memberships. Gun control groups anticipated winning more victories in the years to come.

The November 1994 midterm congressional elections transformed perceptions about the politics of gun control when Democrats lost control of both the House and Senate for the first time in a generation. The Democrats had stumbled through a host of minor scandals, legislative debacles, and political missteps in the first half of President Bill Clinton's first term, from the implosion of First Lady Hillary Clinton's health care reform initiative and an abortive attempt to allow gays to serve openly in the military to the controversy over the firing of several employees in the White House travel office. Despite the role these problems played in contributing to Democratic losses in 1994, the NRA moved aggressively to claim a major victory based on the defeat of several Democrats who had supported the assault-weapons ban.

At first, the NRA's efforts to convince political professionals, journalists, and the public that the assault-weapons vote was largely responsible for the GOP landslide may have been no more than a remarkably shrewd ploy to take credit for the results of an election cycle that undoubtedly was influenced by many factors. Over the next several years, however, the broader consequence of these elections was to incorporate the gun rights movement into the Republican Party's coalition. A symbiotic relationship developed between the leaders of the Republican "revolution" and the leaders of the major gun rights groups, particularly the NRA. In the 1990s, as the GOP worked to cement its hold on power by aggressively courting sympathetic interest groups, no organization has allowed itself to become more closely aligned with the Republican Party—and particularly "movement conservatives" within the party—than the NRA.

Prior to 1994, the NRA behaved more or less like any other interest group in doling out political contributions and other efforts to support its legislative agenda. It gave money to candidates from both parties based on their voting records. By 2002, however, the vast majority of the NRA's political action committee contributions (directly to candidates) and its independent expenditures (on behalf of candidates) took place in support of Republican candidates.[5] The NRA deftly avoided blame for Bob Dole's loss in the 1996 presidential race while moving to claim credit for George W. Bush's narrow Electoral College victory over Al Gore in 2000. Together with the close political relationship between the NRA and top Republican leaders in the House of Representatives, the 2000 presidential election solidified the importance of gun rights among the causes and interest groups that make up the Republican coalition.

On the rare occasions when the NRA supports Democratic candidates, that endorsement does not bring any material amount of cash or volunteer support. Creigh Deeds, a Democrat running for attorney general in Virginia in 2005, learned this lesson the hard way. Although he received the NRA's endorsement, Deeds quickly realized that it was just for show. As he recounted after he lost the election, "The day the NRA endorsement was made public, my opponent's campaign manager quipped to the press that the endorsement was paper thin. Apparently, she knew what she was talking about. In the end the NRA ended up giving my opponent money."[6]

Moreover, the NRA makes a practice of avoiding endorsements of Democratic challengers in races that could affect the balance of power in Washington. In 2006, for example, the NRA refused to endorse Democratic challengers to Republican incumbents in Texas and Florida even where the challengers had higher NRA ratings.[7] The NRA has no interest in being bipartisan when there is a risk that Democrats could actually challenge "conservative" control of the policymaking apparatus. This may not be a bad political strategy—from 2000 until 2006 it served the group exceptionally well—but it locks the NRA and the gun rights movement into a symbiotic relationship with reactionary elements of the Republican Party that ties gun rights organizations closely to a host of partisan and ideological battles far removed from firearms policy.

The NRA is so valuable to the GOP because unlike most other interest groups and corporate donors, it has something beyond money to influence elections: a highly motivated core of supporters accompanied by an elaborate communications infrastructure. Insurrectionists represent a small minority of gun owners, but they are active in political campaigns. Many of them spend countless hours handing out political literature, and they often appear at legislative hearings and other public events. Together with the ability to reach gun owners by setting up booths at gun shows and shooting ranges, sending out millions of e-mails to supporters, and spending heavily on direct mail and other forms of advertising, NRA and like-minded gun groups have an impressive ability to mobilize activists.

Of course, the GOP includes interest groups and individuals from a variety of ideological perspectives. Contrary to the assumptions of some progressives, divisions in the Republican base are not limited to disputes between libertarians and religious fundamentalists over social issues such as abortion. Libertarians, for example, are unhappy about the Patriot Act and electronic surveillance by the National Security Agency, while national-security hawks in the party think these measures are of paramount importance. The coalition that brought the Republicans to power in 2000 and 2004 is sometimes divided on important questions of policy, and the NRA works to keep gun owners (whose interests may diverge sharply from the rest of the GOP base on other issues) in the fold by tying gun rights politically and intellectually to the "conservative" movement.

The Iraq war and its aftermath have proven to be a major setback for Republicans, but through 2008 their strength has been not so much finding mutually reinforcing priorities as building a collection of supporters whose interests are not mutually antagonistic. As Grover Norquist, the leading right-wing political operative outside the Republican Party apparatus, explains, the GOP coalition includes at least three distinct spheres: religious conservatives, gun rights enthusiasts, and opponents of taxes. Norquist has observed that fundamentalist Christians who own guns and hate taxes might be an important voting bloc, but a party that brings together people who fit in any one of these three categories (rather than all three at once) can dominate politics.[8]

The faith/guns/taxes coalition is cohesive because each group believes that the government's sovereign powers should be limited in favor of the individual, the family, and God. Gun rights enthusiasts represent the smallest element of this coalition, but they are perhaps the most politically active. The NRA can leverage its influence over its most committed activists and reach substantial numbers of more moderate gun owners without an effective response from the opposition, making it a highly valued ally. While moderate antitax Republicans and the probusiness wing of the party don't think allowing the assault weapons ban to expire or allowing criminals easy access to guns without background checks is good public policy, they are not so deeply opposed to these changes that they get in the way of building a winning coalition.

In this vein, Wayne LaPierre has been quick to make the case that the business community needs the muscle of NRA members to fight the dangers posed by the Democratic takeover of Congress in November 2006. As the 110th Congress got to work, LaPierre wrote, "Only the NRA energizes the powerful pro-freedom voting bloc, resulting in election outcomes good for both American gun rights and for American business. Candidates who support the Second Amendment also support you. They're typically pro-business people who fight for free-market issues, from tort and estate tax reform to immigration policy and the global war on terror."[9] This assessment that gun rights enthusiasts and "pro-business people" share the same attitude toward immigration is highly questionable, which makes LaPierre's statement a telling example of how gun rights leaders work to smooth over differences of opinion among members of the conservative coalition.

As the belief that the NRA is an important cog in the "conservative" movement's ability to win elections has grown, the NRA and its leaders have developed strong formal and informal relationships with Republican legislators, operatives, and opinion leaders. The NRA board of directors includes Joe Allbaugh, who served as the Bush-Cheney campaign manager in 2000 (and as a consultant to 2008 presidential candidate Rudy Giuliani); U.S. Senator Larry Craig, an Idaho Republican and outspoken gun rights proponent; Grover Norquist, who heads Americans for Tax Reform; and David Keene, leader of the American Conservative Union. With the possible exception of Norquist, Keene is probably the preeminent activist among movement conservatives.

None of these Republican stalwarts is without controversy. Norquist, for example, has been tied to disgraced lobbyist Jack Abramoff, who allegedly used Americans for Tax Reform as a "conduit" to move money "surreptitiously" to support lobbying campaigns for his for-profit clients.[10] Allbaugh was George W. Bush's first director of the Federal Emergency Management Agency, and Allbaugh brought in his old friend, the now infamous Michael Brown, as his deputy. When Allbaugh left the agency, Brown stepped in just in time to take charge of managing the federal government's response to Hurricane Katrina. But in light of the dependent relationship between the right-wing ideologues who have seized control of the Republican Party and the leaders of the gun rights movement, the presence of several right-wing heavyweights at the highest levels of the NRA is not surprising. (Craig, of course, lost his clout within the party in 2007 after he pleaded guilty to a misdemeanor conviction for disorderly conduct in a Minneapolis airport bathroom.)

Remarkably, the major gun rights groups have maintained close relationships with the leaders of what can only be described as extremist organizations and causes. Prominent figures from conservative politics such as Allbaugh, Craig, Norquist, and Keene seem not to be disturbed at the prospect of associating with these fringe figures. The NRA board, for example, also includes Bob Brown, publisher of *Soldier of Fortune* magazine, and Peder Lund, publisher of Paladin Press. These publications cater to readers who fantasize about becoming mercenaries, going "off the grid" by avoiding the use of credit cards and other activities that might allow the government or private debt collectors to track them down, or simply immersing themselves in a subculture where everyone is endlessly fascinated by firearms. Paladin published *How to Be a Hit Man*, a book used in at least one real-life contract killing,[11] and other instructional manuals, including *.50 Caliber Construction Manual* and *Acquiring New I.D.: How to Easily Use the Latest Technology to Drop Out, Start Over, and Get on with Your Life*. These directors connect the NRA directly to the underground network of white supremacists and survivalists and to a wide range of other causes on the outer edges of the American Right. Other controversial figures include current board member Ted Nugent and Sanford Abrams, a gun dealer who was recently forced to resign his NRA board seat.

Nugent, a rock musician best known for his 1970s hit "Cat Scratch Fever," has reemerged in public life as a gun rights zealot. He appears at NRA events and on right-wing talk radio shows preaching to the faithful about the salutary effects of firearms on public safety and self-reliance. Nugent has a long history of making raw, crude, and blatantly racist and sexist comments. For example, in a 1994 interview with *Westword*, a Denver weekly, Nugent said of Hillary Clinton, "You probably can't use the term 'toxic cunt' in your magazine, but that's what she is. Her very existence insults the spirit of individualism in this country. This bitch is nothing but a two-bit whore for Fidel Castro."[12]

At his speech at the NRA convention in Houston in 2005, Nugent showed his respect for the rule of law by encouraging the faithful to shoot first and ask questions later: "Remember the Alamo! Shoot 'em! . . . To show you how radical I am, I want carjackers dead. I want rapists dead. I want burglars dead. I want child molesters dead. I want the bad guys dead. No court case. No parole. No early release. I want 'em dead. Get a gun and when they attack you, shoot 'em."[13] *Rolling Stone* reported that at a 2007 concert, Nugent veered away from music into political commentary: "Decked out in full-on camouflage hunting gear, Nugent wielded two machine guns while raging, 'Obama, he's a piece of shit. I told him to suck on my machine gun. Hey Hillary,' he continued. 'You might want to ride one of these into the sunset, you worthless bitch.' Nugent summed up his eloquent speech by screaming 'freedom!'"[14]

Abrams, a well-known Maryland gun dealer and former officer of the Maryland Firearms Dealers Association, owned and operated Baltimore's Valley Guns. In less than ten years as proprietor of the store, Abrams was cited for more than nine hundred violations of federal firearms laws.[15] ATF inspectors found that he could not account for 25 percent of the guns that were listed in his inventory.[16] Out of almost eighty thousand gun sellers nationwide, Valley Guns ranked thirty-seventh in number of guns traced in connection with criminal investigations.[17] ATF attempted to sanction Abrams and eventually moved to take his license, but Abrams took advantage of loopholes in federal gun laws to hold off enforcement action until 2006. In upholding the revocation on appeal, the U.S. Court of Appeals found that "Valley Gun's violations were not technical; they were serious, and public safety required their correction. Preventing Valley Gun from continuing its history of significant failures goes to the core of ATF's responsibilities under the Gun Control Act. Not only was ATF authorized to revoke Valley Gun's license, ATF meaningfully served the public safety in doing so."[18] Even after his lawless behavior attracted widespread publicity, Abrams was reelected to the NRA Board of Directors.

Abrams was finally forced to resign from the NRA board in late 2006, shortly after he came under scrutiny for additional violations of federal and state firearms laws, and he ultimately was convicted (but not sentenced to serve time in prison). Abrams was charged after he supplied convicted felon Keith Showalter with a Bushmaster assault weapon, a Yugoslavian rifle, and a Remington semiautomatic rifle. During a domestic dispute with his estranged girlfriend, Showalter shot at two police officers who tried to intervene. The officers returned fire and killed him. After the shooting, investigators found that Abrams had never recorded the sale of two of the weapons with the state police, as required by Maryland law, and that he broke federal law by possessing an unregistered machine gun.[19]

So why do legislators and high-ranking Washington insiders feel that they benefit by being associated with an organization that routinely elects survivalists and rogue gun dealers to its board? The answer lies in the NRA's ability to activate a grassroots network on behalf of "conservative" candidates and causes. Norquist is a formidable force in fund-raising for Republican candidates and has substantial influence over business lobbyists and others opposed to taxes and regulation of commerce. He has a limited ability to communicate directly with the activists who listen to Nugent or Bob Brown, however. The price that Republicans and their political allies must pay for the assistance of the Insurrectionist-led gun rights groups is having to do their bidding from time to time. And while right-wing populists are a relatively small voting bloc, gun rights groups are among the most effective at reaching and energizing them, using appeals to the defense of freedom that also are attractive to more moderate gun owners who do not necessarily accept or even understand the subtext of the Insurrectionist message.

The NRA's grassroots infrastructure can be a potent force even outside of election campaigns. It is also a weapon that can be used to punish any company or individual in the firearms industry that tries to take steps to limit the flow of guns to criminals through illegal markets. Most gun makers and sellers are happy to follow the NRA's lead on policy questions, but when members of the industry have tried to exercise greater responsibility in curbing the illegal trade in firearms, the NRA has been quick to respond with blacklists and boycotts that have ended careers and bankrupted companies. Although gun control activists often assume that the NRA is a tool of the firearms industry, the gun rights groups drive the industry's political and legislative agenda. The industry takes its marching orders from the NRA, not the other way around.[20]

Firearms sellers are an extremely diverse group. While the NRA likes to portray the industry as a success story for an American manufacturing sector besieged by foreign competition, foreigners control many gun makers. Glock, an Austrian corporation, through a U.S. subsidiary called Glock USA, now manufactures the leading firearm for law enforcement. The sidearm for the U.S. military is manufactured by Beretta, an Italian corporation that once made firearms for Mussolini's fascist regime. It operates through a U.S. subsidiary called Beretta USA. Other brands long associated with the cowboy myth and the American

West, such as Winchester Arms, are now owned by multinational corporations or are out of business.

Conversely, some U.S. gun makers devote themselves to turning out low-quality handguns known as Saturday night specials or "junk guns" that have been prohibited from importation by the Gun Control Act of 1968.[21] Some manufacturers are mom-and-pop operations that turn out small quantities of specialty guns, such as high-end target pistols or low-end assault weapons. The entire U.S. firearms manufacturing and ammunition industry is quite small, generating approximately two billion dollars in gross annual sales.[22]

Gun companies benefit from the political organization and clout of the NRA and other gun rights groups but are also held hostage to the Insurrectionist worldview that guides gun rights advocacy. Until the late 1990s, the firearms industry maintained an independent trade association to push its agenda on Capitol Hill and in statehouses across the country. Through the American Shooting Sports Council (ASSC), gun makers and dealers had a voice on public policy issues that sometimes deviated from the gun rights movement's party line. For example, legitimate firearm sellers were unhappy about the failure to regulate sales by "collectors" and "hobbyists" at gun shows, because many of these unlicensed sellers distribute large numbers of guns without being required to perform background checks, maintain insurance, or pay for the routine overhead associated with running a gun store. During the Clinton administration, the ASSC endorsed closing the loophole that allows criminals to avoid background checks at gun shows by purchasing from these unlicensed sellers.[23]

The NRA responded to this turn of events by orchestrating the dismantling of the ASSC, eliminating the industry's only independent trade association.[24] Most gun owners support requiring background checks on all firearm sales at gun shows, but Insurrectionists insist on retaining the option to conduct transactions outside the FBI background-check system, and they were unwilling to allow the firearms industry to support legislation that would establish a system of universal accountability for gun purchases.

Again contrary to the common assumption that the NRA does the industry's bidding, this incident illustrates that the gun rights group tail wags the industry dog. Firearms makers and dealers deviate from the Insurrectionist line at their peril. The NRA's bark is much worse than its bite when it comes to threats to boycott businesses outside the firearms industry, but it has enormous economic leverage over gun dealers and manufacturers. Bucking the NRA, Smith & Wesson worked closely with the Clinton administration even after the ASSC was silenced. The NRA responded by crippling Smith & Wesson's business, eventually forcing the company into bankruptcy. Today, without exception, the industry toes the NRA line even when doing so is bad for business. In exchange for the industry's acquiescence in its leadership, the NRA has used its political power to win legislative favors for gun companies, such as federal legislation that immunizes gun dealers and manufacturers from civil liability for distribution and sales practices that make it easier for criminals to buy guns.

Allied Gun Groups

The NRA is by far the largest gun rights group in the world, but a host of smaller players fill every conceivable demographic and geographic niche in the gun rights movement. State-based gun rights groups such as the Virginia Citizens Defense League and the Gun Owners of California primarily focus on legislatures in their home states and generally are most concerned with self-defense issues, such as loosening restrictions on the ability of individuals to carry concealed weapons. Certain groups cater to distinct categories of gun owners, such as Jews for the Preservation of Firearms Ownership (JPFO) and the Pink Pistols, whose motto is "Armed Gays Don't Get Bashed."

Of course, these organizations strongly oppose any new gun control laws and advocate further weakening ATF and repealing the Brady law, but the NRA does not really need their help with lobbying; in some cases, the involvement of these groups in lobbying serves merely to highlight the extremism of the Insurrectionist-inspired gun rights agenda.[25] Some niche groups seem to have few members and exist primarily to create the appearance that support for gun rights extends beyond the Right. The larger and better-organized allied groups earn their keep by maintaining a steady stream of communications with gun own-ers, who are bombarded relentlessly with Insurrectionist rhetoric de-signed to persuade them that the government is evil and that gun own-ers must prepare to resist confiscation of their firearms. The most prominent allied groups articulating this position include the Gun Owners of America (GOA), the Second Amendment Foundation (SAF), and JPFO. These organizations can aggressively and more explicitly in-culcate gun owners with Insurrectionist ideology that the NRA must couch in softer, more general terms that link guns and freedom.

JPFO paints itself as America's fiercest defender of firearms owner-ship, while GOA claims that it is "the only no-compromise gun lobby in Washington." The leaders of GOA and SAF, Larry Pratt and Alan Gottlieb, respectively, are colorful characters, to say the least. Pratt has in the past had ties with the militia and white supremacist move-ments.[26] Gottlieb is a convicted felon who spent a year in prison on fed-eral tax-evasion charges in the late 1970s.[27] These allied groups skill-fully mix gun rights with antigovernment ideology in an effort to warn gun owners about the threat of gun control. "This Second Amendment right . . . is not about hunting or target shooting, it's about freedom and defense. It is the great insurance policy against tyranny, and it has kept our country free for more than two centuries," Gottlieb said in a 2006 press release. "Today's gun grabbers don't march in red coats down country roads. . . . They skulk through the halls of Congress and state legislatures. Yet, their goal is the same. They would disarm us, steal our liberty and destroy our way of life."[28]

JPFO echoes the Insurrectionist theory of the Second Amendment. In a document designed to persuade Jews that they should support a constitutional right to bear arms, JPFO says that "the Second Amend-ment does not aim at protecting hunters. So, there is no reason for a Jew—or anyone else—to say, 'I don't hunt, so why should I own firearms?' It's simple: Jews' history of murderous persecution by gov-ernments means that Jews should spearhead efforts to expand the indi-vidual civil right to be armed."[29]

The allied groups are not content to protect us merely against leg-islative encroachment on the right to bear arms. The courts are part of the plot against liberty as well. In a 2005 newsletter article, "The

Supreme Court Has Declared Itself above the Law," the GOA's Pratt claimed that the courts are out of control and that states should be able to overturn the decisions of Congress and the federal courts: "To save our gun rights, indeed, to save all of our freedoms, the time has come to bring courts back under control. States need to study the history of nullification. Congress needs to do its part to rein in the judges. In the words of the defenders of freedom on Flight 93, 'Let's roll.'"[30]

Pratt has repeatedly emphasized the nullification doctrine that was a key rationale invoked by the Confederacy to justify secession. Of course, the Union was saved when Lincoln refused to let the southern states decide for themselves which federal laws to obey and which ones to reject as inconsistent with their conception of federalism. Pratt appeals to the same doctrine to defend the proposition that armed citizens are entitled to ignore federal laws they find objectionable and that America is not in fact one country. He then has the temerity to invoke the phrase famously used as a rallying cry by real patriots who sacrificed their lives to stop terrorists from crashing an airplane into a building during the September 11 attacks.

But it is far from patriotic to advocate the use or threat of armed violence against a democratic process that has been available to settle grievances and advance common interests for more than two hundred years. In fact, it is precisely the opposite of patriotism. Appeals to prepare for conflict with the government or to nullify federal laws are fundamentally inconsistent with a commitment to core democratic values—that is, to the idea that disputes are settled through debate rather than force within a framework that provides political accountability at the ballot box, not at the barrel of a gun.

Not satisfied in trying to undermine the legitimacy of the federal government in the United States, GOA has interjected itself into the gun debate in other countries. Pratt has helped launch gun rights groups in Brazil and South Africa. He has written that he was happy to be on hand at a conference organized by the new Gun Owners of South Africa organization. South Africa has a major gun-violence problem, and the government has been grappling with measures to reduce the killings, including licensing gun owners. When a South African police chief, Robert McBride, remarked that it was not constructive or accurate for gun owners to compare the licensing law in South Africa to Hitler's actions to lay the groundwork for the Holocaust, Pratt swung into action, writing,

> As in the United States, gun banners are simply unwilling (and unable) to deal with the mountains of data that disprove their arguments. Maybe they are really not concerned about crime after all. If that is the case, maybe we are getting close to understanding why they don't want opponents to keep bringing up countries where gun control led to confiscation and was then followed by genocide. Do you suppose that is what terrorist-now-police-chief McBride has in mind when he wants no talk of Hitler and Pol Pot?[31]

The allied groups use simple tactics. First, discredit the government and gun control supporters as bent on genocide and repression. Second, idealize gun owners as über-patriots prepared to fight tyranny wherever it rears its ugly head. Both Gottlieb and Pratt are experts in using these arguments to build support for their groups.

These organizations inhabit two worlds. To casual observers, they appear to be simply another set of issue-advocacy groups funded largely by direct-mail solicitations from small donors. Their leaders demonstrate their absolutist bona fides by generating mainstream media attention for their support for repealing the de facto ban on machine guns and by staking out other extreme positions on gun policy.

These groups have another, less public, role as conduits to Insurrectionist ideology that is not acceptable in polite company. The allied groups are responsible for managing the hard-core extremists in the gun rights fold without getting so close to the NRA as to damage its credibility inside the Beltway.[32] For example, Pratt is known to have met with white supremacists, neo-Nazi leaders, and state militia groups in Estes Park, Colorado, in response to the shootout at Ruby Ridge between federal agents and Randy Weaver.[33] Pratt has lived a double life that allows him to associate with racists and radical antigovernment activists who openly discuss overthrowing the government at the same time that he maintains close relationships with senior members of Congress and appears regularly in the mainstream media.

Sometimes these worlds collide, as when Pratt was forced to resign from Pat Buchanan's 1996 presidential campaign because his ties to white supremacists had become an embarrassment. Pratt shook off the resulting bad publicity and remains a fixture in Washington. He is a regular on the cable talk show circuit, and one of the authors appeared opposite Pratt in an MSNBC segment in which he objected to a proposal to stop people on the terrorist watch list form purchasing firearms. After the taping, he clarified to the host that one of his objections was that the list could be used to prevent people like his "friends at Ruby Ridge" from acquiring firearms.[34] The siege at Ruby Ridge started when ATF agents attempted to serve a warrant on Weaver for selling two illegally sawed-off shotguns.[35] In Pratt's world, no firearm should be illegal and the federal government is an occupying force attempting to confiscate all the guns in America. He is tolerated and even welcomed in "conservative" circles, however, because he is politically useful.

The allied groups ultimately serve as conduits to the people on the extreme right of the political spectrum. These are people who think the NRA is too mainstream, too willing to compromise. They are tolerated by "movement conservatives" because every vote counts in a country where national elections are often decided by razor-thin margins, and the allied groups appeal to group of voters that are highly engaged in politics because they view it as a life-or-death contest between good and evil. In Norquist's values-plus-taxes-plus-guns equation, the allied groups make sure that the gun owners of every stripe—including those who want to use their guns to fight a race war—are included in the final tally on Election Day.

The Gun Show Circuit

The NRA and the allied groups are by no means the only entities preaching Insurrectionism to grassroots activists. Each weekend in America, Insurrectionists with a similar message meet in civic centers, VFW halls, and fairgrounds to distribute their message at gun shows. Gun shows are among the most important gathering places for Insurrectionists, and they provide a distribution network for propaganda from Far Right causes. Visitors can usually buy anything from a single-shot .22 to a military-style semiautomatic assault weapon, along with instructions on how to convert it into a fully automatic machine gun. Although it is illegal under federal law to sell a machine gun to a purchaser without a special license, vendors on site often offer kits to convert a semiautomatic firearm into a machine gun. A consumer without the special license can legally purchase a semiautomatic assault rifle at one booth and then go to another booth and buy the parts to turn it into a fully automatic machine gun. The sheer volume and variety of guns and ammunition for sale can be overwhelming for the uninitiated. Hundreds of tables with every imaginable type of weaponry: semiautomatic shotguns, target pistols, autoloading pistols, and .50 rifles are all available at gun shows.

As noted previously, many states allow gun owners to sell firearms at gun shows without conducting background checks on the buyers. Unlike federally licensed firearms dealers, who must perform background checks on all sales, "private sellers" are not subject to the regulations applicable to licensed gun dealers, even though these private sellers may be involved in a high volume of firearm transactions. This results in a strange anomaly at gun shows. At one table, a federally licensed dealer who has left his store for the day to come to the gun show will be dutifully filling out paperwork to record a gun sale and run a background check, while at the next table a "hobbyist" with dozens of guns for sale will be offering cash-and-carry service without background checks or a sales record.

If a criminal attends a gun show in search of a firearm, which vendor will he choose: the licensed dealer who is required to conduct a background check that could stop the purchase and will certainly leave a paper trail, or the "hobbyist" offering sales with no strings attached? At a gun show in Nashville, Tennessee, one of the authors was perusing the wares of an unlicensed vendor and saw a Bushmaster semiautomatic assault rifle similar to the one used by John Muhammad and Lee Malvo during their 2002 killing spree in the Washington, D.C., area. When the vendor was asked what needed to be done before the gun could be purchased, the vendor responded that all he needed was to make sure that the purchaser was a Tennessee resident. Since the author looked like a Tennessee resident, he said, there was nothing else to do. It is no wonder that ATF reported (before the Republican-controlled Congress cut off the funding for such reports in 2004) that its investigations determined gun shows to be the second-leading source of illegally trafficked guns recovered in criminal investigations.[36]

A few women and minorities attend gun shows, and one of the authors has witnessed the incongruous sight of an African American browsing the available firearms at a table immediately adjacent to another vendor selling racist bumper stickers and books, but the crowds are invariably composed largely of white men. A careful observer sometimes sees some young women who appear to be making straw purchases for boyfriends who are prohibited from purchasing firearms from licensed dealers, perhaps because of drug convictions or other disqualifying felonies. The chances that a purchase will be stopped are slim. ATF, due to its limited resources, conducts investigations at about 2 percent of the more than five thousand gun shows held each year in the United States.[37] But when ATF does investigate, it often finds that prohibited purchases are taking place. An investigation of seven gun shows in Virginia, for example, resulted in dozens of arrests of purchasers who made false statements on the forms required to conduct background checks, were in possession of marijuana and cocaine, or were fugitives from justice. The NRA promptly responded by persuading its friends in Congress to pressure ATF to halt the investigations.[38]

Firearm sales are only one part of the commerce and conversation at these shows. Amid the guns and gun paraphernalia, vendors do a brisk business in antigovernment propaganda and political material. In fact, gun shows are the only place in most communities where people can purchase books such as the *Turner Diaries,* an apocalyptic novel describing how white American gun enthusiasts can organize themselves to overthrow a U.S. government dominated by black thugs and their Jewish puppet masters. In 2005, one of the authors purchased a copy of the *Turner Diaries* at the Nation's Gun Show, a quarterly event held just outside Washington. Other literary staples on the gun-show circuit include books describing how to make homemade incendiary devices, escape capture by law enforcement, carry out contract killings, and avoid paying income taxes.

Anyone not steeped in Insurrectionist ideology would likely find the mix of unregulated gun sales and extremist political materials disturbing, but for gun owners accustomed to thinking of firearms as symbols of "freedom" (understood as the power and willingness to resist a government that is essentially an occupying force), the combination seems perfectly appropriate. In principle, the Insurrectionist idea does not logically require the embrace of racism or anti-Semitism, but racists, anti-Semites, and others on the political margins have a strong attraction to the Insurrectionist theory of gun rights, for obvious reasons. The people who hold these views believe the U.S. government represents alien values by supporting the welfare state and protecting the rights of racial and religious minorities at the expense of whites and Christians, a variant on the basic Insurrectionist account of how our government works.

Mass murderers Buford Furrow, who made a name for himself by shooting young campers at a Los Angeles Jewish community center, and Timothy McVeigh, the Oklahoma City federal building bomber, spent considerable time at gun shows. McVeigh was a regular at gun shows, and although he certainly sold guns from time to time, he seemed to focus mainly on peddling antigovernment propaganda. He made a point of distributing the *Turner Diaries* and referred to it as his bible for the bombing in Oklahoma City. He was introduced to the book through an advertisement in *Soldier of Fortune*. McVeigh also sold Insurrectionist bumper stickers with slogans such as "Fear the government that fears your gun"; "A man with a gun is a citizen, a man without a gun is a subject"; and "Politicians love gun control."[39]

McVeigh formed a deep attachment to firearms, which he saw as "the first tool of freedom." He viewed his actions at Oklahoma City as a patriotic stand against oppressive government. The day of the bombing, he wore a T-shirt with a drawing of Abraham Lincoln on the front and the words of John Wilkes Booth, "Sic semper tyrannis." On the back was an image of a tree with blood dripping from the branches, superimposed over a Thomas Jefferson refrain: "The tree of liberty must be refreshed from time to time with the blood of patriots."[40] Jefferson was not above using overheated rhetoric, but he certainly never meant for the blood of innocent children to be shed in the name of liberty.[41] Nor would he have been pleased by the linkage of his words to those of Lincoln's killer. Few gun owners would try to emulate the bomber's ultimate course of action, but his ideology and political beliefs were typical of a prominent segment of the gun-show community—and entirely consistent with the Insurrectionist idea. At gun shows, McVeigh undoubtedly encountered many kindred spirits.

Furrow made frequent firearm purchases at gun shows in Washington State, including, it is believed, the weapons used in his attack. Furrow was deeply involved in the anti-Semitic and racist Aryan Nations, spending long periods of time at the group's headquarters in Hayden Lake, Idaho. Furrow was a guard at the compound when he met his future wife, Debbie Mathews. Mathews's first husband, Robert, had been part of an Aryan Nations hit team that assassinated outspoken Jewish talk show host Alan Berg in Denver in 1984. Robert Mathews was eventually killed during a shootout with FBI agents. After Furrow's capture in Las Vegas, he exclaimed that he was trying to send a "wake-up call to America to kill Jews." In a court filing, prosecutors said that Furrow, echoing the *Turner Diaries*, told them that he was "at war with the Jewish-controlled federal government."[42]

Both McVeigh and Furrow were part of an extremist subculture that is impossible to miss at gun shows, but most promoters of these events have made little or no effort to make purveyors of hatred and bigotry feel unwelcome. Booths at gun shows in major metropolitan areas routinely sell Insurrectionist material. Bumper stickers adorned with such slogans as "If I had known things would turn out this bad, I would have picked my own cotton" are offered for sale, along with Nazi war memorabilia and even complete SS uniforms. These materials seem to offend few customers, and promoters continue renting space to the vendors who sell them. The First Amendment protects this type of speech from government censorship, but promoters could simply refuse to accept such business. Most people at gun shows are not criminals or racists, but it is no exaggeration to say that these events are a breeding ground for hate and intolerance as well as a ready source of guns for anyone who has a reason—real or imagined—to fear an FBI background check.

Near the entrance to almost every gun show, the NRA operates a booth or table where members are recruited and political literature is distributed. Gun shows provide an opportunity for the NRA and other allied groups to communicate Insurrectionist ideology and spread political messages (and endorsements) among gun owners who may or may not fully understand or support the group's ideological agenda. The NRA has fought tooth and nail to block legislation that would extend the background-check system that currently applies to licensed firearm dealers at gun shows. Its intensive lobbying on this issue can best be understood as an effort to protect those who want to buy untraceable firearms with no law enforcement oversight. The fact that the NRA views this group as a core constituency speaks volumes about its ideology and objectives.

The NRA likes to call itself the nation's oldest and largest civil rights group, but its commitment to civil rights seems strangely stunted. The NRA argues that hostility toward gun possession and toward citizens who own and use firearms is a form of invidious discrimination. Gun rights, they say, should be protected with the same vigor and in the same ways as other civil rights. Yet as they press this expansive view of gun rights on legislators and the public, the NRA and its allies simultaneously stand shoulder to shoulder with racists and bigots at gun shows. This aspect of the NRA's hypocrisy reached its high-water mark when it objected to identification checks conducted by ATF on buyers at gun shows on the grounds that the checks were conducted in a racially discriminatory manner but continued to stand mute as vendors at gun shows openly sold books advocating race war and bumper stickers celebrating the virtues of slavery.

The Gun Rights Grassroots and the Blogosphere

Gun shows are an important distribution channel for Insurrectionist propaganda and other extremist literature, but the Internet is also a major tool for Insurrectionist advocacy. The Insurrectionists have created hundreds of sites for the robust discussion of guns, "gun grabbers," and "government tyranny." It is easy to find fringe sites that mix hostility toward government with gun issues,[43] but the sites set up as "legitimate" undertakings by establishment gun rights supporters are essentially identical in terms of the substance of the views they represent. At popular sites such as www.KeepandBearArms.com (run by Alan Gottlieb and founded by Angel Shamaya, who was arrested in 2006 for threatening his girlfriend and for various weapons violations) the latest gun news is discussed and dissected by hundreds of postings every day. Complaints about excessive regulation of guns and praise for armed citizens who shoot criminals are common. Even more consistent, however, is the presence of heated diatribes on the evils of government. Many of the articles on these sites have nothing to do with guns, focusing instead on the dangers of expansive government power. The same was true for the popular but now defunct site www.packing.org.

A cursory review of a day's worth of postings on the Web site www.KeepandBearArms.com continues to show a deep fear of government and its agents. A user identified as "Tick@Tock," responding to a posted article on federal standards for driver licenses, wrote, "If you think the government isn't our enemy you and I live in different countries. Granted the UN is a big, BIG enemy of ours, but that's not to say that the [U.S.] government isn't."[44] In response to an article about the murder trial of a South Carolina homeowner who killed two law enforcement agents in a property dispute, "Tdoff" wrote, "It's a rare cop that takes his oath to uphold the Constitution seriously, and if he does he'll be bumping heads with his superior. The bulk of them would much prefer a police state."[45] The homeowner, Steven Bixby, was part of the "patriot" antigovernment movement and moved to South Carolina with his family after fleeing an arrest warrant in New Hampshire. In his new hometown, Laurens, he added a domestic violence charge as well as a harassment charge for calling an acquaintance, Noel Thompson, a "fucking nigger" and threatening to kill him, all because Thompson's kids walked across Bixby's property on the way to the school-bus stop. Bixby was known to get drunk at bars and scream "Live free or die!" at other patrons. Bixby's shooting spree was precipitated when a deputy sheriff knocked on his door to discuss road upgrades in front of the house.[46] "Tdoff," however, blamed the police for the shooting, and no visitor to www.KeepandBearArms.com saw fit to point out that "Tdoff" was attacking two dead law enforcement officers who had been murdered while doing their jobs. Unfortunately, this kind of reaction is typical of the Internet echo chamber, where Insurrectionists insist to each other that gun owners are almost universally righteous citizens defending their families from criminals and their country from its government. They are far from alone in their beliefs.

Gun owners are as diverse as America itself, and as a group they are only slightly to the right of non-gun-owners on questions such as gay rights, school prayer, and other controversial social issues (although they are significantly more likely to vote for Republican candidates).[47] Many would never dream of taking up arms against the government, and they own guns for hunting and target shooting or to defend themselves and their families against crime.

If the gun rights movement's agenda were oriented around protecting and strengthening the right of law-abiding Americans to use guns for these purposes, then the scope of disagreement over gun policy would be exceedingly narrow. Public opinion research shows that an overwhelming majority of Americans—including most gun owners— supports policies designed to improve accountability. For example, gun owners strongly support requiring background checks for all sales at gun shows. Even licensing and registration, the bête noire of gun rights fundamentalism, attracts strong support from gun owners, and many Americans assume that federal law already imposes both background-check requirements and licensing and registration for all guns.[48]

Most gun control debates, however, are not really about policy, and the gun rights groups prefer it that way. A major basis for opposition to most gun control laws is the idea that these laws are merely a pretext for gathering information that can be used by the state to seize privately held firearms in the event of a political crisis. The leaders of gun rights groups employ the ideology of Insurrectionism to motivate gun owners to support the broader worldview espoused by such groups. Their leaders and theorists portray the debate over guns as a black-and-white struggle between "pro-gun" lovers of freedom and "antigun" statists.

These advocates define any proposal to regulate access to guns—for example, by requiring all buyers to undergo background checks—as a blow to liberty, even though many gun owners support background checks as a way to make it harder for convicted felons to buy weapons. Similarly, proposals to require licensing and registration so police can trace guns used in crimes to their last owner (and not just their original retail purchaser, who may be several steps removed from the most recent owner in the chain of possession) are immediately dismissed as nothing more than a way to make it easier for the government to seize all guns in private hands whenever it gets the chance. In other words, the gun debate has morphed into a discussion of the role of government, allowing gun rights groups to tap into a broad vein of undifferentiated antigovernment sentiment. For example, Phil Van Cleave, president of the Virginia Citizens Defense League, told Virginia legislators in 2006 that a bill to require background checks on all firearms sales at gun shows was a step toward government confiscation of handguns,[49] even though existing law requires background checks for all firearm sales at gun stores, a system that has neither resulted in confiscation nor created a database that would allow the state to confiscate guns at some point in the future.

Inconvenient facts are never allowed to interfere with the Insurrectionist message: all proposals to regulate any aspect of the manufacture, sale, or use of guns are simply government efforts to take guns away from every law-abiding citizen who wants a firearm for any purpose. Gun control advocates have failed to take seriously this grossly oversimplified and wildly inaccurate view of firearms regulation because they cannot grasp how any significant number of people could be persuaded by such preposterous claims. The problem is not so much the power of the argument, however, as the fact that it has been repeated so often that many gun owners accept it as true, while gun control advocates have failed to answer it.

Insurrectionist rhetoric is now a standard feature of the gun rights movement's support of unrestricted access to firearms and opposition to even the mildest form of gun regulation. At an October 2006 forum sponsored by the NRA at George Mason Law School in Virginia, Shaun Kranish, the founder of www.I-Carry.org, asked the gathered group of gun rights activists whether the onslaught of recent gun regulations is an indication that they should start "the revolution" against government tyranny. The crowd, many of whom were openly carrying sidearms, did not rush out into the streets and attempt to seize control of the municipal government, but no one challenged the premise of Kranish's question—the idea that we stand at the threshold where our government might legitimately be challenged with force. One of the speakers explained that while armed revolution would be justified in principle, things really were not all that bleak for gun owners yet, because six years of solid Republican control of the legislative and executive branches of the federal government had helped to curb some of the most offensive limits on gun owners and individual freedom.[50]

The Insurrectionist leanings of grassroots leaders present at the NRA forum should alarm all citizens who believe that effective democratic government is an indispensable component of real freedom. The uncritical acceptance of Insurrectionist explanations of the role of guns in a free society is profoundly unhealthy for democratic institutions and values. Just a few weeks after the forum, Congress changed hands and the NRA immediately predicted the impending onslaught of "government gun-grabbing." In early 2007, Kranish focused his antigovernment zealotry by becoming an active supporter of New Hampshire couple Ed and Elaine Brown, who embody the sort of crackpot resistance to government that is the natural consequence of Insurrectionist thinking.

The Browns have refused to pay income taxes since 1996, claiming that the U.S. government lacks the authority to levy such taxes. In January 2007, the Browns were convicted of conspiracy and tax evasion.[51] They continue to adhere to their belief that there is no legitimate law requiring the payment of income taxes and that the entire U.S. legal system is under the control of the Freemasons. In April 2007, the Browns were sentenced in absentia to sixty-three months in federal prison, but they forcibly resisted arrest at their fortified compound. They were finally taken into custody six months later.

Ed Brown was the national leader of several organizations dedicated to protecting citizens from the government, including the U.S. Constitution Rangers and the Un-American Activities Investigations Commission.[52] He has been an outspoken detractor of the United Nations and the power of the U.S. government, especially with regard to the income tax and gun control. The Browns have gained a great deal of support because of their involvement in these Insurrectionist groups. Kranish, one of Ed Brown's most outspoken supporters, created the Browns' official Web site, MaketheStand.com, and was a frequent surreptitious visitor to their New Hampshire residence, providing them with supplies and links to the outside world after law enforcement cut off access to their compound after their convictions. Randy Weaver, who precipitated the Ruby Ridge standoff, also has been outspoken in his support for the Browns and his belief that the government has unlawfully brainwashed American citizens.[53] Ron Paul, a libertarian Republican who represents Texas in Congress and mounted a surprisingly strong campaign for president in 2008, has compared tax evaders like the Browns to Martin Luther King Jr. and Mahatma Gandhi.[54]

This support enabled the Browns to prevent U.S. marshals from entering their fortresslike residence until October 2007. Despite government efforts to force the Browns out by cutting off their power, phone lines, and Internet, they managed to live in relative comfort because supporters provided them with solar generators, disposable cell phones, surveillance equipment, and food.[55] In September 2007, four of their primary supporters, Jason Gerhard, Cirino "Reno" Gonzalez, Dan Riley, and Robert Wolffe, were arrested and charged with providing firearms to the Browns and conspiracy to prevent officers of the United States from discharging their duties. A number of firearms were found at the residences of these supporters, including .50-caliber high-powered rifles and assault rifles, including AK-47s.[56]

Kranish played a pivotal role in their arrest by unknowingly leading a deputy U.S. marshal to their doorstep. Early in the standoff, Kranish formed an Internet friendship with "Dutch," a U.S. marshal posing as a Brown supporter. After months of correspondence, Dutch and Kranish met in person and decided to visit the Brown residence. Kranish brought Dutch to the Browns' Plainfield compound, enabling the U.S. marshal to spend time with Ed Brown and gain a great deal of insight into his plans to evade arrest indefinitely. The next day, Dutch led a small group of U.S. marshals, disguised as supporters, into the Brown residence, where they peacefully took the Browns into custody.[57]

The Browns and their supporters have threatened the lives of numerous judges involved in the case and their family members. Prior to his arrest, Ed Brown took to the airwaves on his radio show, *Ed Brown under Siege,* and openly threatened the judges: "Once this thing starts, we're going to seek them out and hunt them down." He later reaffirmed the threat, announcing, "We're going to bring them to justice. So anybody who wishes to join them, you go right ahead and join them. But I promise you, long after I'm gone, they're going to seek out you and your bloodline."[58] After two judges recused themselves from the case because of these death threats, pretrial hearings were moved to Maine.

The Browns' supporters said they believe that the couple's arrest was an act of war and that they retain the right to retaliate against the U.S. government. Kranish asserts that the U.S. government's efforts to bring the Browns to justice warrant a revolution: "If you corner us, you give us no option."[59] He had been recorded numerous times on *Ed Brown under Siege* urging other gun owners to take up the fight against the American government.

While few people actually stop paying taxes or gird themselves for an impending war with the government, the ideology that supports these actions is an integral part of the contemporary gun rights movement and its Insurrectionist ideology. When the Browns and others like them begin to take the Insurrectionist idea seriously and decide to act on it, the NRA and others who have worked to popularize it—for whatever reason—ultimately bear some responsibility for the results.

In newspapers, blogs and public forums across the country, run-of-the-mill gun rights supporters have learned to frame the issue of gun control as a menace to individual liberty and as a species of government tyranny and oppression. The currency of Insurrectionist conceptions of gun rights was evidenced in the responses to a January 2007 article in the *Northwest Arkansas Morning News* detailing the arrest and impending trial of Hollis Wayne Fincher, the self-appointed leader of a county militia, on a charge of possessing several unregistered machine guns. The story quickly focused on government oppression. Fincher said he had armed himself to protect against "illegal aggression by federal authorities, including the Bureau of Alcohol, Tobacco and Firearms." Using the e-mail comment section provided by the newspaper, a Fincher supporter with the user name "felon" wrote, "This country is a dictatorship under the guise of dem[ocracy]. [T]he feds care less for what the people want or vote for. [A]ll that matters to them is power to control we the people. [L]ook how they ignore the immigration laws."[60]

A supporter writing under the name "Beefree" wrote, "WHEN YOU

LET PEOPLE DO WHATEVER THEY WANT, YOU GET WOOD-
STOCK. WHEN YOU LET GOVERNMENTS DO WHATEVER THEY
WANT, YOU GET AUSCHWITZ." Responding to "Beefree," another
user wrote, "I say when you let Government do what ever they want,
you get Waco." Other postings spun the intent of the framers in drafting
the Second Amendment and the original authority of the Declaration of
Independence in an effort to defend Fincher's actions and assail the
power of the state.[61] A few voices argued that Fincher was a problem,
but most responses contended that in this effort to enforce the firearm
laws, the government had effectively become a police state that had
stripped Fincher of his basic rights, even though Fincher would stand
trial before a jury of his peers and be represented by counsel of his
choosing.

A federal jury eventually convicted Fincher. His lawyer, Oscar Stil-
ley, vowed that Fincher would appeal all the way to the Supreme Court
if necessary. Picking up the Insurrectionist points, he argued that government has become oppressive. "Basically, the Second Amendment
got defined away so that if the government can tell us what's affected by
the Second Amendment, if anything, I'd like to know what it is," Stil-
ley said. "If this case holds up, the federal government has gone from a
government of limited powers to a government that's absolutely unlimited by the Constitution, by the grant of power (by the states to the federal government) or anything else except politics." The first comment
in response to this article instructs Fincher sympathizers to "support
the Gun Owners of America, NRA, JPFA [sic], etc., hoping that they
may have some counsel be willing to take this case pro bono."[62]

Fincher's defenders did not attempt to make an argument about the
public-safety implications of unrestricted access to machine guns—
they cannot sustain that claim. Instead, they employed the rhetoric of
opposition to government power and support for liberty that plays into
current "conservative" themes of reducing taxes and reducing the size
of government. Moreover, the discussion this case engenders among av-
erage citizens in a regional newspaper picks up many of the major Insurrectionist themes advanced by more sophisticated gun rights advocates, including the claim that Hitler relied on gun control and that the
founders enshrined a right to armed revolt in the U.S. Constitution. The

supporter "felon" even found a way to incorporate the claim that law enforcement should focus on immigrants rather than on machine guns.

Many other gun rights enthusiasts have picked up the Hitler theme. The argument about Nazis and gun control has become a common part of the general discourse about guns. For example, at NoSpeed-Bumps.com (subtitled "Expanding American Freedom in the 21st Century"), blogger Captain Colin wrote from the United Kingdom,

> Why did we all bother to stop the Nazi's in WW2 by using guns and then let them control us by voting for the buggers!
>
> United Nations, United Nazi's more like.
>
> Pro gun = pro human rights, anti gun = Nazi's! (Or just plain stupid).[63]

The Nazi theme is also prominent in the hate mail received on a regular basis by the Coalition to Stop Gun Violence. In one e-mail, a woman wrote, "Shame on you for your Nazi-inspired agenda!!! Hitler was also a big supporter of 'gun control,' and everybody knows what the result of that was! Shame on you!"[64]

On Web sites dedicated specifically to gun rights, calls for actual armed resistance against the government are often debated. At the defunct www.packing.org, one of the most popular gun rights sites at the time, the comments in the "Gun Talk" section got to the essence of the Insurrectionist line of reasoning. One user, "Woody," wrote on November 26, 2006, "I don't think anyone here is advocating revolution, but please know that it is not off the table, nor will it ever be off the table—as long as we retain the arms necessary to the task. . . . However, these people need to know—until we get a Congress that will repeal the unconstitutional law, or a Court that will shoot it down, these people need to know there is a cost if they go any further." Responding in the same thread, "Brentt" congratulated "Woody" on his excellent points and added, "Will we as Americans be able to draw the line at confiscation? I sure as hell like to think so. Isn't having the will and the ability to resist tyranny what makes us Americans? Isn't that what made us free and has kept us free up to this point in our history? Many others in other nations have not been so lucky. They have had neither the will nor the ability to resist tyranny. Need I go into the many examples in the 20th century and even the 21st century where millions upon millions of citizens have been slaughtered by their own governments? Can't happen here you suppose? Keep living in your dream world if that is what you think."[65]

This thread is not at all unusual, and it typifies the thought process of gun rights advocates who take the Insurrectionist idea seriously and are moved to consider the appropriate time and reason to begin the revolution. On www.packing.org under the topic, "Violating the 2nd Amendment is treason already," "Mod 658" wrote on October 23, 2006, "It is treason to not use the Second Amendment when its [sic] needed. I believe its [sic] treason to let this and other rights be frittered away in the name of security and public safety. Yet here we are. Are we ready for the fight?" In response, "Robie Cagle" wrote approvingly of the Confederacy's resistance to the Union and added, "We have an inherent right to self protection, and a responsibility to defend our freedom to the last. As pointed out by another, insurgencies cause a great deal of mayhem, especially if the initial blows come from many sides, and cover the land. One good, coordinated blow could create the opportunities needed to force the [U.S.] government to act, hopefully to correct the errors of their ways."[66]

We are not suggesting that more than a few of these bloggers and message board posters will ever actually act on their fantasies, but the larger and more dangerous problem is the antidemocratic sentiment that is part and parcel of the Insurrectionist idea. These bloggers are, in effect, claiming that their possession of firearms makes them supercitizens ready to take the initiative to confront the government with violence. As we will discuss later in this book, the essence of our democracy is equality, and an armed citizen does not get special veto rights over legislation or have a special or more legitimate claim on freedom.

Liberal Law Professors and *D.C. v. Heller*

In a remarkable case of strange bedfellows, the Insurrectionists have been aided by some of the intellectual elites that they so frequently vilify—liberal law professors. Writing in law reviews and casebooks, a handful of legal academics with left-leaning political attachments have given the Insurrectionist idea a patina of intellectual respectability. Until the 1990s, few law professors paid any attention to the Second Amendment. If the subject was addressed at all in law school classrooms, it was described as a collective right of the states to organize militias as they saw fit. Until the U.S. Supreme Court's decision in *District of Columbia v. Heller*, described in depth in chapter 9, the federal courts had uniformly upheld gun control laws against constitutional attack on the basis of a 1939 case, *U.S. v. Miller*, that arose from a challenge to the federal ban on sawed-off shotguns. *Miller* upheld a conviction because in the absence of a showing that the weapon in question has "some reasonable relationship to the preservation or efficiency of a well regulated militia, we cannot say that the Second Amendment guarantees the right to keep and bear such an instrument."[67]

As we have described, Nelson Lund, David Kopel and other right-wing lawyers—some with academic affiliations—have worked for years to churn out law review articles and hold symposia designed to challenge the received understanding of the Second Amendment and elaborate its Insurrectionist roots. These efforts would have come to naught if a group of liberal law professors had not decided to dabble in Second Amendment scholarship. These quick forays into the field started with the University of Texas law professor Sanford Levinson, author of "The Embarrassing Second Amendment," and continued with such well-known law professors as William Van Alstyne of the College of William and Mary, Akhil Reed Amar of Yale, and Laurence Tribe of Harvard. These professors generally did not immerse themselves deeply in the primary source material used to justify Insurrectionist claims about the original understanding of the Second Amendment, and some of these treatments of the issue were appallingly superficial.

Partly as a result of the interest generated by these academics, the Second Amendment discussion in law schools today is more complex. In the most recent update to his constitutional treatise, Tribe, a liberal legal icon, for the first time describes the Second Amendment as an individual right: "The amendment achieves its central purpose by assuring that the federal government may not disarm individual citizens without some unusually strong justification consistent with the authority of the states to organize their own militias. That assurance in turn is provided through recognizing a right (admittedly of uncertain scope) on the part of individuals to possess and use firearms in the defense of themselves and their homes—not a right to hunt for game, quite clearly."[68] Tribe made it clear that he now believes that the Second Amendment may well establish an individual right to own guns "to protect the people of the several states from an all-powerful national government."[69] Insurrectionists have lauded Tribe's "conversion," and his failure to consider the implications of the theory he endorsed (such as how and when an individual exercises a right of self-protection against the federal government in practice) added fuel to the fire.

Unfortunately, the liberal law professors who have lent support to the Insurrectionist theory of interpretation of the Second Amendment have not parsed the various possible scopes of an individual right to own guns, and they approve an Insurrectionary reading of the amendment's purposes without much discussion and often on the basis of nothing more than an argument about the grammatical construction of the text.[70] The contours of an individual right could vary greatly, of course. For example, an individual right to participate in a state militia would be among the most narrow of interpretations; an individual right to bear arms against criminals (traditionally a common law, not a constitutional right) would be broader; while the broadest and most radical interpretation would be an individual right to take up arms against the government.

The third interpretation is exactly where these liberal law professors would lead us. Levinson and Van Alstyne, for example, have argued that the framers intentionally diverged from the centralized power of contemporary European states and deliberately created a different model with armed citizens as a check on government power. Van Alstyne writes that "the Second Amendment represented not an adoption, but a rejection, of this vision—a vision of the security state."[71] Van Alstyne pontificates, "Specifically, [the Second Amendment] looks to an ultimate reliance on the common citizen who has a right to keep and bear arms rather than only to some standing army." Moreover, he adds, "There are doubtless certain national constitutions that put a privileged emphasis on the security of 'the state,' but such as they are, they are all *unlike* our Constitution and the provisions they have respecting their security do not appear in a similarly phrased Bill of Rights."[72]

We attribute the wave of endorsements for an Insurrectionist reading of the Second Amendment by liberals to a failure to analyze the legal and political history surrounding the adoption of the Bill of Rights with anything like the seriousness that is applied to other subjects. The academics who have embraced the Insurrectionist theory of the Second Amendment have tended to rely heavily—and for the most part uncritically—on the scholarship/advocacy of the right-wing lawyers who pioneered the Insurrectionist theory by cutting and pasting selectively from primary sources to give their conclusions the appearance of fidelity to the historic record.[73] The liberal adherents to the Insurrectionist theory of the Second Amendment do not intend to induce ordinary citizens to take up machine guns and revolt, but they unthinkingly lend their credibility to a warped and dangerous conception of how our system of government works.

The framers would have recognized the claims advanced by Insurrectionist lawyers as the same arguments advanced by radical Antifederalists and flatly rejected by the Federalist majorities that dominated the Constitutional Convention and the first Congress, which adopted the Second Amendment. These were the same framers who scrapped the Articles of Confederation in favor of the Constitution expressly because the latter gave the national government the ability to maintain domestic tranquility and compete economically and militarily with the great powers of Europe. In an otherwise thoughtful article about the structure of the Bill of Rights, Amar argues that "history also connected the right to keep and bear arms with the idea of popular sovereignty. In Locke's influential *Second Treatise of Government*, the people's right to alter or abolish tyrannous government invariably required a popular appeal to arms. To Americans in 1789, this was not merely speculative theory. It was the lived experience of their age. In their lifetimes, they had seen the Lockean words of the Declaration made flesh (and blood) in a Revolution wrought by arms." In a footnote, Amar explains that the Constitution did not actually countenance violence: "Between 1776 and 1789, Americans domesticated and defused the idea of violent revolution by channeling it into the newly renovated legal instrument of the peaceful convention. Through the idea of conventions, Americans legalized revolution, substituting ballots for bullets."[74] The point made in the footnote undercuts the claim that the framers intended to enshrine in the Constitution a right to engage in political violence, and Amar's nuanced discussion of the Second Amendment has been interpreted as a defense of Insurrectionist theory.

Citing Amar's "right to alter or abolish" language, Brent McIntosh, writing in the *Alabama Law Review*, constructs an argument that goes well beyond Amar's thesis and finds a clear right to revolution in the Second Amendment. McIntosh laments that the power of private citizens to assert their political views with firearms has been eclipsed by the power of the U.S. military. According to McIntosh,

> The federal government can now muster war-waging capabilities that, though they might be used only at a terrible cost in American lives, could not be overcome by even the most determined of popular uprisings. With modern weaponry and the diminished interest of American civilians in things martial, gone is the era when a concerted popular effort could have deterred even the most destructive resistance of the government to its own overthrow.
>
> With these two passings—the disappearance from Second Amendment doctrine of the revolutionary focus and the death of the American citizenry's absolute ability to overthrow the government by force—so has gone the deepest, most profound, and most vital function of the Second Amendment.[75]

When such arguments are taken seriously in legal academia, it is little wonder that many gun owners have come to believe that they are the modern incarnation of the spirit of revolution that led the founders to break with the British monarchy. Even if taking down the government is not really possible now, why shouldn't patriots who object to higher marginal tax rates or permissive immigration laws breathe new life into the Second Amendment's promise of a right to shoot disagreeable politicians? It is not uncommon to see the work of the liberal legal academics plastered on Insurrectionist Web sites offering justification and cover for anyone with a grievance against the government.

Of course, many of these left-wing academics belatedly realized the implications of embracing a right to insurrection and have tried to downplay their positions, asserting that their writings should not be used as a justification to find gun control laws unconstitutional. Tribe has suggested that the challenge to the District of Columbia's handgun ban in *D.C. v. Heller* should have failed because "under any plausible standard of review, a legislature's choice to limit the citizenry to rifles, shotguns and other weapons less likely to augment urban violence need not, and should not, be viewed as an unconstitutional abridgment of the right of the people to keep or bear arms."[76] Amar has written that "to rail against central tyranny today is to be considerably more paranoid than were the Founders, given the general track record of the United States since 1787. Put another way, given that ballots and the First Amendment have proved pretty good devices for keeping the feds under control, bullets and the Second Amendment need not bear as much weight today as some pessimists anticipated two centuries ago."[77] Moreover, none of these liberal scholars ultimately agreed to sign any of the briefs urging the Supreme Court to strike down the District of Columbia's gun laws in the *Heller* case. Unfortunately, the horse has left the barn. Professor Carl Bogus has noted that the flirtation with Insurrectionist theory by the liberal law professors who endorsed the "individual right school was politically important. These . . . important scholars gave this position respectability, and their membership in the individual right camp was loudly trumpeted by the gun rights community."[78]

In June 2008, in a 5–4 opinion written by Justice Antonin Scalia, the Supreme Court ruled in *Heller* that the Second Amendment guarantees an individual right to own firearms.[79] Scalia (like Tribe in his treatise) declined to articulate the scope of the right other than to say that it definitely included the right to have a handgun to protect "hearth and home."[80] Scalia alluded to the Insurrectionist idea, hinting that the right to own and use guns may be far broader than self-defense in the home. In his majority opinion, he suggests that the Second Amendment could not simply have been intended to protect the organized state militia, because that interpretation would exclude the possibility of individual citizens with their arms banding together and acting as a check on government: "If . . . the Second Amendment right is no more than the right to keep and use weapons as a member of an organized militia . . . if, that is, the *organized* militia is the sole institutional beneficiary of the Second Amendment's guarantee—it does not assure the existence of a 'citizens' militia' as a safeguard against tyranny."[81] This rather circular argument assumes that the Second Amendment must not be limited to service in a militia because otherwise the right would apply only to service in a militia.

In the ultimate case of buyer's remorse, within hours of the release of the *Heller* decision, Levinson wrote a posting for the Huffington Post Web site complaining that he was "dismayed" by the Court's opinion and decrying the historical methodology in both the majority and dissenting opinions.[82] He complains about the same "law-office history" in service of advocacy that he employed in his "Embarrassing Second Amendment" article. In many ways, Levinson's article was responsible for making gun rights revisionism intellectually respectable in the academy and ultimately among jurists, and the article—as much as any other single event—laid the groundwork for the *Heller* decision.

Maybe Levinson and Tribe and the others were not serious when they argued that Americans should have an individual right to take up arms against the U.S. government. Maybe they should have tried a little harder to untangle the complicated history of the Second Amendment before renouncing established interpretations of the right to bear arms. Backed by a grassroots conservative political movement, their arguments got out of control and are now enshrined in a Supreme Court decision—which, by Justice Scalia's design, is clearly just the first in what will be a series of future decisions to flesh out the breadth of the Second Amendment. The lower federal courts have just began to hear challenges to gun laws under *Heller*, but the progressive legal theorists who aided and abetted the revolution in constitutional doctrine that produced *Heller* clearly have unleashed a theory with no clear limiting principles and have helped ensure that this theory would be put into practice, with troubling implications in the real world.

Dissenters and Enforcement of the Insurrectionist Orthodoxy

Anyone who doubts that the Insurrectionist idea now operates as the central animating force behind the modern gun rights movement need only consider what happens when firearm enthusiasts dare to question the Insurrectionist idea in public.

A recent example is the experience of one of America's most famous hunters and outdoor enthusiasts, Jim Zumbo. Zumbo has written thousands of articles for hunting magazines, hosted a television show, and served as a board member for many conservation and hunting organizations, including the Outdoor Writers Association of America, the Rocky Mountain Elk Foundation, and the U.S. Sportsmen's Alliance. He has had professional affiliations with the NRA, Remington Arms Company, *Outdoor Life* magazine, and a host of other outdoor-oriented products. All this came crashing down on him after he had the audacity to question whether assault weapons should be viewed as necessary and appropriate for sporting uses. On February 16, 2007, after a day of testing a new Remington .17-caliber Spitfire bullet while hunting coyotes in southeastern Wyoming, Zumbo wrote on his *Outdoor Life* blog,

> I must be living in a vacuum. The guides on our hunt tell me that the use of AR and AK rifles have a rapidly growing following among hunters, especially prairie dog hunters. I had no clue. Only once in my life have I ever seen anyone using one of these firearms.
>
> I call them "assault" rifles, which may upset some people. Excuse me, maybe I'm a traditionalist, but I see no place for these weapons among our hunting fraternity. I'll go so far as to call them "terrorist" rifles. . . .
>
> Sorry, folks, in my humble opinion, these things have no place in hunting. We don't need to be lumped into the group of people who terrorize the world with them, which is an obvious concern. I've always been comfortable with the statement that hunters don't use assault rifles. We've always been proud of our "sporting firearms."
>
> This really has me concerned. As hunters, we don't need the image of walking around the woods carrying one of these weapons. To most of the public, an assault rifle is a terrifying thing. Let's divorce ourselves

from them. I say game departments should ban them from the prairies and woods.[83]

The response was fast and furious. In just a few days, the blog drew six thousand comments excoriating Zumbo and calling for his removal from *Outdoor Life*. One commenter, "dan55362," wrote, "I sure hope that all of Mr. Dumbo's sponsors drop out of all association directly or indirectly with this Idiot. If you didn't know any better you would think Mr. Jim Zumbo was sleeping with Sarah Brady. This truly is a Sad time for all!!!!"[84] The Zumbo story shot across the Internet. Visitors to chat sites catering to gun enthusiasts went after Zumbo with venom. A Web site called Dump Zumbo (now Zumbo Dumped) appeared and demanded his head. Dump Zumbo's main contributor, BCR-Shorty, explained on another Web site that "The 2nd Amendment isn't about gun ownership for 'Sporting Purposes' to protect your hunting rifles & shotguns. The spirit and intent of the 2nd Amendment is about ensuring that the current 'Arms of the Day' are in the hands of the general populace to deter tyranny from enemies abroad & within from depriving any U.S. citizens of our life, liberty, property and our great country."[85] The story had morphed from a discussion about appropriate hunting weapons into a defense of the Insurrectionist idea.

As soon as the discussion turned to Zumbo's assault on freedom, he did not stand a chance with the Insurrectionist crowd. Within a few days of making the comments, Zumbo was dropped by all his outdoor sponsors and lost his television show and magazine deals, including one with the NRA. In terminating its relationship with Zumbo, the NRA made it clear that challenges to the Insurrectionist worldview (even from gun enthusiasts such as Zumbo) would not be tolerated and used the opportunity to threaten Congress:

> The ensuing wave of grassroots response in support of the Second Amendment is a clear indication that America's gun owners will act swiftly and decisively to counter falsehoods or misrepresentations perpetuated by any member of the media—whether it is one of the major networks or a fellow gun owner.
> That depth of feeling and the unanimity of the response from the na-

tion's firearms owners sends a message to the new Congress. It says that millions of people understand the issue of semi-autos and will resist with an immense singular political will any attempts to create a new ban on semi-automatic firearms.[86]

Other outdoor writers tried to come to Zumbo's defense but were treated with an equal degree of hostility. Pat Wray, an outdoor writer from Oregon, used his column to ask Zumbo's critics to think about their actions: "Something very strange happened in the world of outdoor communication this week. One of America's best known hunting writers slipped and metaphorically cut himself—so a few thousand of his closest friends ate him alive." Wray continued,

> For decades the NRA has fostered a climate of fear and paranoia among gun owners. They have hammered home the message that everyone is out to take our guns and that compromise is tantamount to treason. They created an attitude within their membership that anyone who disagreed was an enemy and the best defense was a good offense. Nowhere has that message taken root as strongly as within the owners of the military style rifles, and it was they who came after Zumbo in their thousands.
>
> It is ironic—and tragic—that the NRA's message, so effectively delivered for so many years, has come back to ruin the professional life of one of their own.[87]

While some gun owners reflected on the situation and concluded that efforts to punish dissenting points of view within their ranks would be inconsistent with a professed commitment to individual freedom, Wray quickly found himself in the crosshairs of firearms-rights advocates who uncritically accept the idea that challenges to the Insurrectionist idea are tantamount to the repudiation of democracy and freedom. On KeepandBearArms.com, a leading gun rights Web site, the response was addressed to "Zumbo" Pat Wray. One person commented, "Oh yeah Patrick? We're zealots now! Maybe Pat needs a little zealots treatment as well. He can go join Zumbo in the unemployment line."[88] In a comment on the online version of Wray's article, an angry reader got to the heart of the matter:

Jim Zumbo didn't get it and now Pat Wray doesn't get [it]. . . . What Zumbo's words amounted to was an attack on your and my 2nd Amendment rights which was never about hunting. The 2nd Amendment was put in place to guarantee that the Citizens of the United States are armed and to give them a fighting chance in case someone declared themselves dictator of the United States and declared our Constitution along with all Amendments null and void. Enemies of our Constitution want to get rid of the 2nd Amendment first because it would in effect pull the teeth on the Citizens of these United States. We would no longer have a fighting chance.[89]

For having the temerity to suggest that there is room for debate about civilian use of weapons designed for the military, Zumbo and to a lesser extent Wray (who in fact opposes banning assault weapons) endured vicious personal attacks and loss of livelihood. For Insurrectionists, the world is divided into black and white, with the good guys defined by their support for the proposition that Americans should stockpile armaments for use against their own government. A posting from "quoteman" on KeepandBearArms.com makes this point: "The one good thing that came out of this is how I now honestly believe that gun owners as a whole have actually drawn their line in the sand. If Congress passes anything remotely close to the [19]94 [assault weapons] ban it might just ignite a nation. And our little group of 20 will be right on the front lines. Molon Labe!"[90] "Molon labe" is Greek for "Come and take them!" According to the Firing Line, the self-proclaimed "leading online forum for firearm enthusiasts," owned by *S.W.A.T. Magazine*, gun owners

have adopted this defiant utterance as a battle cry in our war against oppression because it says so clearly and simply towards those who would take our arms.

It signifies our determination to not strike the first blow, but also to not stand mute and allow our loved ones, and all that we believe in and stand for, to be trampled by men who would deprive us of our God-given—or natural, if you will—rights to suit their own ends.[91]

It is past time to take the Insurrectionist idea seriously and create a cogent and compelling response. The failure of progressives to do so has allowed the gun rights movement to chip away at this country's most important values.[92] The core belief that supports American democracy is that each vote has equal weight, so anyone who dislikes a particular elective or legislative outcome is obliged to work through democratic institutions such as the courts or future elections to change the outcome. The Insurrectionists reject this premise in favor of a political value system in which might makes right and the people who are willing and able to bring armed force to bear are entitled to compel the resolution of political controversies according to their preferences.

In essence, Insurrectionists are trying to cultivate the antidemocratic citizen, echoing the sentiments of the Civil War rebels who decided to fight rather than to abide by election results they found not to their liking. This line of thinking was played out with disastrous results in the nineteenth century. If we allow this idea to be resuscitated as a respectable approach to politics and citizenship, we will regret that decision in the twenty-first.

PART TWO

HISTORY ACCORDING TO
THE INSURRECTIONISTS

CHAPTER FOUR

THE FOUNDING

Insurrectionist propagandists often try to tie their theoretical account of the relationship between guns and government to historical episodes in which, they claim, egregious violations of human rights or even mass murder could have been avoided if only the victims had been armed. With regard to the founding of the United States, they claim that our forefathers wisely chose to guarantee a right of insurrection as a check on the excesses of centralized power, with the result that our system has kept the inevitably oppressive tendencies of government under control. In this chapter, we argue in favor of a competing interpretation of the period surrounding the framing of the U.S. Constitution and point out why the Insurrectionist account of the relationship between guns and democratic government was as untenable at the time the Constitution was adopted as it is today.

Any firearms regulation, according to the Insurrectionists, is at odds with the tradition of respect for freedom that our founders bestowed on us. In the eccentric lexicon of the Insurrectionists, a self-styled "pro-freedom" faction is amply justified in defying not only the most modest forms of firearms regulation but any public policy choice they find contrary to their conception of liberty. This interpretation of the meaning of the Second Amendment casts some of our greatest statesmen in the role of conspirators seeking to deprive our government of the tools it needs to function effectively. By advancing the myth that America was founded at least in part on the idea that government is an alien force, the Insurrectionists are trying to legitimize values that are fundamentally hostile to the survival of democracy not only as we have known it but also as our founding fathers knew it.

In fact, the bizarre teaching that the state should be kept as weak as possible to prevent it from oppressing its citizens endangers both citizens' physical safety and individual liberties. As we discuss later in this chapter, most human beings prefer living under government—in some cases, even highly imperfect governments—because anarchy sets the stage for chaos and violence, failing to protect freedom in any meaningful sense. Contemporary Somalis and Iraqis, though abundantly armed, are constantly endangered. They have no freedom worthy of the name— no freedom to move about, no freedom to conduct commerce, no freedom to express themselves in the public sphere. More precisely, they cannot exercise these freedoms without risking their lives, though no government is trying to repress them. Without security, in short, there is no freedom. The United States has succeeded as a free and orderly society not because it is armed to the teeth but in spite of it. Our system of government sustains itself, as Abraham Lincoln knew it must, by ballots instead of bullets. Our vibrant democracy allows room for private gun ownership, yet Insurrectionist ideology denigrates at every opportunity the cultural and institutional safeguards that make it possible.

When this country was born, did our founders bestow on us a special legacy of continuous armed confrontation with a sovereign state? The Insurrectionists insist that the Second Amendment enshrines virtually unlimited rights for every American to own and carry firearms and that those rights form an integral part of the constitutional bulkhead that holds tyranny at bay. Let the Europeans and Asians give up their guns, they say, but for Americans, let private gun ownership endure as a guarantor of freedom.

The Insurrectionist argument that "freedom is not free" appeals to the noble sentiment that sometimes our ideals require sacrifice, including a willingness to die to defend political liberty. For the Insurrectionists, violent crime fueled by easy access to firearms by drug dealers and street gangs is simply one of the sacrifices we have to make to keep our society free. Even if a gun control law might make citizens safer by, for example, requiring background checks on all firearms purchases at gun shows so that convicted felons would have difficulty getting access to weapons, the Insurrectionists would say the law is a bad bargain if it limits citizens' ability to fulfill their responsibilities under the Second Amendment.

The question, then, is whether American history teaches that widespread and unregulated individual access to firearm ownership protects Americans from government tyranny (even if it is anathema to democratic values), and if so, whether that notion is embodied in and protected by the Second Amendment. In other words, is the antidemocratic effect of the Insurrectionist claim an unfortunate but inescapable consequence of the Second Amendment, much as the inadmissibility of evidence in criminal trials is sometimes an inescapable result of the Fourth or Fifth Amendment? The answer depends on the meaning of the Second Amendment and to some extent on the intent behind our constitutional framework more generally. If Americans are guaranteed an individual right to own firearms to perpetually prepare for armed conflict with the state or federal government, then almost any gun law that operates to identify gun owners or restrict access to certain types of firearms, such as assault rifles, is unconstitutional. Automatic weapons might be unsuitable for hunting or fighting off burglars, for example, but they are arguably well adapted to the demands of guerrilla warfare against the government. Nobody would try to take on the U.S. Marines (or even the local police department) armed only with a musket. By the same token, background checks—or even licensing and registration—for firearms purchases do not interfere with law-abiding citizens' ability to acquire and keep guns for target shooting and self-defense, but they might give the government access to information about gun owners that could be used to locate and disarm them during an outbreak of political violence. Conversely, if our guarantees extend to us only the right to participate in a well-regulated and state-sponsored militia—or even the individual right to own a gun for self-defense—then most gun laws are valid and democratic values and institutions take precedence over the martial fantasies of the Insurrectionists.

The Insurrectionists claim that the Second Amendment gives self-anointed patriots the right to resist and even attempt to overthrow the U.S. government by force if they think the country is flirting with tyranny. However, only a gross misreading of our law and our history would conflate the prerogative of the individual to attack the United States, which is in fact insurrection, and the "natural right" of revolution, which never inheres in an individual or even in an individual state.

The Constitution, then, recognizes no right to insurrection. If there is a natural law right to revolution, then no one in the founding generation, except the most radical Antifederalists, would have viewed this right as belonging to individual citizens. The right to revolution, if it exists at all, is a right of the states, and mustering a militia requires keeping track of who is armed, mandates certain types of weapons while prohibiting others, and demands extensive training of members. Any understanding of the right to keep and bear arms that bars the state from effectively using extensive regulation to organize its militia is unsupportable. There is no denying that ours is a nation born of a collective revolution, but our founders were quick to squelch any suggestion that insurrection might be a legitimate form of recourse for any disgruntled constituency in the new democracy. The founders did not bequeath to us a tradition of endless armed political violence or endless preparation to carry out such violence. Far from it. They tried to create a government where change was peacefully played out inside a democratic structure. A firearms free-for-all, therefore, is not an inescapable legacy of our founding but is rooted, at least in part, in Insurrectionist mythology.

Guns and the Revolution

Firearms hold a prominent place in our nation's history. The United States of America was the end result of a revolution that succeeded by force of arms. George Washington's Continental Army and the state militia forces under his direction used firearms along with other implements of eighteenth-century warfare to expel the British from the original thirteen colonies, paving the way for a new nation. Of course, Washington was helped by the French army and navy, sent under the authority of Louis XVI, in the decisive battle of Yorktown; bumbling and inept British military leadership; and his mastery of the colonial terrain. The fact remains, though, that firearms played an important role in winning American independence.

From the time we are in elementary school, Americans learn about the brave men who formed the companies of Minutemen at the battles of Lexington and Concord and who offered the British their first taste of defeat at the hands of the colonists. Even today, the link between these original citizen-soldiers and their guns has been carefully preserved at a host of Revolutionary War battlefields, monuments, and museum exhibits. Appropriating this history in service to their ideological agenda, the Insurrectionists declare that firearms are an integral part of America's revolutionary history and that had the colonists not been well armed, the revolution would have sputtered. The principle they derive from this experience is that even today, every American has a part to play in protecting our freedoms, gained as they were through violent revolution, by stockpiling private arms.

This oversimplified account misses the point that the American Revolution was not an individual undertaking or the project of a group of disaffected zealots who failed to persuade their fellow citizens of the merits of their cause. The men who declared a new country and then fought to establish it did so collectively on behalf of a broad set of political interests that were denied representation by the British government. The Minutemen who fired the first shots of the American Revolution in April 1775 predated the formal declaration of American independence by more than a year. While they are often depicted as a group of farmers[1] "who responded to a spontaneous call to arms," the reality is that the Minutemen were part of a collective structure that dated to 1645.[2]

The Minutemen were part of the militia tradition, based on the English system that was modified to meet the requirements of the early American condition.[3] Based on the need for quick mobilization to respond to threats from Native Americans on the western frontier, "a specific portion of the militia, well trained, well equipped, and set aside as a ready force" was created.[4] This select portion of the militia was known by various names over the colonial years but by the time of the fighting at Lexington and Concord was known as the Minutemen. These men, far from waiting in anonymity for an opportunity for action, were mustered regularly and provided with arms and gunpowder by their towns. Each town was responsible for its militiamen as part of an overall command controlled by the royal authorities.[5]

In the fall of 1774, with a standing British army occupying Boston and General Thomas Gage limiting the power of town meetings, the Massachusetts colonists dismantled the king's militia and developed their own militia on the old framework. Towns collaborated through a provincial congress to organize their militia and Minuteman companies. "Towns, not individuals, decided to fight,"[6] and fight they did. When the British under Gage attempted to seize common stores of gunpowder and arms, they faced a combined force of Minutemen and regular militia numbering fourteen thousand men, who had been called out on a few hours' notice.[7] As all American schoolchildren learn, the British took massive casualties and had to fall back all the way to Boston.

An obvious, essential truth about the first battle of the war is often lost, and not only on the Insurrectionists. This nascent revolution was no spontaneous uprising of individuals feverishly reacting to British provocations. It was the deliberate and thoughtful action of a people, working collectively through their local governments, to rebel against a political system that denied them representation. As John R. Galvin notes, "It is ironic that the militia and the minute men, who together wrested their army from the control of the Crown, doubled it in size, equipped it with 20,000 muskets and 10,000 bayonets, and trained it secretly all one winter, are praised as an example of soldiers who fought well with no organization, no equipment, no training, and no planning."[8]

Not all of the colonial militia organizations shared such glorious success or were as effective as the Massachusetts militia. Both Washington and his military protégé, Alexander Hamilton, observed the militias at close quarters during the war and generally thought them worse than useless as a fighting force.[9] As Washington famously stated about the militiamen, they "come in, you cannot tell how; go, you cannot tell when, and act, you cannot tell where, consume your provisions, exhaust your stores, and leave you at last at a critical moment."[10] The militias' effectiveness and focus varied from state to state. The South Carolina militia, for example, was so focused on its role as a slave patrol that it lost its usefulness as a military force.[11]

One thing stayed constant: the militia was not a group of individuals banding together on an ad hoc basis. It was fully a creature of the community. Historian Saul Cornell notes, "Colonists who bore arms did not act as isolated individuals, but rather acted collectively for the common defense, and did so within a clear set of legal structures established by colonial and British law."[12] The community thus had no compunction about regulating the use and storage of firearms or membership in the militia. After independence, the "regulations could be quite intrusive, allowing government not only to keep track of who had firearms, but also requiring citizens to report to muster or face stiff penalties."[13] As one would expect, blacks and Native Americans remained outside the militia structure, but in colonial America, so were "white servants and apprentices, and free white men on the move."[14] In short, at the dawn of American Revolution, firearms played a role in fighting British tyranny but did so only within the context of the institution of a well-regulated militia, which was wholly controlled by and accountable to the community through a legislative body.

The right to resist tyranny served a political function, so it could be exercised only within a structure provided by a sovereign—as in a militia—and was understood as a political or structural right. Voting is a good example of this type of right. Each citizen in a democracy has an individual right to vote, but not without limits. An individual, for example, cannot vote any time he or she pleases or at any place he or she chooses but can vote only at the intervals and in the manner established by the legislature or constitution.

The right to arms for self-defense, conversely, was a natural right modified and limited by centuries of common law and was seen as an individual right. The right to self-defense was not open-ended, either, and the common law imposed an obligation on an individual who felt threatened to take advantage of reasonable alternatives to violent confrontation with an aggressor. But when that same individual had his or her back to the wall, he or she was allowed to "turn on his assailant." By contrast, revolution, which is an effort to deliberately pit one political unit against another, is a decision that a citizen has no legal authority to make.[15] As Cornell points out, "Without legal authority, a group of armed citizens acting on their own was little more than a riotous mob."[16]

This does not mean that colonial Americans frowned on private ownership of firearms, only that the right to use firearms to defend against tyranny was, as Lord Blackstone, the eminent legal thinker, put it, "a public allowance, under due restrictions."[17] Blackstone categorized the right to bear arms as a necessarily "auxiliary" right to protect the great rights of life, liberty, and property. Professor John Goldberg outlines Blackstone's four other auxiliary rights: "(1) the right to parliamentary government; (2) the right to clear limits on the royal prerogative; (3) the right to apply to the courts of justice for redress of injuries; (4) the right to petition the King, or either house of Parliament, for redress of grievances." Goldberg clarifies that these were rights that Englishmen enjoyed to protect their primary rights and that the king was bound by the customs of England's unwritten constitution to provide a structure under the appropriate conditions for their exercise.[18]

After the fighting broke out in Massachusetts and the Crown's authority had disintegrated, a new government needed to be formed. But as historian Gordon Wood observes, "The Massachusetts Congress was reluctant 'to assume the reins of civil government' on its own authority and perhaps thereby to disrupt the unity of the colonies. Therefore in May 1775, Massachusetts applied to the Continental Congress for the 'most explicit advice, respecting the taking up and exercising the powers of civil government,'" and other colonies followed, seeking "the sanction of the Congress to form governments."[19] This revolutionary movement's purpose was not a return to the state of nature but, as John Adams put it, "to glide insensibly, from under the old Government, into a peaceable and contented submission to new ones."[20]

At each step on the march to Independence, the delegates to the Continental Congress and similar revolutionary bodies sitting in the colonies (soon to be states) cloaked their actions in laws, deliberation, and collective decision making. Revolution was not a private grievance and could not be executed individually. The American Revolution did not rest on the backs of citizens disgruntled about a tax law or land-use issues. This revolution was the work of a people intent on protecting their collective liberty. Relying on Adams, Wood argues, "No specific acts of the government against the people could sanction revolution. Only 'repeated, multiplied oppressions,' placing it beyond all doubt

'that their rulers had formed settled plans to deprive them of their liberties,' could warrant the concerted resistance of the people against
their government."[21] The actions taken by the Americans were carried
out as a whole people.

Yes, some British loyalists opposed the stance taken in Philadelphia,
but the decision had legitimacy because it rested not on private grievance but rather on collective oppression and was advanced by the people
as a whole. Ron Chernow quotes Alexander Hamilton to show that the
"American Revolution had succeeded because it was 'a free, regular and
deliberate act of the nation' and had been conducted with 'a spirit of justice and humanity.' It was, in fact, a revolution written in parchment
and defined by documents, petitions, and other forms of law."[22]

Our founding document, the Declaration of Independence, thus ex-
presses the idea of revolution in a context of legal change and collective
action. The Insurrectionists often refer to the Declaration as a statement of first principles.[23] Daniel Polsby and Don B. Kates Jr. take this
argument a step further, calling the Declaration a "code of revolutionary procedure" and arguing that by applying this code, it is easy to distinguish the Timothy McVeighs of the world from the founders. While
Polsby and Kates acknowledge that revolution is never a private right,
they concoct an individual right of self-defense against government
tyranny out of this most public right.[24] This is little better than
sophistry. While revolutionary in nature, the Declaration of Independence is not an individualized call to arms to vindicate personal grievances. The signers were no anarchists; they yearned not to create perpetual revolution but to form the basis for a new government that could
vigorously protect liberty.

The Declaration includes a laundry list of wrongs inflicted by the
king on the colonists. These complaints are not individualized but apply to the people as a whole and affect their most fundamental liberties—liberties that they had come to expect as British citizens. The
grievances detailed include, "He has called together Legislative Bodies
at Places unusual, uncomfortable, and distant from the Depository of
their public Records, for the sole Purpose of fatiguing them into Compliance with his Measures"; "He has dissolved Representative Houses
repeatedly, for opposing with manly Firmness his Invasions on the

Rights of the People"; and "He has obstructed the Administration of Justice, by refusing his Assent to Laws for establishing Judiciary Powers." Such a litany shows the total breakdown of representative democracy as understood by eighteenth-century Englishmen and the total inability of any forum provided by the Crown to vindicate the colonists' rights. Seen through modern eyes, these grievances make a compelling case for a change of government. What is remarkable about the document, though, is that it is not a bill of rights or a plea for individual protection. It declares with great lucidity that liberty is best protected in a representative system.

We all know Thomas Jefferson's majestic phrase from the Declaration, "We hold these Truths to be self-evident, that all Men are created equal, that they are endowed, by their Creator, with certain unalienable Rights, that among these are Life, Liberty, and the Pursuit of Happiness." But we are less familiar with the next phrase, which clearly indicates the early American view that representative government best protects liberty: "That to secure these Rights, Governments are instituted among Men, deriving their just Powers from the Consent of the Governed." Jefferson noted not only that the people have the power to abolish oppressive government but that the object was "to institute new Government" with enough energy to protect the people by "organizing its Powers in such Form, as to them shall seem most likely to effect their Safety and Happiness."

The founders were not a collection of antigovernment zealots seeking to undo the oppressive yoke of government. They believed that representative government is the protector of individual liberty. The Declaration itself shows the intent to give government the "power" to protect liberty. Wood documents that getting rid of government was not the point of the revolution. "Liberty," good Whigs continually emphasized, "does not consist in living without all restraint"; "without the pooling of each man's liberty into a common body, no property would be secure."[25] The men who signed the Declaration of Independence were not seeking to get rid of laws altogether. They simply wanted to live under laws initiated by them or by their elected representatives. Far from seeking a return to the state of nature, where factions had to have arms and where might made right, they wanted a government that would be both representative and energetic. Unfortunately, the new state governments and the Articles of Confederation came nowhere close to giving the government enough power to protect the people's liberties. In a few years, the founders realized that the government needed much more authority to curb the excesses of the states and their citizens.

The path to independence that started at Lexington and Concord was sealed with the British defeat at Yorktown. The path took many unexpected and dangerous turns, and even in victory, a number of deep flaws in the new confederation of states were exposed. All of these flaws stemmed from a lack of central government power. As Americans went about the business of setting up new state governments, they grappled with how states should work together. They understood that fighting the British could not succeed on a state-by-state basis but needed coordination. Yet in the process of shedding the oppression of a distant government, citizens were not enthusiastic about pledging allegiance to a national government that could seem equally remote in the days when the fastest communication was by horseback or sailing ship. As a result, the compact between the states, documented in the Articles of Confederation, left Congress without the basic mechanisms to administer a country. Lacking the authority to tax or recruit troops, Congress was without much of the power of contemporaneous European countries, against which it was forced to compete for military and commercial supremacy. The Articles left the new Congress completely dependent on the state governments.[26]

This arrangement severely hampered the war effort. In 1776, the colonists had no professional fighting force. From the beginning, Washington never had enough troops or supplies to prosecute the war effectively. In accordance with the republican ethic against a standing army, most of the Massachusetts militiamen that locked up the British in Boston were volunteers uninterested in extended military service in the Continental Army.[27]

Under the Articles of Confederation, Congress had the authority to decide on the number of troops needed, but the states could decide whether to fill the requests. States that turned to the draft when volunteerism failed, as it often did, gave potential draftees the option of finding substitutes or paying fines, and "the men hired were generally those most in need of the money, that is, at the economic bottom of society."[28] Washington's army, then, consisted of fighters who were there solely for the money as well as untrained state militias and short-term enlistees, at least in the beginning. Washington had no faith in the militia units that came in and out of his army and remained concerned about the quality of his army throughout the war. "A year before the decisive victory at Yorktown, [Washington] wrote that 'I most firmly believe that the Independence of the United States will never be established till there is an Army on foot for the war.'"[29]

In addition to the lack of a professional army, Washington was hampered by shortages resulting from the inability of Congress, which had no power to directly levy taxes, to collect the necessary revenues for the war. The suffering of Washington's troops in the winter of 1777–78 is well known, but it is worth reflecting on how a country that had abundant resources and was generally prosperous could let thousands of its revolutionary soldiers slowly die from malnutrition and exposure. As Wood sees it, "The war with Britain had scarcely begun before the nature and tendency of American behavior was frighteningly revealed. The self-sacrifice and patriotism of 1774–75 soon seemed to give way to greed and profiteering at the expense of the public good."[30] The public virtue that had characterized the years leading up to independence quickly seemed to dissipate. It was not that the new country was too poor to support an army but that "the financial demands of a centralized army recruited in this way were simply too great for the fiscal system to handle; it was not a problem of war being too much for available resources."[31] Congress was incapable of arranging the necessary logistical support for the war effort, forcing Washington literally to scavenge the land for food and clothes, even resorting to cattle rustling to support his troops in some meager way. In addition, the lack of a reliable revenue source made it difficult to borrow money, float currency, or even pay the troops and officers.[32]

Fortunately for the Americans, the British, after initially underestimating the broad-based support for the rebellion, changed course and tried to encourage social division within the colonies by arming Cherokee Indians, encouraging slaves to turn against their masters, and arming and activating the loyalist minorities. This strategy ultimately backfired by "providing the motivation for continued American resistance when the initial enthusiasm seemed to have burned out." With the help of the French, who were determined to turn a "colonial war into a global war," a conflict that could have dragged on even longer shuddered to a merciful conclusion.[33]

The Articles of Confederation

The war accomplished its objective of driving the British and their oppressive policies out of the former colonies, yet it was nearly a disaster. Government bankruptcy caused a crisis in the latter part of the war that pushed the administration of the effort down to the state and local levels. This weakness was not lost on Washington and his brethren who served in the war. They had been forced to cope with Congress's inability to support a real army and learned firsthand what happens when a government is too weak to efficiently sustain a military campaign. Washington warned his departing troops that "unless the principles of the federal government were properly supported and the powers of the union increased, the honour, dignity, and justice of the nation would be lost forever."[34] In December 1783, as Washington made his way to the temporary capital in Annapolis, where the Continental Congress was still in session, to resign his commission as commander in chief, he was honored with many galas and feasts. At Wilmington, Delaware, after listening to thirteen toasts, he offered his own: "Competent powers to Congress for general purposes."[35]

After the war, the military weakness created by the unworkable division of power between Congress and the states persisted. Under the Articles of Confederation, Congress was unable to protect the "union's commercial and territorial interests,"[36] and the Continental Army was reduced to eighty men. In 1787, as the Constitutional Convention got under way, a mere seven hundred men were in the military service of the new nation.[37] The men who gathered to draft a new constitution understood that the union desperately needed to strengthen its military and fiscal powers.[38] John Shy maintains that "the harsh realities of a protracted war, more than anything else, explain the difference between

the euphoria at Philadelphia in 1776, when Congress declared independence, and the hard-headedness of many of the same men, when eleven
years later, in the same city, they hammered out a federal constitution."[39] But other serious issues also brought these men back to
Philadelphia.

If the Articles of Confederation hamstrung the Congress, the state
governments were not in much better shape. It was not that their constitutions left the state legislatures powerless; in fact, fear of monarchy
and centralized power in general had allowed the drafters of the state
constitutions to create legislatures with almost no executive or judicial
checks and balances. The accumulation of all powers in the legislatures,
even though they were thoroughly democratic in the purely majoritarian sense of the word, created a situation where the rule of law was applied according to "crude notions of equity."[40] States confiscated private property and prevented creditors from collecting debts, passed ex
post facto laws, and violated basic principles of justice. Wood has found
that "an excess of power in the people was leading not simply to licentiousness but to a new kind of tyranny, not by the traditional rulers, but
by the people themselves."[41]

If the states through their legislatures were exercising arbitrary
power, the citizens were trying to collect power directly in their own
hands. Lacking any real redress in the face of laws that seemed onerous
or unfair, the people often used extralegal activity such as committees,
conventions, and even mob violence to accomplish desired ends. Wood
calls this phenomenon "the people out-of-doors" and explains that it
was a common feature of the prerevolutionary colonies. Immediately
prior to independence, mob violence had decreased as revolutionary associations came to control and regulate almost all aspects of daily life.
But by the late 1770s, when Congress and the state legislatures started
passing laws that negated some of the economic rules adopted by the
revolutionary associations, ad hoc local and state committees tried to
assert the "real will" of the people against the legislatures. These committees instigated serious and recurrent riots in all of the major cities.[42]

Wood reports that by 1784, even the radical Samuel Adams "had
come to believe that 'popular Committees and County Conventions are
not only useless but dangerous.' When they were used in place of royal

legislatures, they had served 'an excellent Purpose,' but 'as we now have constitutional and regular Governments and all our Men in Authority depend upon the annual and free Elections of the People, we are safe without them. . . . Bodies of Men, under any Denomination whatever, who convene themselves for the Purpose of deliberating upon and adopting Measures which are cognizable by Legislatures only will, if continued, bring Legislatures to Contempt and Dissolution.'"[43] Nowhere were the people out-of-doors creating more chaos than in western Massachusetts, where Shays's Rebellion had dragged the people back to the state of nature. Mob rule was the only source of law.

Shays's Rebellion brings into sharp relief the changes that guided America's leading men to rethink their theories about government and ultimately to produce the new constitution with its expanded role for the central government. If it is true that revolutionary ideology played an honorable role in helping the Americans win freedom from the British, then it is equally true that the same ideology contributed to the chaos of lawlessness and mob rule that characterized the 1780s. And because Americans were well armed, when this ideology turned inward, it had ugly and dangerous consequences. Modern-day "revolutionaries" who believe that individuals should be prepared to topple tyrannical government acknowledge only half of our historical experience. America was born by revolution, but our founders, having witnessed the horrors of the mob, opposed creation of a permanent condition of revolution. Citizens with guns who challenged the laws of legitimate government were considered criminals, not revolutionaries, even before the Constitution was finalized. The fatuous idea that the Constitution and its amendments legitimized armed insurrection ignores altogether the purpose of the Constitutional Convention. The men gathered at Philadelphia clearly wanted to create a stronger central government. They knew a government that could not cope with insurrection would put the liberties for which they had just fought so hard at risk.

In 1786, farmers in western Massachusetts, led by, among others, Daniel Shays, asserted their natural right to take up arms against a tyrannical state government to protest the heavy taxation and tight fiscal policy that were causing financial hardship and foreclosures. The rebels took on the trappings of a militia, even though they were operating in opposition to state authority, and invoked the symbols of the revolutionary militia in an effort to distinguish themselves from an ordinary mob. Using their muskets and other weapons, they closed the courts in Northampton and other western Massachusetts cities to prevent further foreclosures. In doing so, the Shaysites relied on their perceived natural right to bear arms, which they claimed did not depend on the state constitution. When Governor James Bowdoin called out the militias, many of the towns' militias declined to act against the protesters. The governor, with the help of the Continental Congress, eventually raised an army to quell the rebellion. In response, the Shaysites moved toward Springfield in an attempt to seize the federal arsenal there. The government troops, under the direction of Secretary of War Henry Knox, used artillery to drive off the rebels and protect the arsenal. He then gave chase and forced Shays's forces to scatter. Through state and federal force, the rebel movement collapsed.[44]

Shays's Rebellion clearly illustrates the distinction between insurrection and revolution. The Shaysites believed that they were the true "body of the people" rising together to resist a tyrannical government. Shays did not see his uprising as one of individuals but rather as a local "communitarian" reaction to a distant and unresponsive government. Shays's opponents, who called themselves the Friends of Order, believed that the Shaysites were nothing more than an armed mob. According to Cornell, "In their view, American Independence had banished the right of armed resistance against constitutional government. . . . In a situation in which representative institutions and courts of law were functioning, the rule of law, not arms, was the primary guarantee of life, liberty and property."[45] Not only did the Friends of Order carry the day militarily, but the fear of mobs engaging in insurrectionary activity was a major impetus for the Constitutional Convention in 1787.

Washington, already deeply concerned by the weakness of Congress, found himself compelled by the rebellion in western Massachusetts to return to public life, and he made the difficult decision to attend the Constitutional Convention in Philadelphia. This was not an uncommon move among the men who gathered to write the new constitution.[46] "Bitter experience of fighting from weakness had all but obliterated the naïve optimism of 1775, and had sensitized Americans to their own political peril. Fearful prophecies, based on dismal fact, functioned to defeat those prophecies by channeling political energies into the struggle against anarchy. . . . Nothing was feared more by leaders in the postwar era than disunion, and most people felt the same way."[47]

Americans in 1776 may have thought that their virtue and goodness would exempt them from the need for strong government, but by 1787 their experience with war and domestic unrest convinced leading citizens to go about building a state in earnest. Wood chronicles the opinions of some of these citizens as they faced the task of writing a new constitution: "'We were, at the commencement of the late war, but novices in politics,' wrote Thomas Tudor Tucker of South Carolina in 1784, 'and it is to be wished that we may not now be too indolent to correct our mistakes.' After lopping off 'the monarchical part' of the English constitution, 'we vainly imagined that we had arrived at perfection, and that freedom was established on the broadest and most solid basis that could possibly consist with any social institution. That we have in some points been mistaken, is too evident to be denied.'" Wood quotes Benjamin Franklin: "We have been guarding against an evil that old States are most liable to, excess of power in the rulers, but our present danger seems to be defect of obedience in the subjects."[48]

This thinking represented a dramatic change from the idea of 1776 that liberty required only the removal of a powerful government. By the mid-1780s, it seemed apparent that a strong government was needed to preserve the precious liberties for which men had died in the revolution. According to Wood, "The early state constitutions had rendered government too feeble. 'The principal fault,' constitutional reformers agreed, 'seems to be, a want of energy in the administration of government.' In nearly all of the states there were growing demands that the libertarian bias of 1776 be corrected, that the apparent licentiousness of the people be offset by an increase of magisterial power in order to provide for the 'execution of the laws that is necessary for the preservation of justice, peace, and internal tranquility.'"[49] Max Edling quotes America's third Supreme Court justice, a drafter of the Constitution, to make a similar point: "'We combine in society, with an expectation, to have our persons and our properties defended against unreasonable exactions either at home or abroad,' Oliver Ellsworth said. If the government cannot do so, 'we do not enjoy our natural rights.' "[50]

The Constitution

At the dawn of the new constitutional government in America, then, the issue was not how to perpetuate conditions where armed revolution would remain available as a permanent check on overreaching by the central government but rather how to create a society stable enough to protect liberties. Of course, some prominent citizens remained fearful of centralized power, and the debate between the two sides was played out in the course of drafting the Constitution. To a large degree, however, the group favoring a stronger government, known as the Federalists, succeeded in their goal. A constitutional guarantee for an individual right to armed insurrection would have been wholly inconsistent with the purpose of the constitutional gathering. Any attempt to read these events differently must come to terms with the fact that a major reason the Constitution was organized was to give the government the power to put down armed insurrection. The Insurrectionist contention that the framers intended to protect the accumulation of artillery and cannon and the stockpiling of small arms in private hands to protect against potential government tyranny is counterfactual.

Of course, the Insurrectionist worldview is not informed entirely by historical argument, accurate or otherwise. The Insurrectionists say that no matter what the historical context may have been, the Second Amendment enshrines our right to have guns free from government regulation. This argument does not stand up to scrutiny. The Constitution formed a new basis for governing in America. No longer would Congress have to rely on requests to the states because it would have the authority to act on its own. The Federalists sought to create a polity that had enough power to ensure stable government.[51] The Federalists were determined to vest the new country with the fiscal and military authority to defend commercial interests and territorial integrity, including the power directly to levy taxes and to raise a standing army. In addition, the Constitution gave Congress direct if not exclusive power over the militia. Historian Garry Wills makes a persuasive case that the Constitution has a series of clauses that were "framed and passed precisely to put down domestic insurrections," including, among others, Article III, Section 3, Clause 1, which makes treason a constitutional offense; Article I, Section 8, Clause 15, which specifically provides for the calling forth of the militia to "suppress insurrections," not to acquiesce in them; and Article I, Section 8, Clause 16, which requires that Congress train and discipline the militia.[52]

At the Constitutional Convention, the debate about the military clauses was relatively brief, but it framed the objections that would arise at the state ratifying conventions. Edling observes that "anti federalist critique against the Constitution's army clauses centered on the transfer of military power from the states to Congress. To them, the centralization of power brought about by the Constitution threatened the continued existence of two institutions which they believed to be vital to the preservation of liberty: the militia and the state assemblies. These provided the people with the means to withstand the possible abuse of power by the central government. Should the militia and the state government be swallowed up by Congress, this would tip the balance of power decisively in favor of the national government, which would then be able to pursue whatever actions it chose regardless of popular opposition."[53] Ellsworth, who went on to become a great defender of the national government, insisted that "the authority over the Militia ought by no means to be taken away from the States whose consequence would pine away to nothing after such a sacrifice of power."[54]

Obviously harkening back to the disrepair of the militia in the Revolutionary War, James Madison responded to this concern by stating that "the primary object is to secure an effectual discipline of the Militia. This will no more be done if left to the States separately than the requisitions have been hitherto paid by them. The States neglect their Militia now, and the more they are consolidated into one nation, the less each will rely on its own interior provisions for its safety & the less prepare its Militia for that purpose; in like manner as the militia of a State would have been still more neglected than it has been if each County had been independently charged with the care of its Militia. The Discipline of the Militia is evidently a National concern, and ought to be provided for in the National Constitution."[55] Let's be clear. The debate about the militia played itself out within the broader debate about federalism. This was a battle not about individual rights but about whether the state or federal government would control the militia.

The state ratification debates forced the Federalists to defend their consolidation of military power. In truth, the leading Federalists had no use for the militia. Ill-trained and unprepared, with few exceptions, the militia would not be an adequate force to help build the new nation. The Antifederalists were concerned that Congress would either use its power to remove the militias from state control or neglect the militias. The Antifederalists worried not that individuals would lose their right to own guns but that Congress would interfere with state prerogatives regarding the militia. For example, according to Cornell, "Virginians were especially worried that federal control of the militia would threaten their state's ability to put down insurrections, a particularly frightening prospect for a state with a large slave population."[56]

These federalism concerns were captured in a debate between Patrick Henry and James Madison at the Virginia ratifying convention. Henry complained that since the draft Constitution prohibited states from using their own militias to go to war unless they had been invaded, he believed that states would not be able to suppress insurrections.

> If you give this clause a fair construction, what is the true meaning of it? What does this relate to? Not domestic insurrections, but war. If the country be invaded, a state may go to war, but cannot suppress insurrections. If there should happen an insurrection of slaves, the country cannot be said to be invaded. They cannot suppress it without the interposition of Congress. . . . The State legislatures ought to have power to call forth the efforts of the militia, when necessary.[57]

Madison responded by showing that dual sovereignty over the militia was the ultimate protector of the people's liberty:

> Let me ask . . . what we are to understand from [Henry's] reasoning. The power must be vested in Congress, or in the state governments; or there must be a division or concurrence. He is against division. It is a political

monster. He will not give it to Congress for fear of oppression. Is it to be vested in the state governments? If so, where is the provision for general defence? If ever America should be attacked, the states would fall successively. It will prevent them from giving aid to their sister states; for, as each state will expect to be attacked, and wish to guard against it, each will retain its own militia for its own defense. Where is this power to be deposited, then, unless in the general government, if it be dangerous to the public safety to give it exclusively to the states? If it must be divided, let him show a better manner of doing it than that which is in the Constitution.[58]

Of course, the Constitution was ratified by the states, but some, like Virginia, offered amendments to be considered in the first Congress. Despite the evidence that the Constitution was crafted specifically to prevent insurrection, the Insurrectionists claim that what eventually was ratified as the Second Amendment changed the equation, preserving not only the right of insurrection but making it personal and individual. We cannot look here at every argument surrounding the Second Amendment, but we believe that there is one "right" it does not protect: a decision by individuals to take up guns against the state or federal governments. The Second Amendment reads, "A well regulated militia being necessary to the security of the free state, the right of the people to keep and bear arms shall not be infringed." The first clause clearly talks about the necessity of a militia and even links this need with the protection of freedom. The second enumerates a right of the "people" but does so in a way that clearly links it to a military purpose, "keep[ing] and bear[ing] arms." Even a cursory reading indicates that this was not intended simply to be a guarantee of personal protection.[59]

Dissenting delegates in Pennsylvania issued a document that is most often associated with an individual right to bear arms outside of a militia, and Insurrectionist "scholars" frequently cite it. The Pennsylvania dissent stands as one of the very few instances in which that right was described in terms that arguably contemplate an individual right. But as Cornell points out, the "dissent" was issued by a minority of delegates that had failed to garner enough support in the Federalist-dominated Pennsylvania convention to stop the Constitution from being affirmed or even to get the convention to add a list of suggested amendments.[60]

The complaints emanating from the state conventions and the Antifederalist commentators, like those that arose during the Constitutional Convention, were directed not at the absence of a guarantee of an individual right to own or use firearms (for whatever purpose) but at Congress's power to raise a permanent military force under the control of the central government. Antifederalists opposed the idea of a standing army in times of peace and the threat that centralized control over the nation's military posed to the role of the various state militias.[61]

These concerns about the relationship between a national standing army and the state militias were raised and were a subject of serious debate, but there is no basis for concluding that the Second Amendment represented a decision to give the Antifederalists what they wanted. During the debates over the Second Amendment in the first Congress, the overwhelming Federalist majorities ensured that the powers delegated to the national government in the body of the Constitution were left intact. The records of the debate make it clear that the goal was to ensure that the state militias would not be displaced, and there was no discussion at all about the merits of protecting an individual right to own or use a gun, much less about the purposes that might be served by recognizing such as right in the Constitution. "The amendment, as revised, would still assuage Anti-Federalist concerns by stating a principled commitment to the value of a militia. But it would not hinder Congress in using its best judgment to determine how to organize, arm, and discipline an effective militia."[62] Constitutional historian Paul Finkelman adds,

> Madison and the great Federalist majority in the First Congress rejected any amendments that undermined the power of the national government. Is it conceivable that they failed to follow this philosophy with the Second Amendment? That they meant to implement the demands of the Pennsylvania anti-Federalists and, in effect, eviscerate the power of the national government? Such an argument goes against the entire history of the period.

> Hence, the Second Amendment prevents Congress from abolishing

the organized or "well regulated" state militias. . . . Madison and his colleagues provided for an amendment dealing with the militia because most of the states that proposed amendments wanted some guarantee that Congress would not destroy their militias.[63]

Of course, there was no shortage of Antifederalist criticism of the Constitution. Patrick Henry, for example, wanted the Constitution revised to give more power to the states on the grounds that they were most likely to protect the people's liberties. Henry did not see the Bill of Rights as achieving any new distribution of power. Henry had used the lack of a bill of rights to campaign against the Constitution,

> but when offered the Bill of Rights in 1789 he balked. Henry fully understood that a bill of rights would destroy the possibility of achieving his real goal, which was to destroy or completely undermine and remake the new Constitution. Henry and his cohorts correctly realized that if the lack of a bill of rights was no longer an issue, many of the softer anti-Federalists would be satisfied with the Constitution and accept the new government.[64]

This is exactly what came to pass. Madison and most Federalists were unwilling to go along with any more significant limitations on the powers delegated to the new national government. Madison was willing to consider a bill of rights because he did not think it altered the constitutional relationship between the states and the federal government. Finkelman writes, "The Bill of Rights did not shift any political power from the national government to either the states or 'the people.' In Madison's mind it merely clarified the constitutional powers, rights, and responsibilities of the national government."[65]

The structural amendments favored by many of the leading Antifederalists were defeated in the first Congress, including the amendments that would have limited the federal government's military power. "The Antifederalists had lost. They wanted the militias as an alternative to a standing army. When they got militias and a standing army, they were not satisfied."[66] Instead of a major body blow to the federal structure, a bill of rights was added as the first ten amendments, among them the

Second Amendment, which the Antifederalists did not support. The In-surrectionists are fond of quoting from Henry, Jefferson, and other An-tifederalists to buttress the contention that the framers of the Constitu-tion were intent on limiting the power of the federal government but neglect to acknowledge that the Antifederalists were on the losing side of the argument about whether to entrust the central government with more authority, both in general and with regard to the control of mili-tary forces.

Moreover, Cornell shows that with few exceptions, even those on the losing side of the constitutional debates did not consider the "right to keep and bear arms" to imply an individual right to take up arms against the government. For example, Cornell analyzes the thinking of St. George Tucker, one of the leading Antifederalist jurists of the revo-lutionary period. Tucker was a law professor at the College of William and Mary in Williamsburg, Virginia, and was well acquainted with the happenings at the Constitutional Convention. His treatise on Black-stone, published in 1803, was an important commentary on the laws and constitution of the new republic.[67] In Tucker's notes to his law lec-tures, which were made contemporaneously with the adoption of the Constitution and the Bill of Rights, he "accepted the common view that most citizens would own their own muskets, or other militia weapons. In the case of Cavalry officers, one might own a horsemen's pistol, but the constitutional protection accorded these weapons was clearly con-nected to their function as standard militia weapons. Guns without any connection to the militia were subject to the full scope of the individual states' police powers."[68] Tucker believed that the Second Amendment embodied the ancient right to resist government tyranny, but that right could only be exercised within the context of state law.

This idea, of course, was anathema to the Federalists, who had re-mained adamant that "an appeal to arms" would destroy the Constitu-tion.[69] The important point here, though, is that even those Antifeder-alists who claimed that the Second Amendment guaranteed a right to use violence against the government thought that this right was limited to the states. They understood that the state "enjoyed tremendous lati-tude to legislate on a broad range of issues that could restrict individual liberty. As long as government's actions were a product of the people's own representatives, government was entitled to limit the actions of its citizens in a manner consistent with the public good." Leading Antifederalists such as Maryland lawyer Luther Martin believed that arbitrary power could be resisted by arms but "did not advocate a permanent right of revolution or an individual right of resistance." Instead, they believed that "state control of the militia was the proper check on . . . arbitrary authority."[70]

"Brutus," a widely reprinted Antifederalist commentator, clarified the point that the constitutional debate with the Federalists was a discussion over federalism itself and whether power should reside in the state or federal governments. Responding to Hamilton's contention in Federalist 23 that the national government should retain unlimited military power, "Brutus" wrote,

> The *protection and defence* of the community is not intended to be entrusted *solely* into the hands of the general government, and by his own confession it ought not to be. It is true this system commits to the general government the protection and defence of the community against foreign force and invasion, against piracies and felonies on the high seas, and against insurrections among ourselves. They are also authorised to provide for the administration of justice in certain matters of a general concern, and in some that I think are not so. But it ought to be left to the state governments to provide for the protection and defence of the citizen against the hand of private violence, and the wrongs done or attempted by individuals to each other—Protection and defence against the murderer, the robber, the thief, the cheat, and the unjust person, is to be derived from the respective state governments.[71]

Of course, variations existed among the Antifederalists, and Cornell's groundbreaking work, *The Other Founders: Anti-Federalism and the Dissenting Tradition in America, 1788–1828,* details the distinctions among the elite, middling, and plebeian views of the Constitution. The majority of the Antifederalists agreed, however, that the states were the guardians of liberty. Although the middlebrow Antifederalist essayist "Federal Farmer" wrote "that the militia, when properly formed, are in fact the people themselves," Cornell points out that "Federal Farmer" believed that "state control of the militia 'places the sword in the hands of the solid interest of the community, and not in the hands of men destitute of property, or principle, or of attachment to the society and government.'"[72] This writer's view of protection against government tyranny was not to spread guns around indiscriminately and hope for the best. He believed that the militias should remain tightly under state control.

Of course, some Antifederalists saw armed resistance to government as an individual right. In December 1878, as the Pennsylvania convention ratified the Constitution, Federalists attempted to mark the victory with a celebration in Carlisle. Antifederalists were determined to stop the festivities and rioted for several days, burning and executing effigies of leading Federalists. When several of the rioters were arrested, local militia units marched through the streets and secured their release.[73] For Antifederalist "plebians" (Cornell's word) who organized in militia units, "the right to bear arms included the right of citizens to organize spontaneously as militia units to defend their liberties."[74]

Most Antifederalists, however, were repulsed by this sort of behavior and recognized it as repugnant to the democratic order. "The specter of mobocracy frightened many Anti-Federalists. . . . To members of the Anti-Federalist elite, the right to bear arms and the militia were legal only within the structures provided by the states."[75] It is not surprising, then, that the first Congress soundly rejected any amendments to the Constitution that could change this understanding, such as those proposed in the Pennsylvania minority dissent. The Constitutional Convention was called in direct response to Shays's Rebellion and other mob violence. The Constitution was drafted with those events in mind, and it gave plenty of power to Congress to suppress these kinds of uprisings. The suggestion that the Carlisle riots persuaded the Federalist majority in Congress of a need to curb the power of the central government or to recognize a right of private citizens to use force against it simply makes no sense.

Insurrectionist theorists often argue that the Second Amendment's reference to a right of the people, rather than a right of the states, is an express recognition of a role for armed citizens acting outside of government control in the defense of liberty. Cornell, however, offers a

compelling explanation for the Second Amendment's reference to individual rights in the context of militias under the control of the states—
it was intended to guarantee an individual right to bear arms in a state's
well-regulated militia, free from federal interference. Cornell contends
that the Second Amendment leaves under the control of the states decisions about how the militia is called up, when it drills, and what arms
soldiers can carry and where.

So why is the Second Amendment directed at the right "of the
people" to bear arms and not to the rights of the states to maintain militias? Cornell argues that the Second Amendment guarantees the right of
individuals to participate in a well-regulated state militia in much the
same way that individuals have a right to vote or to be included in the
pool of citizens selected for service on juries: "Perhaps the most accurate way to describe the dominant understanding of the right to bear
arms in the Founding era is as a civic right. Such a right was not something that all persons could claim, but was limited to those members of
the polity who were deemed capable of exercising it in a virtuous manner. Freedom of religion, freedom of the press, trial by jury were gen-
uinely rights belonging to individuals, and were treated differently than
were civic rights such as militia service, or the right to sit on juries."[76]
The right to serve on a jury is an individual right that is exercised collectively. In other words, no individual is entitled to be selected to serve
on any particular jury, but no category of citizen may be excluded from
service on a jury based on an arbitrary classification or invidious discrimination—for example, race or status as a property owner. The Second Amendment is an individual right, but not in the way that the Insurrectionists think.

In any event, the Second Amendment was not a codification of a
natural right of self-defense against our government. David Konig notes
that even Jefferson did not see the Second Amendment as a license for
individuals to amass arms to vindicate their own interests, describing
Jefferson as "consistent in his beliefs about states' rights and civic re-
publicanism, and supportive of the civic right—and thus obligation—of
the individual to keep and bear arms collectively in a manner consistent
with the Second Amendment as a guarantor of a republican revolution."[77] Jefferson thought the state militias needed to be protected from

meddling by the federal government, but not because he believed individual citizens or the states had reserved the right to make war on the federal government. Jefferson understood that the new constitutional government ended any "recourse to arms,"[78] but he also thought that the state militias were an important local training ground for republican virtue, about which he cared deeply. For this reason, Jefferson did not want to see state militias subsumed by the military forces of the national government. Konig concludes that "for Thomas Jefferson the creation of a well regulated militia did not require a virtuous citizenry; rather, the creation of a virtuous citizenry required a well regulated militia."[79]

The states were not clamoring to protect their militias to preserve their ability to depose the federal government. The militias were needed to protect the frontier and to enforce the rights of property owners to control their slaves. The question for the states was not whether to maintain the power to challenge the authority of federal government through force of arms but how to address the need for localized use of police powers.

Many of the academics who have lent some measure of intellectual legitimacy to the Insurrectionist theory of the Second Amendment ultimately agree that there is no individual right to take up arms against government tyranny or are unwilling to face the logical consequences of their position. For example, in a widely cited 1995 article in the *Georgia Law Review*, Nelson Lund claims that the government lacks the authority to regulate weapons in any manner, that individuals can own "grenades and bazookas," and that the purpose of the Second Amendment is to prevent "attempts at political oppression by the government." In a footnote, however, Lund adds that "it obviously does not follow from this proposition that the Second Amendment creates an individual right of insurrection against the government."[80]

Of course, it is not at all obvious that interpreting the Second Amendment as allowing for no restrictions whatsoever on the private ownership of weapons of war does not legitimize an individual right of insurrection. Lund and his intellectual comrades can't have it both ways. They cannot claim an individual right robust enough to allow personal ownership of grenades and bazookas grounded in the need to check government power and at the same time deny that they have legitimized an individual right of insurrection. The colonial militias so heavily regulated their members because the distinction Lund attempts to draw cannot be maintained in the real world. If citizens are to keep militia weapons in their homes, then they must be regulated. Otherwise, how could the state possibly determine whom to call out to quell an insurrection, what type of weapons will be needed, what kind of ammunition the citizens should bring, who will be officers, who says "March" and who says "Retreat," how enemy infiltrators will be detected and weeded out, and so on. The colonial militias mustered regularly and kept track of who had weapons and gunpowder so that they could perform as a unified fighting force. Even if the Second Amendment is a safeguard against governmental tyranny, it does not follow that individual ownership and use of firearms cannot be regulated. How otherwise can it be subject, as even Lund grudgingly admits it must be, to the control of the states?

The evidence shows that Constitution bestows no individual right to take up arms against the government. The Constitution was created to prevent armed anarchy and insurrection, and the Second Amendment did not negate the hard work that Madison and the other framers put into creating a strong government. But does this mean that Americans must stand idly by if the government fails altogether? For example, what would happen if the government permanently suspended elections and closed the courts? As Wills observes, "One of the principal devices of the insurrectionists is to confuse the right of insurrection under (within) the Constitution with the right of revolution (which would overthrow the Constitution). . . . A people can overthrow a government it considers unjust. But it is absurd to think that it does so by virtue of that unjust government's own authority."[81] Cornell adds that "while the natural right of revolution could never be parted with, the notion that there could be a constitutional appeal to arms was antithetical to the idea of constitutionalism itself."[82]

The revolution was not forgotten, but the framers hoped that because of the Constitution, it could be a thing of the past. There could be no appeal to arms to block enforcement of an unpopular law, such as a tax provision. The Constitution was intended to channel dissent into nonviolent, lawful avenues for political change. When pressed during the ratification debates, both Hamilton and Madison, writing as "Publius" in the Federalist Papers, made it clear that if the Constitution were to fail, the people's original right to self-defense would not be forgotten. According to both men, however, this right was extremely limited and its use should be avoided at all costs.

In Federalist 46, Madison attempted to sell the new Constitution to the country. In response to the fear that the federal government could use a standing army to usurp a state's powers, Madison wrote, in a line the Insurrectionists like to quote, "To these would be opposed a militia amounting to near half a million of citizens with arms in their hands, officered by men chosen from among themselves, fighting for their common liberties." The Insurrectionists neglect, however, to include the rest of the sentence: ". . . and united and conducted by governments possessing their affections and confidence."[83] In context, Madison made it clear that before any resort to violence, states would "open correspondence" with one another, "plans of resistance would be concerted," and "one spirit would animate and conduct the whole."[84]

Federalist 46 does not support the claim that individuals with guns are the guarantors of liberty. It affirms that even if the Constitution fails, the states are the political unit to which people must adhere, and the well-regulated militias under state control are the only vehicle available for armed response. For Hamilton, too, if the federal government were to fall under the control of a despot, the people would resist "through the medium of their State governments," though he admitted that "the apprehension may be considered as a disease, for which there can be found no cure in the resources of argument and reasoning."[85]

While Insurrectionists often use the abridged quotation from Madison to justify taking up arms against the federal government, Madison himself pushed for the Constitution's strong centralized powers. In fact, during the Constitutional Convention, Madison insisted that the new government should have even more muscular powers. He went so far as to propose a federal veto over all state laws—ultimately defeated, of course. When his position on this matter was revealed many years later, during the 1808 presidential campaign, his reputation as a true Federalist, concerned with balancing state and federal powers, suffered.

The bottom line is that both Madison and Hamilton were nervous about the states wielding military power. There is no evidence that they would have gone a step further and given individuals the right to take up arms independent of the states. They were willing to acknowledge that the militia is the vehicle through which the states can employ the use of force. As we have seen, this concept necessarily implies the regulation of individual gun ownership, which was well accepted and uncontroversial at the time. Moreover, both men supported giving broad powers to the new government as a way to prevent politics from turning into armed conflict.

Not surprisingly, the founders, having just fought a war of independence from Great Britain, were not ready completely to do away with the right of revolution. Conversely, their apprehension about the prospect of ongoing revolution in lieu of ordinary politics drove the Constitutional Convention. The framers were eager to put that insecurity behind them. In fact, in Federalist 46, Madison discussed the possibility of a conflict between states and the federal government as an unlikely hypothetical. Clinton Rossiter, a noted American historian and editor of one edition of the Federalist Papers, summarized Madison's conclusion: "No happiness without liberty, no liberty without self-government, no self-government without constitutionalism, no constitutionalism without morality—and none of these great goods without stability and order."[86]

In this context, it is difficult to view "Publius's" words as a justification for individual citizens to oppose their own government with force. As Wood concludes, "The Americans had demonstrated to the world how a people could fundamentally and yet peaceably alter their forms of government. 'This revolution principle—that, the sovereign power residing in the people, they may change their constitution and government whenever they please—is,' said James Wilson, 'not a principle of discord, rancour, or war: it is a principle of melioration, contentment, and peace.' Americans had in fact institutionalized and legitimized revolution. Thereafter, they believed, new knowledge about the nature of government could be converted into concrete form without resorting to violence. . . . The Americans of the Revolutionary generation believed that they had made a momentous contribution to the history of politics. They had for the first time demonstrated to the world how a people could diagnose the ills of its society and work out a peaceable process of cure."[87]

The framers took great pride in the revolution but became disillusioned when political violence continued after the war, threatening to disrupt the consolidation of the new democratic system. The peaceful revolution that accompanied the ratification of the Constitution does not say much about gun ownership but speaks volumes about the use of force as part of the political process. The framers tried to create a system that allowed for radical change without violence. We dishonor that legacy when we prepare for the worst at the expense of the magnificent system that they created. Neither the Second Amendment nor an inchoate right to armed revolution allows for violent opposition to the policies of a democratically accountable government, even if some citizens view those policies as tyrannical. The idea that gun owners are entitled to vindicate an individual right to insurrection is dangerous folly. An individual who claims the prerogative of deciding when violent resistance to a democratic government is justified disenfranchises fellow citizens and substitutes individual judgment for democratic institutions such as the courts.

The Founders and Insurrection

The founders did not believe that violent insurrection against the government is a legitimate avenue of dissent. In fact, many of the founders had a deep aversion to armed rebellion and did not hesitate to use state and federal government forces to crush insurrections. A number of events that transpired shortly after the ratification of the Constitution shed light on how the leading figures of the generation—the men whom Joseph Ellis has labeled the "Founding Brothers"—viewed the power of the federal government under the Constitution. Their actions after taking the reins of power uniformly show the political distance they had traveled from the days of the revolution. Revolutionary ideology served up by opponents of the new government quickly met with opposition from all segments of the political spectrum, and the use of force or the threat of force against the new government evoked not honor but disdain. The Founding Brothers, including Jefferson, did not hesitate to use the full power of the Constitution to enforce the laws of the new government when they took their turn at the helm.

As in so many areas of the presidency, George Washington set the tone for dealing with would-be domestic rebels. When protesters tried to evade the federal excise tax on whiskey in the early 1790s, he labeled them insurrectionists and used force to subdue them. The Whiskey Rebellion forced a confrontation between the revolutionary ideal that citizens have the right to take up arms against unjust laws and the constitutional ideal that there could be no extralegal remedy to prevent enforcement of a democratically enacted law. By the end of the rebellion in 1794, almost all responsible leaders had concluded that a "revolution" against democratic lawmaking was in fact an "insurrection" against legitimate government and deserved to be treated as such.

The first test of this principle resulted from passage of a tax law. In 1791, with bipartisan approval, Congress passed an excise tax on whiskey. Distillers in western Pennsylvania took umbrage at the tax and were determined to stop its enforcement, much as the previous generation had seen opposition to the Stamp Act and other British revenue-raising tactics as a political statement. The ostensible objection to the tax was that it placed an unfair burden on western farmers, who could not ship raw grain over the mountains to markets in the East and had to distill the grain into whiskey, a more durable product. The strong local response may have been symptomatic of a number of other grievances that the westerners believed eastern interests in Washington were ignoring, including inattention to the Indian threat and the failure to open the Mississippi River for trade.[88]

In any case, substantial parts of western Pennsylvania stood in open revolt by the summer of 1794. Turmoil had been escalating since the excise law was passed, and opposition was expressed through protest meetings, large-scale tax avoidance, and violence against tax collectors and distillers who complied with the law. The immediate cause of the revolt was the federal effort to effect service of process on distillers who failed to comply. One of the major sources of discontent was the fact that the trials were to be held hundreds of miles away in Philadelphia. (Although the law was amended that summer to allow local trials, it was not retroactive.) On July 16, 1794, local militia units from Allegheny County, with approximately five hundred men, descended on the home of General John Neville, the inspector of excise for the area, and attempted to force him to resign. Neville defended his home with the help of a few soldiers from a nearby military base. Two of the militiamen were killed and four wounded before Neville escaped. His house was then looted and burned. On August 1, insurgent leaders called a meeting of militia companies, and six thousand men opposed to the tax gathered outside Pittsburgh in a show of force. Some of the protesters recalled the revolution against Britain in justifying their actions. They saw themselves "re-enacting the scenes of the Revolution and resisting an alien sovereign." One rebel supporter, radical Antifederalist William Petrikin, said, "It was time there should be a Revolution—that Congress ought either to Repeal the Law or allow these people to set up a government for themselves—and be separated from us."[89]

After showing considerable patience, President Washington took a two-pronged course of action. On August 7, he made it known that he was calling out the militia to stop the lawlessness and enforce the excise tax. He sent commissioners to the affected counties to offer amnesty to anyone who would offer an oath of submission. After hearing from the commissioners that the rebels remained unwilling to comply with the law, Washington ordered a militia force numbering well over ten thousand men, comprised of units from eastern Pennsylvania and neighboring states, to march on western Pennsylvania. All of the leaders of the insurrection who had advocated violence had escaped the area, and Washington's army, which he personally led for part of the journey, found no one left to engage. The rebellion was over. A handful of men were detained, and all but two were eventually acquitted of any wrongdoing. The two convicted men received pardons.[90]

The Whiskey Rebellion tested the question of whether the Constitution established a right to rebel against the government. Hamilton and Washington, of course, argued vociferously against such an interpretation. Without respect for duly enacted laws, anarchy would reign. On August 28, 1794, Hamilton wrote of the Whiskey Rebellion,

Were it not that it might require too long a discussion, it would not be difficult to demonstrate that a large and well-organized republic can scarcely lose its liberty from any other cause than that of anarchy, to which a contempt of the laws is the high-road. But without entering into so wide a field, it is sufficient to present to your view a more simple and a more obvious truth, which is this: that a sacred respect for the constitutional law is the vital principle, the sustaining energy, of a free government. . . . Those, therefore, who preach doctrines, or set examples which undermine or subvert the authority of the laws, lead us from freedom to slavery. . . . Such a resistance is treason against society, against liberty, against every thing that ought to be dear to a free, enlightened, and prudent people.[91]

Washington added,

I say, under these circumstances, for a self created, permanent body, (for no one denies the right of the people to meet occasionally, to petition for, or to remonstrate against, any Act of the Legislature &ca) to declare that this act is unconstitutional, and that act is pregnant of mischief; and that all who vote contrary to their dogmas are actuated by selfish motives, or under foreign influence; nay in plain terms are traitors to their Country, is such a stretch of arrogant presumption as is not to be reconciled with laudable motives.[92]

For the Federalists, then, no right existed forcibly to resist a lawfully enacted statute, even one that is disagreeable or onerous. Militia units that organized without being called out by the governor or the president were mobs, and taking up arms against the government was treason.

Perhaps surprisingly, the vast majority of the Antifederalists and their heirs, the Democratic-Republicans, agreed with Hamilton and Washington and vehemently opposed violence as a part of the political process after the Constitution had been approved. They may have found the laws distasteful and unfair, but they were appalled at the idea that some citizens would resort to violence to resist the application of those laws. Most Americans, even those who thought the Federalists were accumulating too much power, believed that taking up arms against the state was incompatible with constitutional government. Democratic-Republican societies had been vocal in their opposition to Hamilton's excise program, yet when violence broke out, the rebels were quickly condemned.

Albert Gallatin, an important Democratic-Republican spokesman who later served as President Jefferson's secretary of the treasury, differentiated "between a publication of sentiments and acting." He went further, arguing, "We must distinguish between an opinion merely that this or that measure is wrong, . . . and an opinion to which is annexed a declaration that those who give that opinion mean to act in a certain manner or advise others to act."[93] He thus drew a line between speaking out against a law and inciting a riot against it.

William Findley, a Democratic-Republican member of Congress from western Pennsylvania and a prominent opponent of the excise tax, defended the right of citizens to protest the excise in the public sphere. He did not believe, however, that the right to oppose the tax extended to rebellion: "The great error among the people was an opinion, that an immoral law might be opposed and yet the government respected." Further, "All men of discretion and interest in the country, [realized] that, if they permitted government to be violently opposed, even in the execution of an obnoxious law, the same spirit would naturally lead to the destruction of all security and order; they saw by experience that in a state of anarchy the name of liberty would be profaned to sanction the most despotic tyranny."[94]

Individual Democratic societies outside of western Pennsylvania took great pains to distance themselves from the rebels. A public resolution from the Democratic Society of Newark affirmed as "an essential ingredient in . . . Republican government, that the voice of the majority govern; that a deviation from this rule unhinges every principle of freedom, by setting up the will of the few against that of the many. That the conduct of our fellow-citizen in several counties of a neighboring state, is a flagrant violation of this important principle—the law which they have refused obedience to, having been constitutionally enacted by a majority of the representatives of the people."[95] When the claim that the Constitution and the Second Amendment protect an individual right to use force to contest an unjust law was put to the test, it was rejected by the same people who had just ratified the Constitution. As Cornell puts it, after the Whiskey Rebellion, it became clear that the "right to keep and bear arms and participate in the militia was intended to provide the people with the means to put down rebellions, not foment them."[96]

A great deal of popular and scholarly analysis has been devoted to the rivalry between Jefferson and Hamilton and the differences in their political philosophies. Contemporary Insurrectionists routinely invoke Jefferson's poetic prose in support of their claim that taking up arms against the government follows the best tradition of the founders. Yet the Insurrectionists bind themselves to Jefferson not for what he did as president but for what he did when he was John Adams's vice president. Presiding over the Senate that passed the hated Alien and Sedition Acts that would prove to be the downfall of Adams's presidency and reputation, Jefferson was anonymously framing some of the basic ideas about states' rights (later used by the Confederacy) in his drafting of what has become known as the Virginia and Kentucky Resolutions. The resolutions, passed by their respective legislatures, registered opposition to the Alien and Sedition Acts and asserted that the states had the ability to nullify federal laws.

As in most of Jefferson's efforts, he collaborated with Madison on the resolutions. However, although Madison participated, he cautioned Jefferson against being too assertive. Jefferson nonetheless slipped the concept of state nullification of federal laws into both resolutions. The Virginia and Kentucky legislatures removed the word *nullify* when they passed the resolutions in 1798, but the idea entered public discourse when Jefferson's draft resolutions were printed anonymously in the press. In private correspondence that later became public, Jefferson wrote to Madison that if nullification were not taken seriously, which it never was, "secession" should be an option. Of course, the Virginia and Kentucky Resolutions came back to haunt both Jefferson and Madison after the Democratic-Republicans came to power in 1800, but the resolutions became the backbone of a states' rights ideology that eventually became unsustainable, leading to the Civil War. Madison, for a few moments in 1798, pushed by what he viewed as the gross excesses of the Federalists, took up the Antifederalist critique of the Constitution that he had condemned during ratification. He came to regret this lapse, as Wills makes clear: "Those who admire Madison as a champion of states' rights are not admiring (as they think) the Madison of *The Federalist* but the Madison of 1798—even though he would spend the rest of his life trying to back away from the Virginia Resolutions."[97]

After the 1800 elections, the administrations of both Jefferson and later Madison stood as ready to use the force of the state to suppress an actual or even a latent insurrection as were Hamilton and the other Federalists. After Jefferson's first vice president, Aaron Burr, killed Hamilton during an 1804 duel, Burr's political career was finished, as was his law practice. Hoping to restore his wealth, he ran away (he was under indictment for murder in both New Jersey and New York) to the Southwest, where he came up with a scheme to detach Mexico from Spain and may even have tried (although the historical record is not clear) to establish a new nation composed of several of the western states with himself as the ruler.

Rather than view Burr's actions as a legitimate expression of self-determination based on republican principles, Jefferson had Burr and his two alleged coconspirators arrested and charged with treason. Jefferson was so zealous in his push to prosecute the men that he even allowed the suspension of their right to habeas corpus. All three eventually were acquitted, and Jefferson was left bitter by the experience, blaming the acquittals on what he regarded as one more facet of Federalist chief justice John Marshall's plan to empower the judiciary at the expense of the executive.[98] Burr's mysterious activities in the Southwest may never be adequately explained, but Jefferson was unwilling to countenance any type of rebellion on his watch as president, and he was willing to use the full power of the state to end the threat. Of all the founders, Jefferson had the most sympathies for the Shaysites and the Whiskey Rebels (although he clearly understood that rebellion was not protected by the Constitution),[99] but when he was in charge of the government, he acted as his predecessors had done and permitted no rebellion against the Constitution.

Jefferson also proved willing to expand the standing army and use it for purposes not confined to the defense of the country's borders against foreign aggressors. While he may be the darling of the Insurrectionists, a review of the historical record shows that he was the only president to use the military for day-to-day law enforcement. To implement the Embargo Act, which prevented trade with European powers, Jefferson pressed Congress to give him the authority to call out the army and the navy, which it did. He then deployed the regular army in New York and Vermont to prevent cross-border trade into Canada. Among the founders, Jefferson was probably the most inclined to support an individual right to bear arms, and he offered an amendment to that effect during the drafting of the Virginia Constitution. (The amendment was defeated.) As president, however, he quickly realized that governance required enough force to ensure compliance with the law.[100] Citizens who tried to avoid the embargo were confronted with the full resources of the United States.

Despite Jefferson's statement that "the tree of liberty must be refreshed from time to time with the blood of patriots and tyrants,"[101] neither he nor the other founders hesitated to suppress armed citizen rebellions, including tax revolts, with violence. The founders were reluctant revolutionaries and acted against England not as individuals but as a nascent government with full and representative deliberations. They worked to establish a new republic on the basis of equal representation and a belief in the rule of law. With political representation achieved, no legitimacy could attach to armed rebellion, either by individual or by the state. Insurrectionists of our era who argue for a right to "vote from the rooftops" with sniper rifles and to reject the voting booth as a definitive means of conferring democratic legitimacy on government action have no legitimate ties to our founding spirit. They amount to nothing but the misbegotten rogue armies and benighted vigilantes whose mind-set the best leaders of our nation have always detested.

CHAPTER FIVE

THE CIVIL WAR
AND RECONSTRUCTION

The Civil War

Revisionist claims about the constitutional status of political violence emerged well before the gun rights movement adopted the Insurrectionist idea as a core rationale for opposition to the regulation of firearms. In fact, by the time the attack on Fort Sumter marked the beginning of the Civil War, advocates of secession, the forefathers of the modern Insurrectionists, had worked out elaborate theoretical justifications for their decision to take up arms against the United States. The states had never surrendered their sovereignty to the central government, the argument went, and therefore were free to dissolve the compact that bound them to the United States when they decided the Union no longer served their interests or represented their values. When Abraham Lincoln was elected president, many southerners felt they had no obligation to accept his mandate. Having lost the election, they set out to overturn it by force.[1]

In his first campaign for the presidency, Lincoln made it clear that he viewed secession as a violation of the compact among and between the states and the central government. While the states retained a large degree of sovereignty, their decision to join the Union was binding, and only a decision by a majority of states to rescind the contract could be

valid. As president, Lincoln acted on his view that insurrection was illegal and unconstitutional. He put the resources of the nation and the
lives of its citizens on the line to assert that the United States is indi-
visible.

Lincoln's First Inaugural Address laid out a version of sovereignty
and constitutionalism that identifies that there can be no right of revolution within the Constitution and shows the true folly of Insurrectionism. He did not deny a natural right to revolution but denied that it exists as a moral right that is "against the law."[2] In the inaugural address,
delivered as he was trying to prevent the nation from splintering, he
said,

> I hold, that in contemplation of universal law, and of the Constitution,
> the Union of these States is perpetual. Perpetuity is implied, if not ex-
> pressed, in the fundamental law of all national governments. It is safe to
> assert that no government proper, ever had a provision in its organic law
> for its own termination. Continue to execute all the express provisions
> of our national Constitution, and the Union will endure forever—it be-
> ing impossible to destroy it, except by some action not provided for in
> the instrument itself. . . . It follows from these views that no State, upon
> its own mere motion, can lawfully get out of the Union,—that resolves
> and ordinances to that effect are legally void; and that acts of violence,
> within any State or States, against the authority of the United States, are
> insurrectionary or revolutionary,[3] according to circumstances.[4]

In July 1861, after the Confederacy had already attacked Fort
Sumter, Lincoln needed to justify sending the nation to war. In his July
4 message to Congress, he explained that he saw himself as forced to
choose between

> "immediate dissolution, or blood." And this issue embraces more than
> the fate of these United States. It presents to the whole family of man,
> the question, whether a constitutional republic, or a democracy—a gov-
> ernment of the people, by the same people—can, or cannot, maintain its
> territorial integrity, against its own domestic foes. It presents the ques-
> tion, whether discontented individuals, too few in numbers to control

administration, according to organic law, in any case, can always, upon the pretences made in this case, or on any other pretences, or arbitrarily, without any pretence, break up their Government, and thus practically put an end to free government upon the earth. It forces us to ask: "Is there, in all republics, this inherent, and fatal weakness?" "Must a government, of necessity, be too strong for the liberties of its own people, or too weak to maintain its own existence?" So viewing the issue, no choice was left but to call out the war power of the Government; and so to resist force, employed for its destruction, by force, for its preservation.[5]

Lincoln excoriated those who twisted history to induce the people of the southern states to take up arms against the United States:

It might seem, at first thought, to be of little difference whether the present movement at the South be called "secession" or "rebellion." The movers, however, well understand the difference. At the beginning, they knew they could never raise their treason to any respectable magnitude, by any name which implies violation of law. They knew their people possessed as much of moral sense, as much of devotion to law and order, and as much pride in, and reverence for, the history, and government, of their common country, as any other civilized, and patriotic people. They knew they could make no advancement directly in the teeth of these strong and noble sentiments. Accordingly they commenced by an insidious debauching of the public mind. They invented an ingenious sophism, which, if conceded, was followed by perfectly logical steps, through all the incidents, to the complete destruction of the Union. The sophism itself is, that any state of the Union may, consistently with the national Constitution, and therefore lawfully, and peacefully, withdraw from the Union, without the consent of the Union, or of any other state. The little disguise that the supposed right is to be exercised only for just cause, themselves to be the sole judge of its justice, is too thin to merit any notice.

With rebellion thus sugar-coated, they have been drugging the public mind of their section for more than thirty years; and, until at length, they have brought many good men to a willingness to take up arms against the government the day after some assemblage of men have enacted the farcical pretence of taking their State out of the Union, who could have been brought to no such thing the day before.

This sophism derives much—perhaps the whole—of its currency, from the assumption, that there is some omnipotent, and sacred supremacy, pertaining to a State—to each State of our Federal Union. Our States have neither more, nor less power, than that reserved to them, in the Union, by the Constitution—no one of them ever having been a State out of the Union.[6]

Lincoln staked everything on the indivisibility of the United States. He would allow no rebellion against the Constitution and sent hundreds of thousands of Union soldiers to their death to vindicate the idea that there is no constitutional right to take up arms against the government. Lincoln's words and deeds stand as a permanent rebuke to the self-serving and ahistorical claim that guns represent the tools of political dissent.

Saul Cornell summarizes the implications of the Civil War for the Insurrectionist idea: "The actions of the South Carolina militia took the antebellum states' rights interpretation of the Second Amendment to its logical conclusion. . . . After the defeat of the Confederacy the notion that a state or an individual might exercise such a right was simply no longer tenable."[7] If the political reality was not enough, the Supreme Court flatly rejected an Insurrectionist reading of the Constitution. In *Texas v. White*, the Court ruled that the state of Texas had no power under the Constitution to secede from the Union. "The union between Texas and the other States was as complete, as perpetual, and as indissoluble as the Union between the original States," the opinion said. "There was no place for reconsideration, or revocation, except through revolution, or through consent of the states."[8]

Reconstruction and "Redemption"

Insurrectionists did not invent the selective and oversimplified use of history in service of an ideological agenda. Still, the Insurrectionist interpretation of American history in the aftermath of the Civil War provides a particularly brazen example of how history can be contorted by ideologues. According to the Insurrectionists, the collapse of Reconstruction—and every tragic consequence that followed—could have been avoided if the newly freed slaves had had access to firearms. This explanation of events is a fantasy.

It is easy for Insurrectionists to identify incidents where the victims of racist violence might have defended themselves more effectively if they had been armed with guns. The idea that white racists could have been kept in check by ensuring widespread access to firearms among black southerners, however, is absurd. In fact, the American experience during and after Reconstruction illustrates that the core premise of the Insurrectionist idea—that private ownership of guns safeguards individual rights against the tyranny of the majority—is exactly backward in explaining the relationship between private force and state power in protecting individual rights. The lesson for gun rights and for our country is that private violence—especially when carried out with the acquiescence or even tacit approval of local government authorities—represents the most realistic danger to liberty in our society. Wherever mob violence threatens individuals' rights, a government that is both subject to democratic constraints *and* capable of maintaining a monopoly on the organized use of force is the only hope for the rule of law. A brief review of the broader historical context of Reconstruction will help us to understand why this is so.

Abraham Lincoln could easily have been forgiven in the spring of 1865 for allowing a measure of optimism to color his view of America's future. What had begun as a rebellion to tear the Union apart had set in motion a chain of events that created a stronger central government with new legal and political authority and a Union with a vitality that would have been inconceivable four years earlier. No one person is more responsible for the strengthening of the power of the federal government than Lincoln. Today it is fashionable in many quarters to deride the federal government as overbearing and inefficient. Whatever its shortcomings in our time, Lincoln understood that the central government had to be strong enough to defend the rule of law when private groups—or even the states—defy democratic institutions or trample minorities' rights. The federal government serves this function today because Lincoln consciously strengthened centralized authority as a means to a noble end—that is, to extend and protect freedom throughout the land. Lincoln employed the might of the federal government against the seceding states not only to save the Union but also to advance the cause of individual liberty.

Lincoln believed that only a more powerful federal government could protect the democratic process that was and remains the foundation of political freedom in the United States. In a letter to James C. Conkling, Lincoln wrote, "Among free men, there can be no successful appeal from the ballot to the bullet; and that they who take such an appeal are sure to lose their case, and pay the cost."[9] Conkling did not miss the significance of Lincoln's lucid words, replying, "It indicates another step in the onward progress of our government towards its only true position, and that which it ought always to have occupied viz the establishment and protections of universal Liberty."[10]

In the period following the Civil War, the nation moved in fits and starts toward "universal liberty" for all men. The project ultimately fell far short of its goal. What might have been was lost to history when, on April 14, 1865, John Wilkes Booth used a concealed, single-shot .44-caliber pistol to assassinate Lincoln.[11] Booth could not abide Lincoln's use of federal authority, against the wishes of recalcitrant states and their citizens, to enforce the formal rights recently granted to freed slaves by the government of the United States. As Booth escaped from Ford's Theatre, at least one person heard him scream, "Sic semper tyrannis" (Thus always to tyrants) and then, "The South shall be free." Others thought Booth said, "Revenge for the South."[12]

Whatever his exact words, Booth was deeply committed to the Confederate cause and to the idea that the South had the right to reject the will of the voters regarding slavery—as expressed in the victories of President Lincoln in the national elections of 1860 and 1864—by using armed force to secede from the Union. He viewed Lincoln's expansive use of federal power, especially in Booth's home state of Maryland (which did not secede but whose people were largely sympathetic to the Confederacy), as an affront to freedom. Booth despised Lincoln and after the 1864 elections lamented that Lincoln would turn the presidency into a monarchy and destroy the republic. In a letter to his mother discovered after the assassination, Booth wrote, "I have not a single selfish motive to spur me on to this, nothing save the sacred duty, I feel I owe the cause I love, the cause of the South. The cause of liberty and justice."[13] In his conviction that an armed individual has the right—and even an obligation—to take up arms against democratic government, Booth foreshadowed the logic of Insurrectionism.

If Lincoln had not been assassinated, Reconstruction might well have put the nation on a much more direct path to the goal of civil equality. In *Forever Free*, Eric Foner and Joshua Brown call it "inconceivable" that Lincoln would have botched things as badly as Andrew Johnson did after assuming the presidency.[14]

In any event, Reconstruction was all but dead by 1877. Former slaves were only marginally closer to full legal and political equality than had been the case under formal bondage. Johnson, the man Booth propelled to the presidency, was a Tennessee Republican and the only U.S. senator from a seceding state to pledge his support for the Union and keep his seat. He was nominated as part of the 1864 Republican ticket to reflect "Republicans' determination to extend their organization into the South once the war had ended."[15]

Johnson had supported Lincoln's call to emancipate the slaves but viewed the role of the federal government in a starkly different light. Where Lincoln believed that the central government had an obligation to defend the integrity of the Union, individual rights, and the rule of law, Johnson was an unyielding proponent of states' rights and tight limits on federal power. He argued that the federal government should not interfere in local politics, even if the failure to do so left the freedmen disenfranchised. This perspective is, of course, far closer to Booth's than to Lincoln's.[16]

In 1866, the notoriously stubborn new president sent a message to Congress after vetoing a bill that would have extended the Freedmen's Bureau. (Congress overrode the veto in July of that year.) As Foner puts it,

> In appealing to fiscal conservatism, raising the specter of an immense federal bureaucracy trampling on citizen's rights, and insisting self-help, not dependence upon outside assistance, offered the surest road to eco-

nomic advancement, Johnson voiced themes that to this day have sustained opposition to federal intervention on behalf of blacks.[17]

Johnson and Lincoln's views on the role of government in protecting freedom and individual rights are part of a debate that is as old as the republic and has raged on to the present day. As we have explained, the Insurrectionists share with Johnson the belief that robust federal power should be equated with tyranny. The Insurrectionists fail to account for the major contributing factors in the rise of Jim Crow laws—the development of *private* militias and the *diminished* role of federal power. Whether they find these factors ideologically inconvenient or simply have never bothered to study the history they are so quick to appropriate in the name of gun rights advocacy, the Insurrectionists have spun a tale so misleading and incomplete that it is essentially a lie.

Of course, a few scholars have argued that gun control was an integral part of the system of control imposed by whites on slaves and later on freedmen and -women. These writers assert that the federal government's unwillingness or inability to protect former slaves during Reconstruction demonstrates that private access to guns was and is crucial to safeguarding democratic rights and that gun control therefore originated in racist impulses. They further claim that without gun control legislation, the waves of political violence perpetrated by white southern Democrats during Reconstruction would have been prevented and that Reconstruction itself would have been dramatically more successful. To take but one example, in "Of Holocausts and Gun Control," Daniel Polsby, dean of the George Mason University School of Law and a beneficiary of grant funding from the National Rifle Association (NRA), and Don B. Kates Jr. baldly assert that

> over a period of two centuries gun control laws played an indispensable part in Southern control of slaves and—after the Civil War—of freedmen. This legacy to the Second KKK from the triumph of the first Klan was enlarged when in 1911 New York followed Southern states by conditioning handgun ownership on obtaining a police license. The purpose of this requirement was to disarm Italians, Jews, and other supposedly criminous immigrant groups.[18]

Polsby and Kates draw a straight line from gun restrictions on slaves to the Holocaust, without pausing to examine the other circumstances and factors contributing to these events.

Another illustrative article, Robert J. Cottrol and Raymond T. Diamond's "The Second Amendment: Toward an Afro-Americanist Reconsideration," argues,

> The willingness of blacks to use firearms to protect their rights, their lives, and their property, alongside their ability to do so successfully when acting collectively, renders many gun control statutes, particularly of Southern origin, all the more worthy of condemnation. This is especially so in view of the purpose of these statutes, which, like that of the gun control statutes of the black codes, was to disarm blacks.[19]

And of course David Kopel, writing for the lay audience of the magazine *Reason*, details a litany of southern gun control laws passed to perpetuate Jim Crow.[20]

We are tempted at this point to paraphrase the NRA's favorite aphorism, "Gun control laws don't lynch people, people lynch people," and leave it at that, but a closer analysis is required. Not only is the claim that gun rights could have stopped the Jim Crow system a falsehood, but it covers up the even more important insight that the Insurrectionist construct is a continuation of a concerted effort, born and nurtured in the antebellum South, to limit the federal government's effectiveness in protecting the democratic rights of the most vulnerable Americans.

Before we examine the historical claims raised by the Insurrectionists in academia, it is important to remember that the "racist" character of any public policy choice depends on its context. In a racist society, all sorts of policies may be racist in their intent and effect—vagrancy laws, zoning restrictions, school boundary decisions, and even livestock-fencing regulations.[21] During Reconstruction and the era of Jim Crow, state legislatures enacted a wide variety of laws designed to deny black Americans political, legal, economic, and social equality. For example, a series of state laws mandated segregated public schools for blacks and whites. It does not follow, however, that all laws governing public education are racist. It simply means that a racist state legislature is capable of using a wide range of public policy choices to achieve the same nefarious ends. Gun laws are no different, and it is ludicrous to contend that the Brady background-check law is racist simply because an unrelated gun control law from another era was passed with the intention of preventing blacks from defending themselves.

None of this is to say that gun control laws designed to leave blacks defenseless against racist violence are not worthy of condemnation. Any use of state power that seeks to leave unpopular minorities more vulnerable to mob violence than is already the case is an affront to human rights and democracy. Gun control laws, however, were far from the worst affront to democratic values that arose during Reconstruction and Jim Crow. Far more destructive was the rise of private militias, including the Klan, the Knights of the White Camellia, and local rifle clubs that became de facto agents of the Democratic Party and state and local governments in the South. These armed terrorists did not need or wait for racist gun control schemes to do their dirty work. They killed, maimed, raped, pillaged, and yes, disarmed former slaves; they operated in many cases without fear of prosecution or even the opprobrium of their communities. Only the federal government had the capability to address the situation, although its commitment to use this capability proved lacking even in the best of times.

Reconstruction was a complicated patchwork of policies and programs that worked differently in each region of the South. Immediately after the Civil War, President Johnson used his executive authority to craft a set of policies now known as Presidential Reconstruction, which in effect differed little from de jure slavery. Former slaves were required to sign labor contracts and were still restricted in all aspects of their lives. According to Foner, "The entire complex of labor regulations and criminal laws was enforced by a police apparatus and judicial system in which blacks enjoyed virtually no voice whatever. Whites staffed urban police forces as well as state militias, intended, as a Mississippi white put it in 1865, to 'keep good order and discipline amongst the negro population.'"[22]

Even as laws that explicitly singled out blacks for disparate treatment fell by the wayside beginning in 1866, blacks remained excluded from the institutions of power, including service in militias and on juries. As the first wave of Klan violence started, "sheriffs, justices of the peace, and other local officials proved extremely reluctant to prosecute whites accused of crimes against blacks."[23] Johnson had no interest in changing the antebellum social order that included a strong emphasis on states' rights. Yet it became clear soon after the cessation of hostilities that the states themselves were unable or unwilling to give meaning to emancipation and that the federal government would have to step into the breach. This discovery was not lost on the former slaves: "Presidential Reconstruction reinforced blacks' identification with federal authority. Only outside intervention could assure the freedmen a modicum of justice."[24] The nation as a whole would have to protect the rights of the former slaves.

In response to the failures of Presidential Reconstruction and because of the crisis caused by rising violence in the South, congressional Republicans pushed to enact Radical Reconstruction. The radicals believed that traditional principles of federalism and states' rights should not be allowed to stand in the way of a national effort to secure the former slaves' rights and had no qualms about using the full resources of the federal government to make the effort succeed.[25]

Gaining power after the elections of 1866, the radical Republicans overrode a Johnson veto to pass the Reconstruction Act of 1867, which provided the means for former slaves to exercise their political rights. Although the measure did not disenfranchise the rebels and created only temporary enforcement provisions, the radicals pinned great hope on the ballot's ability to transform the South without having to resort to a massive, long-term federal military presence in the region.[26] To a large extent, black suffrage was a revolutionary occurrence. Foner notes, "Alone among the nations that abolished slavery in the nineteenth century, the United States, within a few years of emancipation, clothed its former slaves with citizenship rights equal to those of whites."[27] Suffrage transformed southern black life, with newly freed slaves energetically engaging in the trappings of public life, seeking elected office, and building the institutions of what we today call civil society, including political organizations and self-improvement societies.

Southern Democrats, acutely aware of their lost power and influence, responded with all of the legal and extralegal tools at their disposal to undo what the radicals had achieved. Steven Hahn argues that the Klan and other groups committed to violence were part of a long tradition of the use of brutality to maintain political power in the South: "Paramilitary organization had been fundamental to the social and political order of slavery; it remained fundamental to the social and political order of freedom."[28] In effect, these organizations served as the armed wing of the Democratic Party, and their role was to force the former slaves and their allies out of the political process through violence and intimidation.[29]

They achieved their goal. The Klan and its allies intimidated or killed Republican elected officials at all levels of government and devastated the leaders of the emerging grassroots organizations that supported black political participation. Starting with the elections of 1868, the paramilitary groups suppressed Republican voting, especially in areas where the states did not have federal troops at their disposal.[30]

The Camilla Riot in southwestern Georgia in the fall of 1868 was among the best-known of thousands of acts of intimidation throughout the South that led to voter suppression. The incident began when a lightly armed group of freedmen, "led by a wagonload of musicians playing fifes and drums," tried to enter the town of Camilla to hear Republican congressional candidate William P. Pierce speak at a rally. Racial tensions were high. Whites had harassed Pierce a few days earlier at a rally in a nearby town. As the procession entered Camilla, a local drunk fired on the group and then was joined by white townspeople organized in rifle squads. The freedmen tried to escape, but the white mob followed. The violence continued for days, and nine blacks were killed and many others wounded. More telling, on Election Day, "Only two Republicans bothered to cast ballots in Camilla, and the turnout was so low elsewhere in the district that the Democrats, despite being greatly outnumbered among eligible voters, registered an official victory."[31]

In response to this violence, the federal government put its resources to work. Congress passed the Ku Klux Klan Act of 1871, which provided for federal prosecutions of individuals who deprived former slaves of their civil rights and even called for military intervention if necessary.[32] Under the recently established Department of Justice, hundreds of Klansmen were prosecuted, and the Union Army was used to root out the Klan in South Carolina. The results were impressive. As Foner explains,

> Judging by the percentage of Klansmen actually indicted and convicted, the fruits of "enforcement" seem small indeed, a few hundred men among thousands guilty of heinous crimes. But in terms of its larger purposes—restoring order, reinvigorating the morale of Southern Republicans, and enabling blacks to exercise their rights as citizens—the policy proved a success. "The law on the side of freedom," Frederick Douglass would later remark, "is of great advantage only where there is power to make that law respected." By 1872, the federal government's evident willingness to bring its legal and coercive authority to bear had broken the Klan's back and produced a dramatic decline in violence throughout the South.[33]

Some Republican governors in the South also mounted serious offensives against the Klan, especially where they had a base of white Republicans on whom to rely.[34] According to Foner, the former slaves generally exercised remarkable restraint and preferred to rely on democratic processes to vindicate their rights.[35] But as Hahn points out, the freed bondspersons also organized and took up arms because they knew from bitter experience how politics in the South worked. Even as blacks were deeply committed to democracy, they understood that in the South, "the rites of democracy had been built on the rituals of violence."[36] Hahn chronicles many examples of former slaves organizing and arming in efforts that successfully if temporarily vindicated their political rights. He details how blacks drove the Klan out of Wilmington, North Carolina, in 1868 by taking up night patrols on the streets with guns and fence rails. "Four 'tempestuous' nights later, they had ended the career of the Ku Klux Klan in Wilmington."[37] Blacks exercised their voting rights freely in the fall elections.[38] Blacks in state militias also were part of successful efforts to suppress political violence. The decline in violence made the 1872 elections the most peaceful of Reconstruction.[39]

These small victories were short-lived, however, and proved impossible to maintain after the federal government withdrew its assistance during President Ulysses S. Grant's second term. During Grant's first administration, he went along with Congress and used the power of his office to ease the plight of the former slaves. It was here that the benefits of a strong national government were recognized. "The antebellum, Civil War, and early Reconstruction experiences had proved that various states could be just as tyrannical as many Americans at the Founding had feared the federal government might be. These recent events had also shown that the central government—aided by a national army of both volunteers and draftees—could at times be freedom's best friend."[40]

But during his second term, amid rising Republican political losses, Grant backed off from his support of blacks and left the southern Republicans without federal backing. Asked why he had not sent troops to Mississippi to stop brutal political violence in 1875, Grant maintained that northern Republican leaders had pressured him, insisting that there was no sense in trying to save Mississippi if it meant losing Ohio. The results were disastrous. The Democratic paramilitary apparatus used violence and election fraud to "redeem" the South. Black and white Republicans were again killed and intimidated and prevented from voting or exercising other political rights. "Unlike crimes by the Ku Klux Klan's hooded riders, those of 1875 were committed in broad daylight by undisguised men, as if to underscore the impotence of local authorities and Democrats' lack of concern about federal intervention."[41]

Hahn shows how the former slaves valiantly fought the "redemption" plans by organizing and taking up arms. In late 1874, in Vicksburg, Mississippi, Sheriff Peter Crosby, a black Republican, organized a posse to protest his forcible removal from office by a group of "White-Liners" who had been organized in close association with the Democratic Party and were dedicated to excluding blacks from the political process. Crosby brought together several hundred troops and had the backing of the Republican governor, yet when he attempted to reenter Vicksburg, his men were gunned down by armed whites, who then attacked blacks for another ten days, killing twenty-nine and wounding and intimidating many more. Federal troops finally stepped in to stop the carnage and reinstate Crosby. The White-Liners' tactics spread the following year, however, part of the attempts to intimidate Republican voters throughout the state. "Paramilitary squads terrorized rural districts, county seats, and other polling places, sometimes with the help of counterparts from Louisiana and Alabama, on election eve and election day in most places where an organized Republican constituency was still to be detected." When the White-Liners' campaign was complete, Republicans had lost control of the state legislature, and many Republican holders of local offices were either defeated or forced out.[42]

This pattern was repeated throughout the South, even in South Carolina, which had well-organized and -armed black militias. Hahn estimates that as many as one hundred thousand black men served in the South Carolina Militia.[43] Ultimately, however, the determined plans of the Democratic paramilitary organizations, buttressed by massive election fraud, pushed the Republicans out of South Carolina, leaving a trail of blood. By 1874, "armed whites sought direct confrontations with black militiamen" even in areas with large majorities of former slaves.[44] In Hampton, South Carolina, a clash between a drilling black militia company and two white men who demanded the right of way led to an armed confrontation between the militiamen and the local rifle clubs. Before the fight was over, the town marshal and a militia lieutenant had been killed, and thirty militiamen had been captured, with five of them summarily executed. The reign of terror continued, with whites determined to destroy the former slaves' political power.

Hahn quotes a white paramilitary man to sum up the situation: "By God we are going to take your guns [and] the United States Government hain't got anything to do with it. . . . [T]he Constitution is played out, and every man can do just as he pleases."[45] Foner observes that "the practical obstacles to armed resistance were immense." Not only did blacks tend to have inferior weapons, but those "with military experience were far outnumbered in a region where virtually every white male had been trained to bear arms."[46] During the Colfax Massacre, these obstacles became painfully apparent. In the single-most-devastating incident of Reconstruction, a dispute over a contested election in Louisiana led to a standoff between armed black Republicans and an assortment of white paramilitary groups over the control of local government. The Republicans held the paramilitary forces at bay for several days before being flushed out by the whites' superior force, which included the use of a cannon. When it was over, hundreds of blacks were dead.[47]

While Hahn cautions against underestimating the "extent and tenacity of black resistance," Foner reminds us that "ultimately, of course, the responsibility for suppressing crime rests not with the victim but with the state." Foner and Hahn agree that federal troops were the most important factor in protecting Republican political participation in the South. In the words of members of the Alabama Union League, "Only a standing army in this place can give us our right and life."[48]

For purposes of evaluating the Insurrectionist account of Reconstruction, the salient point is that where federal power was brought to bear, former slaves could exercise their political rights fully and enjoy many benefits of full citizenship, but when federal power waned and political will drained away, blacks—despite their personal bravery and willingness to defend themselves—were overcome by larger and more powerful white paramilitary organizations.

The facile arguments made by Polsby and like-minded right-wing academics assume that an armed populace best protects liberty and that a weak government is less capable of becoming tyrannical. Reconstruction, however, showed something else entirely: a well-armed populace is capable of enforcing its will at the expense of the rights of minorities if the federal government lacks the political or military strength to intervene. When the federal government pulled out of the South, Reconstruction-era state governments lacked sufficient loyal militia or law enforcement resources to protect black citizens and safeguard the rule of law. The crime of Reconstruction, therefore, is not enactment of a few gun control statutes but the fact that under the camouflage of states' rights, southern Democrats were permitted to turn the clock back on freedom and civil rights. The federal power that Lincoln had zealously developed to protect and support former slaves was quickly relinquished after his death. Almost a century would pass before another Republican president's troops stepped in to protect the rights of black Americans in the South.

Former slaves tried to protect their rights—some by using guns—but were overwhelmed by their opponents. Governors who called out state militias quickly learned that white citizens who only recently had fought a war to preserve the institution of slavery were not eager to fight for the civil rights of newly freed slaves. The events leading to the "redemption" of the southern states showed that an uncontrolled mob is just as capable of tyranny as any consolidated government. Yet the Insurrectionist fantasy blames gun control laws—not the despicable conduct of southern Democrats, not the ballot fraud that forced Republicans from power, and not the states' rights ideology of Johnson and Booth—for the repressions of civil rights. Insurrectionists build on this fantasy—the very antithesis of Lincoln's view—even now.

The former slaves should indeed have had the same right to bear arms as their white counterparts. But the Insurrectionists' revisionist history, which puts gun control laws at the center of the struggle against the Ku Klux Klan, misidentifies the real villains—the southerners who put the rights of the states ahead of the rights of their fellow citizens. The revisionist myths about Reconstruction attempt to explain a complex set of events through the prism of a simple slogan for true believers: guns make us free. A more nuanced understanding of history shows otherwise. Not until the federal government acted to fulfill Lincoln's promise of freedom were black Americans able to participate fully as citizens in our democracy. The Insurrectionist claim that restrictive gun laws bore at least partial responsibility for the rise of political violence against blacks after the Civil War may be correct in the narrow sense that some African Americans were left without an effective means of defending themselves when Klansmen arrived at their doorsteps but is 180 degrees from the truth on the broader—and far more important—question of the relationship between centralized power and the rights of the individual in the Reconstruction era.

Indeed, while Reconstruction ultimately failed to deliver on the promise of equality for African Americans in the short term, it achieved legal changes that built the foundation for the protection of a much broader range of rights for all Americans over the long term. As Foner observes, Reconstruction-era changes to the Constitution represented a fundamental reordering of the relationship between the state and federal governments, giving the federal government a primary role in the defense of individual rights. In 1789, it was assumed that the central government's power represented the most important threat to liberty, and powerful state governments were viewed as a buffer to protect the rights of the people against overreaching by the federal government. By 1865, however, it had become clear that that states—or groups of citizens acting with the acquiescence or approval of state and local officials—were at least as likely to oppress unpopular minorities and trample the rights of individuals. In adopting the Thirteenth, Fourteenth, and Fifteenth Amendments, Congress changed the structure of the Constitution to reflect this new understanding, making the federal government the guarantor of individual rights.

The Reconstruction Amendments, and especially the Fourteenth, transformed the Constitution from a document primarily concerned with federal-state relations and the rights of property into a vehicle through which members of vulnerable minorities could stake a claim to substantive freedom and seek protection against misconduct by all levels of government. The rewriting of the Constitution promoted a sense of the document's malleability, and suggested that the rights of individual citizens were intimately connected to federal power. The Bill of Rights had linked civil liberties and the autonomy of the states. Its language— "Congress shall make no law"—reflected the belief that concentrated power was a threat to freedom. Now, rather than a threat to liberty, the federal government, declared Charles Sumner, the abolitionist Senator from Massachusetts, had become "the custodian of freedom." The Reconstruction Amendments assumed that rights required political power to enforce them. They not only authorized the federal government to override state actions that deprived citizens of equality, but each ended with a clause empowering Congress to "enforce" them with "appropriate legislation." Limiting the privileges of citizenship to white men had long been intrinsic to the practice of American democracy. Only in an unparalleled crisis could these limits have been superseded, even temporarily, by the vision of an egalitarian republic embracing black Americans as well as white and presided over by the federal government.[49]

The implications of these changes were not limited to the question of race and slavery. The Fourteenth Amendment, with its explicit authorization for a sweeping expansion of the power of the federal government to enforce the rights of individual citizens to due process and to equal protection of the laws, represented an entirely new understanding of the role of the central government in the protection of liberty. Instead of interposing the states as a shield between individual citizens and a central government assumed to be remote, unresponsive, and unaccountable, the Reconstruction amendments gave the federal government the right and responsibility to enforce individual rights in the face of a wide range of abuses by state and local authorities and even private individuals—armed or not—who pose a threat to individuals' rights. The failure of Insurrectionist theorists and their allies in right-wing politics to come to terms with the post-Reconstruction Constitution reflects a basic logical weakness in their conception of the federal government as a menace to be kept in check by armed citizens capable of resisting its decisions with violence.

CHAPTER SIX

THE RISE OF THE THIRD REICH

"Loyalty to the Fatherland required disloyalty to the Republic."
    adage among the German Right in the 1920s

"I love my country but fear my government"
    bumper sticker in the United States at the
    beginning of the twenty-first century

German Gun Laws and the Holocaust

"How can anyone support gun control after what Hitler did to the Jews?" What began several years ago as a throwaway line used by gun rights activists to suggest that perhaps European Jews could have organized themselves to resist the Nazis if they had been better armed has become a fully elaborated revisionist theory of the history of the Holocaust. One gun rights group, Jews for the Preservation of Firearms Ownership, is dedicated specifically to promoting the idea that Jews have the most to lose if private ownership of firearms is regulated or restricted because persecuted minorities cannot count on the government to protect them. Any government, the story goes, might well be hijacked by anti-Semites bent on exterminating the Jews. The group's logo is a Star of David flanked by a musket on one side and an assault weapon on the other, and its motto is "America's Most Aggressive Defender of Firearms Ownership."[1]

The alleged link between gun control and genocide is now a staple of gun rights advocacy. Gun rights blogs are replete with calls to remember that the "first thing Hitler did was to take the guns from the people."[2] In *Guns, Freedom, and Terrorism*, Wayne LaPierre claims that firearm registration paved the way for the Holocaust.[3] In a later book, *The Global War on Your Guns*, he maintains that gun control laws have enabled governments to murder 169 million of their own citizens. "If every family on this planet owned a good-quality rifle, genocide would be on the path to extinction," he asserts.[4]

Of course, for someone who believes that gun rights are essential to the prevention of genocide, extremism in defense of an absolutist vision of those rights is no vice. For the activists who transformed the National Rifle Association (NRA) from a moderate group representing the interests of sportsmen into an intensely partisan and ideological organization in the mid-1970s, the standard interest-group model of negotiating with opponents to try to find common ground is simply unacceptable. Former NRA lobbyist Richard Feldman's tell-all book, *Ricochet: Confessions of a Gun Lobbyist*, relates how, as early as 1969, Harlan Carter, the father of the modern NRA, "compared the growing gun control movement [and specifically the Gun Control Act of 1968] to the confiscatory actions of Nazi Germany that permitted only a privileged few like Hermann Goering to own firearms and hunt."[5]

Carter and his allies had no patience for the earlier generation of NRA leaders, who at one point endorsed a ban on cheap handguns as a means of limiting the impact of gun violence. After all, when the stakes are as high as stopping state-sponsored mass murder, nothing can be allowed to stand in the way. As discussed in chapter 3, the Carter faction overthrew the weak-kneed old guard at the NRA's 1977 convention, and the Insurrectionist fantasy became the NRA's basic organizing principle.

By now, the genocide claim is tossed out casually, as if its logic were self-evidently unimpeachable and as if it need not even be explained in great detail. David Kopel and his associate Richard Griffiths, for example, have said, "One of the things that [genocidal tyrants such as] Robert Mugabe . . . and Adolf Hitler all have in common is their strong and effective programs of gun control. Simply put, if not for gun control, Hitler would not have been able to murder 21 million people."[6] The lament that gun registration will lead first to gun confiscation and then to tyranny has been repeated countless times in the popular press.[7]

This is not to suggest that the gun control/genocide argument has not been discussed in detail. Robert Cottrol produced a law review article asking, "Could the overstretched Nazi war machine have murdered 11 million armed and resisting Europeans while also taking on the Soviet and Anglo-American armies?"[8] The current dean of the George Mason University law school, Daniel Polsby, and Don B. Kates Jr. wrote an article, "Of Holocausts and Gun Control," in which they state, "It is hardly a secret that lawful governments sometimes do grotesque things, quite often to popular acclaim." They continue, "One thinks, for example, of the *Kristallnacht*. On November 9, 1937, German mobs perpetrated a nationwide 'spontaneous uprising' against the Jews, assaulting and killing hundreds of people, smashing shops and homes, burning synagogues, and inflicting losses of over one billion Reichmarks. . . . Though it may be an extreme example, the Holocaust draws into question precisely the problem of relying exclusively and simply on 'the law . . . your representatives . . . [and] your fellow citizens.' "[9]

Gun Control and the Nazis

The argument tying gun control to the Holocaust has two elements: first, that Hitler and the Nazis enacted laws that restricted private access to firearms; and second, that these laws helped him further his murderous agenda. The work of Stephen Halbrook, a prolific writer and lawyer specializing in firearms litigation, illustrates the general approach taken by gun rights enthusiasts. In reference to the Second Amendment, Halbrook says, "This right, which reflects a universal and historical power of the people in a republic to resist tyranny, was not recognized in the German Reich." He provides a brief history of the rise of the Weimar Republic after World War I and the accompanying violence between the communists and *Freikorps* (right-wing militias) that gave rise to restrictive German gun laws, including the banning of private possession of firearms. Halbrook describes the German gun law of 1928 in detail, noting that it did not include the ban on gun possession but was considered more enforceable because it developed a licensing scheme for manufacturers and "ensured that the police had records of all firearms acquisitions." Halbrook says these laws enacted by a "liberal republic" were "quite useful to the new government that came to power a half decade later."[10]

Halbrook glosses over Hitler's rise but chronicles the Nazi regime's efforts to disarm political opponents immediately after coming to power. He describes a typical incident that followed the shooting deaths of two Nazi Party members by "Communists" the day after Hitler became chancellor in 1933: "The police closed off the street to all traffic while at the same time criminal detectives conducted extensive raids in the houses. Each individual apartment was searched for weapons. The raid lasted several hours." He documents many similar incidents, including the confiscation of 1,702 firearms during the *Kristallnacht* campaign, and describes how Hitler finally took away all weapons in the hands of Jews with his 1938 gun control measure. Halbrook concludes, "Germany's Jews had been disarmed. The process was carried out both by following a combination of legal forms and by sheer lawless violence. The Nazi hierarchy could now more comfortably deal with the Jewish question without fear of resistance."[11]

Halbrook also asks, "How might the course of history been different had Germany (not to mention the countries Germany would occupy) been a country where large numbers of citizens owned firearms without intrusive legal restrictions and where the right to keep and bear arms was a constitutional guarantee?"[12] In other words, did gun control laws enable Hitler's rise to power?

The first element of the argument—the claim that Hitler and the Nazis adopted significant new restrictions on private gun ownership—is actually quite easy to address because it simply arranges the facts backward. Contrary to what Halbrook and others have asserted, Hitler's 1938 gun control act actually made it easier for ordinary Germans to get guns. Bernard Harcourt, a law professor at the University of Chicago, writing partly in response to Halbrook, observes, "The history of gun control in Germany from the post–World War I period to the inception of World War II seems to be a history of *declining*, rather than increasing, gun control. The Weimar Republic gun laws of 1928 represented a liberalization of the draconian post–World War I prohibitions on gun possession." He continues, "With regard to ordinary gun possession, as opposed to manufacture, the 1938 Nazi laws represented a further liberalization of gun control. In fact, most of the changes in the laws with regard to possession and carrying reflected a *loosening* of the regulations, not a tightening." For example, the 1928 law applied a licensing requirement on the acquisition of all weapons, while the 1938 measure applied the license requirement only to handguns, completely dropping rifles and shotguns from the regulatory scheme.[13]

This correction of Halbrook's counterfactual account does not in itself settle the debate, because Germany indeed had gun control laws before, during, and after Hitler's rise to power. Did these laws help the Nazis consolidate power and carry out the extermination of the Jews? The superficial logic of the argument is undeniable, because anyone confronted with the prospect of being carted off to the gas chambers obviously would want to have something—anything—that might be used to fight back. Who would deny the victims of a genocidal regime the means to defend themselves? No reasonable person would want to leave the Jews defenseless.

In the Insurrectionists' ideal world of weak government, the oppressed will own guns to protect themselves. The problem is that the oppressed will need those guns because the state will be in no position to protect them. By itself, access to small arms is unlikely to be of much help to minorities or individuals who find themselves singled out for persecution. Whether the oppressors are agents of the state itself or private militias operating with the state's acquiescence will not matter much one way or the other. Remember, the Insurrectionist dream requires that the institutions of the state be kept in a condition of weakness so that organized force can be used effectively independent of the rule of law. As to minorities—Jews or otherwise—who would look to the state for protection from mob violence, the Insurrectionists in effect say, "Let them eat guns."

In this regard, it is useful to think for a moment about what might have happened—and in fact almost did happen—when the federal courts began to order racial integration of the schools in the United States. In the Insurrectionist view, where centralized power is always to be regarded with suspicion and hostility, the federal government never should have sent troops to ensure the safety of the first African American student at the University of Mississippi. Instead, James Meredith should have brought a gun—and as many armed friends as he could muster—to the Oxford campus. With enough of them, perhaps Meredith would have prevailed. As it was, two people died and thirty National Guardsmen received gunshot wounds in the rioting that surrounded Meredith's enrollment as a student. It is hard to imagine that less violence would have resulted if he had invoked his "rights" under the Second Amendment rather than the Fourteenth to gain admission to a public institution of higher learning.

Returning to the Holocaust experience of the Jews, an attempt to weigh the costs and benefits of an expansive view of gun rights based on the Insurrectionist paranoia about centralized power warrants a short look at the history of the Weimar Republic and Hitler's rise to power.

A Dangerously Weak State

Hitler's ascent was not inevitable. Contrary to popular belief, Hitler was never elected to fill the position of chancellor. Nor did the Nazi Party win a majority of the national vote or have a majority of seats in the Reichstag in any free election. Hitler seized power because by 1930, Germany was no longer a democracy. The fledgling Weimar Republic, Germany's first, short-lived experiment in democracy, had ceased to function when Hitler took control. To gain the office, his main task was to convince a small circle of powerful insiders that he was the man for the job. Hitler certainly appealed to popular opinion as he jockeyed for position, and once in office, he used his private army to consolidate his grip on the state. But he was initially installed through a backroom deal based on one man's approval, sitting Reich president and former war hero Paul Von Hindenburg.

Of course, there is more to the downfall of Weimar democracy than this one mistaken judgment—the seeds of German democracy's destruction were sown in the aftermath of World War I, which created the conditions for the rise of totalitarianism and highlighted the lack of commitment to core democratic values such as equality and pluralism. Prior to World War I, the German constitutional system differed from the more responsive systems of France and Britain. Many parties were represented in the Reichstag but held little real power. Entrenched interest groups, including the army and big landholders, prevented true parliamentary democracy. Foreign policy and military affairs remained outside the Reichstag's jurisdiction. The powerful position of Reich chancellor was appointed by the kaiser and thus "stood above" the political parties. Democratization met stiff opposition.[14]

Germany's path to nationhood accounts in part for its powerful nationalism in the Nazi era. The nation took shape through the unification of a number of smaller states bound together by "culture and language rather than attaching itself to and emerging from the institutions of a pre-existing unitary state as in the case of England or France. This promoted an ethnic definition of nationhood which could easily slide over (though it by no means always did so) into forms of racism." In the 1912 Reichstag elections, the Social Democratic Party, devoted to a Marxist agenda, was the largest party. In its path stood the collective forces of "a highly aggressive integral nationalism aiming to destroy Marxist socialism." After the war, Hitler harnessed this nationalism to exploit "the belief that pluralism was somehow unnatural or unhealthy in a society" and destroyed his enemies, including Jews and Social Democrats.[15]

Germany entered World War I following the assassination of the heir to the Austrian throne, Archduke Franz Ferdinand, with widespread support from most sectors of society.[16] The war caused severe hardship for the German people. About 2,000,000 German soldiers were killed, and 5,000,000 more were wounded. By 1917, food shortages in Germany caused malnutrition on a large scale, killing 750,000 people. Coal shortages left people cold all winter. These developments led to increased social tension and worker strikes.[17] War efforts in the spring of 1918 had gone well, but disastrous reversals, hidden from the people and even from the Reichstag, forced the German government to seek a peace treaty in October. At the armistice, the army was outside German territory, but the situation was hopeless.

In replying to the German request for peace in October, President Woodrow Wilson noted that autocratic monarchs and military rulers posed an impediment to negotiations. By November 7, the Bavarian monarchy had crumbled, and the kaiser abdicated two days later, forced out by a "groundswell of popular demand for radical change."[18] The masses wanted democracy, yet there was no agreement on what that meant in practice. The Social Democratic Party never fully embraced democratic change and even called out government troops and counter-revolutionary *Freikorps* (illegally armed militias, often supported by the army as a means to get around the troop limitations imposed on Germany after the armistice) to suppress radical leftists.[19] Even as a democratic republic was proclaimed, this split in the Left created wounds that never healed. Eventually, it rendered Hitler's opposition too fragmented to stop him.[20]

The destruction of the imperial monarchy led to the "reluctant assumption of power by the democratic parties in the Reichstag. The Republican Government had to bear the odium of signing, first the surrender and then the peace terms." The terms, as enshrined in the Treaty of Versailles, were harsh and included massive monetary reparations to the allied nations and limited the German military to one hundred thousand men. Although the initiative to end the war had come from the Army High Command, "this fact was concealed. The High Command not only left the civil government, hitherto denied any voice in the conduct of the war, to take the full responsibility for ending it, but tried to dissociate itself from the consequences of the decision."[21]

The situation gave rise to the myth that the new republic had stabbed the country in the back. "The fact that its institutions were democratic, that the Social Democratic Party and the working-class organizations supported it, and that there was a demand for more radical action from the Left—finding expression in workers' demonstrations, strikes, and, on occasion, street fighting—added to the hostility with which the extremists of the Right viewed the new regime." Opponents branded the new government the "November criminals" and made it a scapegoat for the failed war effort. The republic was "damned from birth" by the Right and became forever linked with the "shameful" and "treacherous" surrender. "Rarely has a more fraudulent lie been foisted on a people, yet it was persistently repeated and widely believed—because so many wanted to believe it." The Nationalists and the army managed to escape the blame for their rash actions in taking the nation to war.[22] Hitler referred to the defeat and to the democratic revolution as "the greatest villainy of the century."[23] He used the November criminals as targets as he made his rise to power and apparently had a receptive audience. After the war, "it was openly said that loyalty to the Fatherland required disloyalty to the Republic."[24]

Massive civil unrest, including the revolution in Bavaria in the early months of the Republic, tarnished the image of the Left. Although Bavaria had been consolidated into the unified Germany, it kept a great deal of autonomy, as did other states, such as Prussia. The Bavarian Revolution started before the fall of the kaiser, but violent clashes continued into May 1919. For a few days, power was held by a Soviet-inspired communist government (*Raterepublik*), a number of whose leaders were Jewish. The *Freikorps* and troops from other states eventually crushed the revolt amid much bloodshed. The reaction to the communist revolution pushed politics in Bavaria to the right, a trend that was further solidified when the leaders of a failed right-wing coup against the Reich government found sanctuary and support there. To this crowd, "Not just the legend of the 'stab-in-the-back,' but the notion of an international Jewish conspiracy could be made to sound plausible in the light of the Munich Raterepublik."[25] Such an environment was tailor-made for someone like Hitler to exploit.

Hitler toiled in relative obscurity until Germany's economic condition declined precipitously in the late 1920s. A world economic slowdown and severe structural problems with the German economy led to massive unemployment and real pain among the country's people.[26] Hitler's Nazi Party gained strength as the economy worsened, and the Reichstag, its power hopelessly divided among many small parties, failed to stabilize the economy. Through a tireless campaign and the shrewd use of propaganda and agitation by Hitler's private army, the SA, the Nazis scored a major political breakthrough in the Reichstag elections of 1928, improving their position in the body from 12 to 107 deputies. Meanwhile, their archenemies, the Communists, made large gains as well, garnering 77 deputies. This was an ominous development for German democracy. As Alan Bullock points out, "The two parties which had openly campaigned for the overthrow of the existing regime and had deliberately framed their appeal in extremist terms had together won close on a third of the votes."[27]

If there were any doubts about Hitler's determination to get rid of the republic, his statements around the time of the election should have put them to rest. "It is not parliamentary majorities that mould the fate of nations. We know, however, that in this election democracy must be defeated with the weapons of democracy," he said.[28] Hitler stuck to his script of trying to use democracy (along with some clearly antidemocratic tactics) to gain power. His party steadily gained votes and deputies in the Reichstag, and by July 1932, the Nazis had, at their highest free- election level, 37.3 percent of the vote and 230 seats in the Reichstag, still well short of a majority.[29]

Hitler was the most powerful political leader in Germany but was blocked by a cacophony of other parties, including the second-largest party, the Communists, from assembling a parliamentary majority. His appeals to Hindenburg to name him chancellor and let him form a government fell on deaf ears. The lack of a clear majority in the Reichstag led to yet another election in November 1932, and this time the Nazis suffered a setback, losing seats for the first time since 1928.[30]

Hitler's ascent to the post of chancellor at a time when his political support was waning is one of the most profoundly tragic political stories of all time and a cautionary lesson about the need to safeguard democracy. The nationalists who opposed the government as the November criminals never reconciled with the republic. Hitler used the Nazi propaganda machine to excoriate the government for its inability to deal with the nation's economic problems. These dissatisfactions combined to threaten not just a particular group of political leaders but the democratic form of government that had been so recently adopted. "In Germany, the 'system' itself, the very nature of the state, was at stake from the beginning of the crisis. Hitler and his party were the beneficiaries of this systemic crisis of the Weimar state. They were not its primary cause. Even in its 'golden' years, Weimar democracy had never won the hearts and minds of large numbers of Germans. . . . Not a few among the power elites were awaiting the opportunity to discard the democracy they detested so much."[31]

The economic crisis allowed the old-guard nationalists to show their antidemocratic nature. The political fragmentation came to a head in 1930. The fragile parliamentary coalition that had enabled Chancellor Hermann Muller to govern fell apart in a fight over whether employer contributions to unemployment insurance should be increased. Hindenburg refused to give Muller the power to rule by decree, as authorized in the Weimar Constitution. Hindenburg eventually gave such power to Muller's successors, but the president let the government fall as he "was anxious not to miss the chance of creating an 'anti-parliamentary and anti-Marxist' government and afraid of being forced to retain a Social Democrat administration." As historian Ian Kershaw writes, Muller's fall and his "replacement by Heinrich Bruning of the Zentrum [a right-wing political party] was the first unnecessary step on the suicidal road of the Weimar Republic."[32]

Despite a series of elections in 1932, the German people did not get another elected chancellor. Hindenburg appointed chancellors from a small group of ambitious political players, including first Bruning, then Franz Von Papen, and finally General Kurt Von Schleicher.[33] Each of these men wanted to extinguish the democratic republic as well as undermine the other men.[34] Parliament was dissolved and national elections called on more than one occasion, but no parliamentary government could be formed. The chancellors were forced to rule by relying on the president for decrees. That "fatal reliance on the President . . . produced a situation in which governments could be made and unmade by the simple grant or withdrawal of the President's confidence. . . . [I]t was the end of democratic government in Germany. The key to power over a nation of sixty-five million people was now openly admitted to lie in the hands of an aged soldier of eighty-five and the little group of men who determined his views."[35]

During this period, Hitler and the Nazi Party remained on the outside looking in, lacking a majority of the Reichstag that would enable them to claim the chancellor's post outright but remaining the country's strongest party. Papen, eager to regain power and get revenge on Schleicher for replacing him as chancellor, hit on the idea of including Hitler as chancellor in a right-wing coalition cabinet that Papen would control in the role of vice chancellor. He reasoned that he could harness Hitler's popular appeal while controlling him with a strong group of old-guard nationalists in the cabinet. Even though Hindenburg had twice refused to make Hitler chancellor, the request from his close adviser, Papen, changed the president's mind.[36]

How could such a decision have been made? Hindenburg knew that Hitler was filled with hate, probably mentally unstable, and controlled a large private army. There is no way of knowing exactly what went through Hindenburg's mind, but he and his minions clearly did not believe in the basic equalities that are imperative in a democracy. In their view, workers, democrats, and other supporters of the Weimar Republic were not worthy of political power. To wrest the government from those who differed from them, Hindenburg and Papen were willing to get into bed with a madman. The machinations that brought Hitler to power "were the miscalculations of a political class determined to inflict what injury it could on (or at least make only the faintest attempts to defend) the new, detested, or at best merely tolerated democratic Republic."[37]

Every government needs a basis for legitimacy to command the loyalty of its citizens. In principle, democratic governments derive legitimacy from a popular mandate conferred through elections. In Germany, however, a relentless drumbeat of attacks on the legitimacy of the government took its toll as the Right argued that the government comprised November criminals and leftist agitators. "After the First World War, and indeed for the whole of the Weimar period, 'a strong government that had the entire population behind it' was precisely what was absent from German politics. Weimar governments lacked the basis of support, and popular legitimacy, to push through unpleasant but necessary [political] measures."[38]

Overwhelming Private Violence

This lack of support did not develop in a vacuum. The Nazis not only put their propaganda machine into overdrive starting in the late 1920s but used a carefully crafted campaign of violence to limit the effectiveness of their political opponents who supported the state. These campaigns were carried out by the storm troopers of the *Sturmabteilung*, better known as the SA, the armed wing of the Nazi Party.

The SA was originally formed in 1925 as a protection squad for Nazi Party events but did not grow significantly until late in the decade. Members of the SA received military training, and many leaders were former military officers and veterans of *Freikorps* units. Instruction included "practice with grenades and machine guns." Police raids "often revealed considerable numbers of weapons in the hands of the SA." The SA was a beast different from the *Freikorps* units that were active at the founding of the Weimar Republic because the SA's violence was employed in service of the Nazis' political goals, which Nazis intended to achieve with at least the pretense of legality. Not that the Nazis were above using illegal tactics—they did so all the time—but Hitler hoped to gain power through a constitutional and legal process.[39]

The SA's main duties "revolved around violence and the threat of violence, and this was directed primarily against the Left. The *raison d'etre* of the SA was not, in the first instance, to act as anti-Semitic crusaders or to shape the policy of the Nazi movement, but to challenge the Nazi party's left-wing opponents."[40] The SA gained members as the Nazi Party grew and developed more electoral support. In January 1931, the SA stood approximately one hundred thousand strong, but by August 1932, just after Nazi support in a free election had peaked, its ranks had grown to more than four hundred thousand.[41]

These men were not interested in sitting around and blowing hot air; they were ready to fight. In fact, in a country racked by indecision, "the willingness of the Nazi movement—and, in particular, the SA—to engage in this kind of politics was an important drawing card. Among the strengths of the Nazi movement was the fact that, unlike its rivals either on the Left or on the Right, it appealed both to roughness *and* respectability." The SA used violence to quell dissent at Nazi rallies as well as to disrupt opponents. Any event planned by the Social Democrats or other left-wing parties became an opportunity for SA intimidation and harassment. In 1931 and 1932, the SA destroyed opposition newspapers and political headquarters and in some instances even killed opponents. Political violence spread across Germany. Brawls and street violence became common in "every city neighborhood and town, and in the countryside as well."[42]

As the country prepared for the July 1932 Reichstag elections, dozens of Germans were killed and hundreds injured. "In the worst incident, the Altona 'Blood Sunday' of 17 July, seventeen people were killed and sixty-four injured as shooting broke out during an SA parade seen as a direct provocation by the town's Communists."[43] While the Communists seemed better able to respond, when "Weimar politics became the politics of violence, the Social Democrats no longer could compete." The police initially tried to quell the violence but often found themselves overwhelmed. In 1932, as the Nazis gained more power, especially at the local level, the police became less strict with the SA.[44]

After Hitler was installed as chancellor, he persuaded Hindenburg to dissolve the Reichstag and call for new elections. Hitler was determined to use his new power to purge his enemies in the Reichstag and gain a solid majority there. He needed that majority to support his plans for an enabling bill that would allow him to rule by decree and obviate the need for support from the Reichstag. In effect, he intended to create a dictatorship. None of his new partners in the cabinet, including the defense minister, General Werner Von Blomberg, who presumably could have called on the armed forces to defend democracy, thought to stop him. They were "as keen as he was to end parliamentarism and eliminate the Marxist parties." The other cabinet members assumed that they would be participants in a new, strong right-wing government that could rule without interference from the Left. Surely enough, the Left lost, but cabinet members, with the exception of the defense minister, who was rewarded with a promised buildup of the armed forces, did not share in the spoils.[45]

New elections were set for March 5, 1933. The SA immediately swung into action, attacking other political parties. "Their meetings were broken up, their speakers assaulted and beaten, their posters torn down and their papers continually suppressed. . . . This time the Nazis were inside the gate, and they did not mean to be robbed of power by any scruples about fair play or free speech." Now the SA was under the control of the chancellor, and its members were not only totally immune from the criminal justice system but sometimes had active assistance from the police.[46]

During the last week of February, the Nazis "uncovered" a plan for a communist revolution and a mysterious fire burned down the Reichstag. Some historians believe the fire was set by the Nazis themselves but skillfully blamed on the Communists. These events provided ample political cover for the cabinet to declare a state of emergency and suspend the individual liberties guaranteed by the Weimar Constitution. The rights to free speech and free press, free association, and privacy, among others, no longer existed. The SA stepped up its campaign to brutalize leftists and arrest their leaders.[47]

Even with the power of the SA and the state at their disposal, the Nazis could not get a majority of the electorate to support them. When the election results came in, the Nazis had taken only 43.9 percent of the vote. Even with the support of other right-wing parties, Hitler barely had a majority in the new Reichstag.[48] Hitler's first order of business after the election was to seek passage of the Enabling Act, which would free him from the restraints of the constitution or the Reichstag and allow him simply to rule by decree. Amending the constitution through the Enabling Act required the support of two-thirds of the deputies in the Reichstag. Hitler's dictatorship was within reach if he could summon the necessary votes in a session scheduled for March 23.

One pesky obstacle had already been eliminated. The Communists had eighty-one deputies in the Reichstag, but since the fire, most of the party's representatives had been arrested, and the rest faced certain detention if they showed up to vote. Entering the building on the day of the vote, the remaining opposition deputies must have sensed that their days were numbered, too. The Reichstag met in temporary quarters at Kroll Opera House. Hitler's elite SS units had circled the building in a "solid rank." Brown-shirted SA troops lined the corridors and the walls inside. "They were giving a hint to opposition deputies of what would be the outcome were the Enabling Act not to find the necessary level of support."[49]

Hitler opened the debate with a restrained speech and was followed by the leader of the Social Democrats, Otto Wels. As Wels walked to the tribune, the SA troopers chanted, "We want the Bill—or fire and murder." In Bullock's words, "It needed courage to stand up before this packed assembly—most of the Communists and about a dozen of the Social Democrat deputies had already been thrown into prison—and to tell Hitler and the Nazis to their faces that the Social Democratic Party would vote against the Bill." Hitler returned to the assembly and, abandoning all pretense of moderation, attacked the Social Democrats to "wild cheering."[50]

The result was never in doubt, but the outcome was still shocking. "With 441 votes to the ninety-four votes of the Social Democrats, the Reichstag, as a democratic body, voted itself out of existence."[51] The Enabling Act gave Hitler all the power he needed to create the Nazi war machine and terrorize his enemies. While Hitler had yet to consolidate power after 1933, the cards had been dealt, and stopping Hitler would turn from an internal to an external affair. As Bullock put it, "The street gangs had seized control of the resources of a great modern State, the gutter had come to power."[52]

So where, if at all, does the private ownership of firearms figure into this equation? By the time Hitler became chancellor in January 1933, German democracy had long since ceased to exist. Hitler quickly suspended most civil rights and within a few months had gained the power to issue laws without the Reichstag's approval. He controlled a private army of four hundred thousand men as well as the police and the regular army and had banned all other political parties. Hitler simply did not need gun control laws to disarm and brutalize his enemies.

The Jews and other opponents of the Nazi regime were not disarmed through record checks and court revocations of handgun permits but rather by unruly mobs of SA storm troopers and police ransacking and searching houses at random. And even if his opponents had resisted with force, they could not have held out for long. The German people gave up democracy without a fight, and most even favored getting rid of it. Without a broad base of popular respect and support for democratic institutions, it is almost impossible to protect individual rights.

Halbrook's assertion that a constitutional guarantee protecting the German people's right to keep and bear arms would have stopped Hitler is laughable. Long-standing rights such as freedom of the press and assembly had summarily been extinguished as soon as the Nazis took power, a power grab that was supported by the German people. A right to keep and bear arms would have been as meaningless as other suppressed rights in the Third Reich. As far as Germany's Jews were concerned, gun control or no gun control, they were the enemies of the state, and as a tiny minority, they could do little to stop the Nazis' terror. Their only recourse was desperate attempts to leave the country.

The 1938 gun law did include special restrictions applicable only to

Jews, but they were a tiny percentage of the German population at that time. For Halbrook's argument to make sense, he must assert that gun control deprived a broad cross-section of political opponents of the Nazis with the means of resistance, because the Jews alone could not have mounted meaningful armed opposition. The historical record makes abundantly clear that whatever barriers to armed resistance may have prevented more Germans from fighting the Nazis, legal impediments to the ownership of firearms were not among them.

Of course, Jews throughout Europe did arm themselves and fight the Nazis, most famously in the Warsaw Ghetto but also in Eastern Europe and in the French underground. Many used firearms to fight the Nazi war machine, but access to guns was not a decisive factor in any of these efforts. Jews take pride in these events not because they stopped the Nazis, for that was well beyond their control, but because they stood and fought evil in impossible circumstances, knowing that the most likely outcome was death. The post-Holocaust admonition "Never again" refers not to gun control but to ensuring that Jews have a country where they are not merely guests dependent on the goodwill of their hosts and not subject to the whims of a political system where they can be disenfranchised and turned into the enemy. Moreover, the modern state of Israel has a gun control regime that includes comprehensive licensing and registration laws.[53]

The awful truth is that the Jews were a small minority that a demagogue defined as the enemy of a large nation. The Nazis were going to disarm and isolate the Jews through any means necessary, and they had ample means at their disposal to do so no matter what steps—up to and including the acquisition of private arsenals—the Jews could have taken to defend themselves. Looking to answer the question about Hitler's position on gun control, Harcourt sums up the issue: "Truth is, the question itself is absurd. The Nazis sought to disarm and kill the Jewish population. Their treatment of Jewish persons was, in this sense, orthogonal to their gun-control views."[54]

Like the myth that gun control was a crucial factor in permitting the Ku Klux Klan to terrorize newly freed slaves, the parallel fantasy that gun control enabled Hitler to complete his terrible deeds is a powerful way to frame opposition to gun control. The argument aligns gun rights with a fight against tyranny and unbridled government power. But the argument that gun control led to the Holocaust is baseless.

Conversely, the rise of the Nazis teaches some important lessons about the dangers that can result when private arms are mixed with Insurrectionist ideology. In post–World War I Germany, powerful segments of society deeply distrusted the Weimar Republic and the democratic process that brought it into being. Well-armed and -organized private militias acted on this distrust. Democracy requires that citizens regard each other as equal, that they respect and tolerate their differences, and that they resolve conflicts through the democratic process. Those seeds were never sown in the Weimar Republic. Powerful interests were scheming to topple the democratic order almost as soon as the republic was founded. Hitler's was just one among a cacophony of voices on both the far right and left who wanted to overthrow the new democratic system of government. The republic was a problem for these extremists because it blocked a radical agenda. As the economic crisis in Germany worsened, it created an opportunity for the extremists to gain support from the increasingly frightened people.

The Weimar Republic lacked the benefit of a democratic tradition forged from a common experience to weather the challenges from both left and right, and when these attacks turned violent, the republic was ill equipped to cope. Most of the political parties had military wings, but the Nazis' SA was especially violent and well-armed. The SA used force to destabilize the republic and threaten the other political parties. When the use of violence becomes routine in partisan politics, the democratic process falls apart, and with it the belief that citizens are equal, because force becomes a substitute for representative mechanisms of political expression. Insurrectionist rhetoric holds that an armed citizenry provides a bulwark against government tyranny, but the SA, began in much the same way as our own Michigan Militia or the Militia of Montana, with private resources, worked to undercut democracy.

To add insult to injury, when the Weimar Republic fell, the SA did not stay outside of government as a guardian of the people. Instead, it switched sides and became the most dangerous instrument of Hitler's state. Private gun ownership proved to be an illusory protection to the citizens of the Weimar Republic. Faced with a four-hundred-thousand-man private army, freedom's response needed to be swift and certain, but the Weimar Republic was incapable of responding. A free state cannot survive without popular support for democratic institutions and a monopoly on force so it can control its streets and protect the integrity of the political process. Hitler's success in seizing power was the product of many factors, but laying responsibility for his murderous ways at the feet of gun control is absurd. The structural breakdown of democracy comes when "the people" become separated from "the government" and when loyalty to a faction or political party trumps loyalty to representative government.

Viewed in this light, the cavalier contempt expressed toward the federal government by right-wing populists in the United States should give all Americans pause. The casual willingness to use language that casts the U.S. government as the enemy of the people threatens to corrode respect not just for people who happen to be in office during any particular election cycle but for our democratic system. When gun rights enthusiasts ask us to remember that Hitler supported gun control, we should remember the real historical record: Hitler castigated democratic institutions and values such as pluralism, and he built a private militia to intimidate and assault political opponents. When gun rights enthusiasts describe their romanticized vision of an America where armed private citizens must be urged continuously to stay on the alert for some new incarnation of the November criminals, we should recall the nightmare experience of the Weimar Republic.

Democracies and Genocide

At the beginning of this chapter, we recounted Wayne LaPierre's assertion that gun control helped governments murder 169 million people. He bases this assertion on Professor Rudy Rummel's work on democide—the act of government killing its own citizens.[55] LaPierre never mentions that Rummel believes that totalitarianism, not gun control, leads to genocide. In an e-mail to the authors, he wrote that while he supports the idea that individuals should be permitted to own guns to defend themselves, guns are "not to take on a democratic government, but for personal protection." He believes that a healthy democracy is the best insurance against genocide. "I do not agree that gun control generally is a precursor—this ignores the fact that democracies do not commit genocide and murder their own citizens, and thus gun control for democracies does not mean that genocide is down the road."[56]

Many of the governments that LaPierre charges with democide came to power through armed overthrows of existing governments. As noted earlier, in *The Global War on Your Guns*, he wrote, "If every family on this planet owned a good-quality rifle, genocide would be on the path to extinction."[57] But isn't that exactly the path such tyrants as Mao Zedong in China and Fidel Castro in Cuba took to obtain power? In *The Essential Second Amendment Guide*, LaPierre even lauds the accomplishments of such men: "The 20th Century provides no example of a determined populace which had access to small arms being defeated by a modern army . . . Chiang Kai-shek and [Fulgencio] Batista lost."[58] Mao and Castro, armed insurgents fighting what they believed were tyrannical governments, did not turn out to be such good guys after all. They were both after power, and once they used their weapons to get it, they had little interest in creating democratic states. In these two examples as well as in a host of other countries, armed revolutionaries did not foster democracy but rather totalitarianism, and that is what makes genocide possible. In fact, no democratic government has ever committed genocide against its own people.

Apart from the United States, the countries with the most freedom worldwide are democracies with two things in common: (1) strong regulation of firearms and (2) a lower firearms death rate than the United States.[59] Democracies regulate guns not simply to control violent crime but more fundamentally because unfettered access to firearms poses a threat to democratic institutions. The most sinister threat to freedom is not from gun control but from the imperishable impulse to jettison freedom's noblest traditions in favor of force. Avoiding that eventuality is the duty of all democratic government. Hitler's rise to power offers a prime example of what happens when private arms are turned against the democratic state.

PART THREE

INSURRECTIONISM, DEMOCRACY, AND FREEDOM

CHAPTER SEVEN

THE MEANING OF FREEDOM

The relationship between gun rights and democracy is more complicated than the Insurrectionist account would suggest. Any consideration of the political theory of gun rights, moreover, requires at least a cursory review of some of the broader issues in political theory in general, because democracy and freedom mean different things to different people at different times. We submit that no system can claim to be democratic unless it protects, among other things, individual rights, pluralism, and the right to vote in elections decided by majority rule. To defend freedom on a sustained basis, democratic life must draw on both legal and cultural resources with both formal and informal dimensions. The liberty our democracy was designed to protect—and has largely succeeded in protecting over the course of more than two hundred years—is something more than the false freedom of the state of nature.[1] We have in a mind a particular conception of democracy that protects the political equality of individual citizens as the foundation of liberty.

Without political equality, no country can be truly free. And while other definitions of democracy are possible, the American experiment in democratic government is based on political equality:

> Jefferson's seemingly matter-of-fact assertion in the Declaration—"all men are created equal"—announced a truly radical principle, whose full

implications no one could anticipate. . . . Henceforth, American freedom would be inextricably linked with the idea of equality (at least for those within the circle of free citizens): equality before the law, equality in political rights, equality of economic opportunity, and, for some, equality of condition.[2]

Democracy is an effort to thread the needle between anarchy and despotism and create a space where individual freedom is protected by collective security. The only way to maintain the stability of such a system over the long term is to harness the awesome power of the modern state to consolidated democratic values and structural mechanisms with a range of strong political, legal, and cultural checks. For those who value freedom, a robust democracy is essential. As Robert A. Dahl notes, a

democratic culture is almost certain to emphasize the value of personal freedom and thus to provide support for additional rights and liberties. . . . To be sure, the assertion that a democratic state provides a broader range of freedom than any feasible alternative would be challenged by one who believed that we would all gain greater freedom if the state were abolished entirely: the audacious claim of anarchists. But if you try to imagine a world with no state at all, where every person respects the fundamental rights of every other and all matters requiring collective decisions are settled peacefully by unanimous agreement, you will surely conclude, as most people do, that it is impossible.[3]

The countries that guarantee the most freedom in terms of political and civil rights all are consolidated democracies.[4] In addition, all of these countries have adopted much more restrictive gun laws than the United States, a situation that by itself should be sufficient to discredit the Insurrectionist claim that unfettered access to guns is necessary to keep people free. Robust democratic institutions in the United States have thus far warded off the political dangers that animate Insurrectionist nightmares as well as the political dangers inherent in legitimizing the use of armed force as a means of expressing dissent in an open society. If Insurrectionist ideology weakens our democratic institutions, however, our government and society's ability to safeguard the individual rights Americans take for granted will be gravely compromised, because our shared belief in democratic norms constrains both the state and private groups that might otherwise be tempted to disregard the rights of political dissenters and the interests of unpopular minorities.

While the concept of freedom appears simple, it has often been the rallying cry for partisans of diametrically opposed positions. Freedom was the rallying cry for both the North and the South in the Civil War and for both Democrats and Republicans during the 1930s as the country debated the New Deal. "Freedom has been a battleground throughout our history,"[5] and those who can convincingly claim freedom's mantle have perhaps the most powerful political ideal of all on their side.

In terms of political power, legal rights can protect individuals from government action, but in some cases the protection of individual freedom requires the government to act. For example, the First Amendment bars government interference with speech, but the Thirteenth Amendment requires that the government intervene to prevent the perpetuation of slavery. As historian James McPherson explains,

> Nearly all of the first ten amendments to the Constitution apply the phrase "shall not" to the federal government. In fact, eleven of the first twelve amendments placed limitations on the power of the national government. But beginning with the Thirteenth Amendment in 1865—the Amendment that abolished slavery—six of the next seven amendments radically expanded the power of the federal government at the expense of the states.[6]

These amendments increased the power of the federal government not simply to recalibrate the balance between centralized and local government authority but also to interpose the federal government between the states and their citizens to protect individual rights from abuses by state and local authorities. Even before the Civil War, commentators observed that the American political tradition was grounded in the idea that the protection of equality is vital to individual autonomy. Eighteenth-century writer Joel Barlow said that we need only to "let the people have time to become thoroughly and soberly grounded in the doctrine of *equality*, and there is no danger of oppression either from government or from anarchy." He concluded that the American notion "that all men are equal in their rights" sustained the nation's freedom.[7]

In light of the extensive work by political scientists on the conditions that are most conducive to democracy and freedom, the Insurrectionist insistence on the primacy of a link between the unfettered access to guns and political liberty is not only wrongheaded but dangerously counterproductive. The gun rights groups tell their members that they should participate in politics but only to maintain the political leverage needed to keep government in a condition of perpetual weakness. By insisting that the ability to use private force is the best check—and ultimately the only guarantee—against overreaching by the state, the Insurrectionist idea encourages the misconception that a well-maintained gun collection is a substitute for the hard work of citizenship in a democracy.

CHAPTER EIGHT

ONE GUN, ONE VOTE?

As we have said, the essence of any democratic system is the idea that each person is an equal citizen. This equality extends to, among other things, political and civil rights. This does not necessarily mean that equality in the distribution of wealth or condition is required for a successful democracy—although some scholars have argued that drastic economic inequality makes democracy difficult or impossible to sustain—but democracy requires, at a minimum, that all citizens enjoy the same rights. In many ways, equality is the founding value of our republic, and while equality was not always universally honored in practice, the principle was recognized from the founding as a basic element of the American system's claim to legitimacy.

Not coincidentally, equality is the first principle enshrined in the Declaration of Independence: "We hold these truths to be self-evident, that all men are created equal." This assertion was truly revolutionary in a world where the vast majority of people were serfs, vassals, and slaves. Eric Foner notes, "In rejecting the crown, as well as the principle of hereditary aristocracy, many Americans also rejected the very idea of human inequality and the society of privilege, patronage, and fixed status that these venerable traditions embodied."[1] But once equality was accepted as the basis of governance, it changed everything, because the forms of governments that existed at the time were ill suited for true equality. The ongoing experiment in American democracy is an attempt to create a state that is actually governed by the equal—in other words, by all of us.

The Constitution never explicitly mentions equality. The need to accommodate the southern states and the institution of slavery undercut the commitment to equality articulated in the Declaration of Independence. The document itself, however, was ratified not by the state legislatures but by the people acting through convention assuring that "Americans from all walks of life would be drawn into a wide-ranging public debate about its merits."[2] As Bernard Schwartz points out, "Nowhere in the basic document is there any guarantee of equality or even any mention of that concept. Yet, whatever may have been the Framers' intent, their work disseminated the ideals of Liberty and Equality throughout the world."[3] And of course, the implications of these ideals were not lost on those excluded from such equality.

The Civil War, the defining struggle of American history, was not merely about ending slavery but was also about the broader ideal of political equality. Prior to the war, Abraham Lincoln, adding his voice to that of the abolitionists, made it clear that expanding our founding principle to include all men was necessary to realize the founders' aspirations. During an 1858 debate, Lincoln condemned Stephen A. Douglas's view that the founders meant the phrase "all men are created equal" only to equate British subjects born in the colonies with British subjects born in Great Britain. The founders, Lincoln argued,

> intended to include *all* men. . . . They meant to set up a standard maxim for free society, which should be familiar to all, and revered by all; constantly looked to, constantly labored for, and even though never perfectly attained, constantly approximated, and thereby constantly spreading and deepening its influence, and augmenting the happiness and value of life to all people of all colors everywhere.[4]

Immediately after the Civil War, political equality became enshrined first in the Civil Rights Act of 1866, which clarified that all persons born in the United States were entitled to equal rights as national citizens, and then in the Fourteenth Amendment, ratified in 1868, which elevated the equal protection of the law to a constitutional guarantee. "What is Liberty without Equality?" Charles Sumner asked in 1866, answering, "One is the complement of the other. . . . They are the two vital principles of republican government."[5] The authors of these documents knew the importance of equality to the health of our democracy. The hard-fought struggles for equal rights by the disenfranchised in the twentieth century—African Americans, women, immigrants, and others—offers a continuing testament to America's most important idea.

Even with a history replete with successful struggles to expand the scope of political rights, Americans still tend to view political rights narrowly, in terms of the ability to vote in elections. The fact is, however, that equality in the political process requires more than the right to vote once every two or four years. Academics who study democratic government have identified the elements necessary to make political equality a reality. These elements include effective means of participation, enlightened understanding, the ability to control the agenda, and a franchise that is broad enough to avoid excluding significant interest groups.[6]

In a consolidated democracy such as the United States, some of these elements must be preserved through representation. In a country with three hundred million people, not all citizens will have an opportunity directly to shape the congressional agenda. Democracy requires, however, that citizens have the opportunity to vote for officials on a regular and timely basis; petition their elected representatives on the same footing as other citizens (something to think about in these days of well-funded lobbyists and fifty-million-dollar campaigns for the U.S. Senate); and obtain enough information about the issues being debated to make informed decisions.

The seminal struggles for equality in our history, including those for enfranchisement of African Americans and women, were not simply about voting but also about equal inclusion in the larger political process. During Reconstruction, for example, the former slaves were quite aware that to protect their rights, they needed to do more than simply vote. Thousands ran for office, participated in public life, and demanded their civil and legal rights. As Robert A. Dahl points out,

If you are deprived of an equal voice in the government of a state, the chances are quite high that your interests will not be given the same attention as the interests of those who do have a voice. If you have no voice, who will speak for you? Who will defend your interests if you cannot? And not just your interests as an individual. If you happen to be a member of an entire group excluded from participation, how will the fundamental interests of that group be protected?[7]

Equality forms the backbone of any democracy and confers legitimacy on the products of democratic decision making. Those with an equal opportunity to participate, whether directly as elected officials or as indirectly as voters, may grumble about their point of view not being accepted by the majority of other equally participating citizens, but they have no legitimate grounds to challenge the system as unfair or unjust as long as countermajoritarian institutions and values provide respect for pluralism and legal protection for minorities' rights.[8]

So what does all of this have to do with guns? The fundamental premise of the Insurrectionist idea conflicts with the conception of political equality we have just outlined. In a democracy where all citizens are equal, elections—not insurrections—are the means by which the people select or reject political programs and the officials who carry them out. The decision of a group of private individuals to take up arms against a government elected by the people is in effect an attempt to veto the decision of the majority (as expressed through elections) with violence. By definition, a veto by violence implies an assertion that the individuals resorting to the use of force against the government are entitled to impose their political preferences in place of the majority. In other words, a political theory that posits the legitimacy of armed violence as a tool of dissent in a democracy necessarily legitimizes the idea that the choices of the people as a whole sometimes should yield to the choices of the people with guns who are willing to use them to get their way.

For this reason, the popularization of the Insurrectionist idea is corrosive to respect for democratic means to achieve political ends. After all, democracy depends not only on the formal recognition of the political equality of all citizens by the state but also on a broadly shared belief in equal citizenship by Americans across social, geographic, and economic groups. A strong state does not become a threat when the people have a strong cultural commitment to political equality and the police and military have a deeply ingrained tradition of deference to and respect for civilian authority.[9] "Liberalism demands that people without guns be able to tell people with guns what to do," wrote researcher Stephen Holmes.[10] If armed citizens, whether military or civilian, start to believe they have special rights or are entitled to vindicate their interests at the expense of others with the use of force, then political equality based on citizenship is impossible.

Countries with a long history of sectarian violence or with armed citizens willing to use force to get their way have a difficult time establishing and maintaining democracy. If one group strongly believes its claim to political power to be morally superior to another's, a commitment to political equality and its enforcement is likely to be elusive. Disagreement in a democracy is to be expected, but effective guarantees of political equality provide a legal and moral basis for accepting decisions with which we may disagree. Without a consensus on the importance of political equality and the values that underpin it—pluralism and tolerance—the seeds of democracy are unlikely to grow.

Iraq is an excellent example of this point. The concepts of political equality and pluralism are unfamiliar to the combatants in the ongoing civil war. Sunnis under Saddam Hussein's reign had extra rights and privileges that the Shia majority wanted. After forty years as subcitizens treated with brutality, the Shia impulse toward vengeance is understandable. But a diverse country cannot become a modern state unless all become equal citizens, not just by law but, more important, by belief. The current conventional wisdom among analysts of the situation in Iraq that there will be no security unless a political solution is reached is just another way of saying that if Shia and Sunni do not respect each other as political equals, they cannot work together to find practical compromises to their competing claims on power and resources.

Insurrectionists mock liberals for invoking values such as tolerance and pluralism (along with the conservative bête noir, multiculturalism), but a commitment to these ideas lies at the core of what makes democracy work in the real world.[11] Countries whose citizens and military have internalized these values are more likely to be both democratic and free; countries that lack these values cannot be democracies. In denigrating the ideas of mutual responsibility and community and the corollary values of pluralism and tolerance, respect for the values that support democracy is eroded.

Insurrectionists are not content to disagree with others on policy matters. The Insurrectionists seek to win by portraying those who disagree with them not just as incorrect but as traitors—that is, as unworthy of respect as political equals. Gun control advocates are portrayed not as misguided fellow citizens but as one-world government conspirators whose values and political goals are alien to what it means to be an American. In the Insurrectionist ideology, those who support the power of the state to protect its citizens are seeking to enslave the rest of the population. The National Rifle Association's (NRA) *Freedom in Peril* brochure conjures a far-flung cabal running from the New Orleans police department through the United Nations that seeks to undermine our nation:

> Second Amendment freedom today stands naked in the path of a marching axis of adversaries far darker and more dangerous than gun owners have ever known. Acting alone and in shadowy coalitions, these enemies of freedom are preparing for a profound and foreboding confrontation in which they will not make the same mistakes of their predecessors. We'd better be ready.[12]

The goal here is not just to change policy but to debase civic discourse. Not satisfied with critiquing policy prescriptions they dislike, the Insurrectionists have drawn an elaborate caricature that says if you are against us, you cannot be a patriot. You are an enemy of freedom, and you certainly are not as American as we are. In short, they identify acceptance of their conception of gun rights as the essential litmus test of every individual's patriotism and commitment to democracy.

As we observed in the discussion about the NRA and its allied gun groups, Insurrectionist rhetoric is often hostile to pluralism, consensus, and tolerance. The Insurrectionists frequently try to marginalize their opponents with personal attacks or by suggesting that gun control advocates are enemies of freedom itself. When Charlton Heston famously warns that gun control advocates will have to pry his gun out of his "cold, dead hands"[13] or when David Kopel describes guns as "the tools of political dissent,"[14] they mean that whenever they strongly disagree with a decision produced by democratic means, they feel no obligation to respect or abide by it. The overwrought, pseudopopulist rhetoric employed by the Insurrectionists is more than divisive. It attacks the idea that holds us together—the idea that in a democracy, everyone is entitled to political equality.

As a mature democracy, America can handle the occasional lapse into "us versus them" rhetoric in our political dialogue. Still, the idea that certain people in a democracy are the true patriots (and thus have special insight as to when force may be appropriately deployed to back their ideals) is the same idea that gave us the Civil War, allowed Nazism to flourish in Germany, and still fuels the fires of sectarian and ethnic conflict in Iraq. Lamenting the decline of liberal democracy, especially constitutionalism in the former communist states of Eastern and Central Europe, Professor Jacques Rupnick wrote in 2007, "The common pattern here is one of acute polarization: Eastern Europe's populists do not act as if they face a political opponent (or ethnic, religious, or sexual minority) with whom they can negotiate but rather an enemy whom they must destroy." He cites the example of Slovakia, where the leader of a member of the governing coalition, the Slovak National Party, "has said he would not mind sending the leader of the Hungarian minority to Mars 'with a one-way ticket.'"[15]

It is easy to dismiss this type of statement—whether from a gun rights group in the United States or a political party in the Balkans—as no more than an example of overheated rhetoric in the midst of a political struggle, not to be taken too seriously, but, as Rupnick points out, this kind of attitude is a sign of an unhealthy democracy. The Insurrectionists are so committed to their belief that unfettered access to firearms is the magic key to freedom that they seem to have forgotten that treating one's political opponents (or even friends who disagree) as human beings entitled to a basic level of respect is the essence of a healthy democracy.

Insurrectionists suggest that if peaceful political activism fails to head off proposals to regulate firearms, armed confrontation would be an appropriate response. This sentiment is fundamentally antidemocratic, because it assumes that individuals can claim political power outside of government and decide which rules they will follow. Individual sovereignty is easy to romanticize as part of the grand tradition of Washington and Jefferson, but that would be a historical error. As chapter 4 explains, the founders did not decide for themselves when it was time to opt out of the British empire. They put it to a vote and acted in accordance with legal process.

CHAPTER NINE

DEMOCRACY AND THE MONOPOLY ON FORCE

Against the backdrop of the decision in *District of Columbia v. Heller*, the only Second Amendment case to reach the Supreme Court in seventy years, the presidential candidates in the 2008 election cycle competed against each other to burnish their gun rights bona fides. On the Republican side, a number of candidates explicitly endorsed the concept of an individual right to insurrection and made it clear that if they were to become president, they would take us back to a simpler and better time when the "people" held the federal government in check through force of arms (see chapter 1). Even more striking was the support expressed by the leading Democrats for an individual right to bear arms, although they were less specific about their understanding of how far such a right should extend or on what theoretical basis it should rest. Barack Obama, for example, endorsed the *Heller* decision, explaining, "I have always believed that the Second Amendment protects the right of individuals to bear arms." He continued, "As President, I will uphold the constitutional rights of law-abiding gun-owners, hunters, and sportsmen," but he was never specific about exactly what those rights entailed.[1] A careful look at the *Heller* decision reveals that those specifics are important because the scope of the right identified in the ruling goes well beyond protection from criminals or the ability to use guns for hunting.

Until the *Heller* decision, neither the Supreme Court nor the federal appellate courts had ever struck down a gun control statute on Second Amendment grounds.[2] In *Heller*, though, the court found that the District of Columbia's ban on handguns was unconstitutional because the Second Amendment protects the right of an individual to bear arms without regard to whether the gun owner is part of a well-regulated militia.[3] The Court concluded, among other things, that the fear of government tyranny was part of the basis for an individual right to possess firearms.[4] As we pointed out in the introduction, Justice Antonin Scalia's opinion for the majority states, "If . . . the Second Amendment right is no more than the right to keep and use weapons as a member of an organized militia . . . if, that is, the *organized* militia is the sole institutional beneficiary of the Second Amendment's guarantee—it does not assure the existence of a 'citizens' militia' as a safeguard against tyranny." Scalia insisted that the Second Amendment establishes a right to take up arms against the government even as he attempted to address the objections of the four dissenting justices by assuring them that individuals will not have access to sophisticated weaponry: "Indeed, it may be true that no amount of small arms could be useful against modern-day bombers and tanks. But the fact that modern developments have limited the degree of fit between the prefatory clause and the protected right cannot change our interpretation of the right."[5] In other words, a rifle, pistol, or shotgun might not be a match for the military and police forces at the disposal of the government, but the Second Amendment gives every citizen a right to take his or her best shot, both literally and figuratively.

Under *Heller*, private individuals and groups seem to have at least a limited right to prepare for armed confrontation against the state, and the majority opinion suggests that under the Constitution, the threatened or actual use of force against the government may be appropriate in some circumstances. We take little comfort in Scalia's attempt to avoid the radical implications of his reasoning. Individuals with small arms and improvised explosives have been the mainstay of the resistance in Iraq and Afghanistan, and a religious sect that stockpiled a cache of firearms kept federal law enforcement agents at bay at the Branch Davidians' compound in Waco, Texas, for weeks. The D.C.

sniper episode illustrates how much damage one or two individuals can do with a single firearm. If even a tiny fraction of the U.S. population decided that the time to fight government tyranny had arrived, chaos would ensue.

Until the *Heller* decision, the Insurrectionist theory of gun rights had been expressly disavowed by the Supreme Court and other federal circuits. In *Presser v. Illinois* (1886), the Supreme Court found that no body, other than the officially organized Illinois militia, could bear arms and organize itself militarily, concluding that a group of German nationalist organizations had no right to assemble with their rifles. The Court specifically rejected the idea that there was a right to prepare for armed insurrection against the government:

> Military organization and military drill and parade under arms are subjects especially under the control of the government of every country. They cannot be claimed as a right independent of law. . . . The constitution and laws of the United States will be searched in vain for any support to the view that these rights are privileges and immunities of citizens of the United States independent of some specific legislation on the subject.[6]

By decoupling the militia purpose from the Second Amendment and ascribing an individual right to resist tyranny, the Supreme Court has waded into dangerous waters. The logic of a right to prepare to take up arms against the government is that at some point, private individuals are entitled to take the next step and use violence to achieve political ends. The *Heller* decision, like most Insurrectionist writing, does not make it clear who gets to decide when armed resistance is justified or what criteria they should be expected to use for such a decision to enjoy legal or moral legitimacy. Insurrectionists like to refer to the right of "the people" to confront their government with force when officials acting in the name of the people overreach, but what looks like tyranny to some may look like effective government to others. As we have seen, some Americans feel that an attempt to ban the sale of assault weapons to civilians would by itself constitute a tyrannical act justifying violent resistance. Others believe that such a ban would constitute an entirely reasonable and legitimate exercise of the state's power to protect the public from violent crime. If a law appears tyrannical to some but not to the majority, when does the minority have the right to take up arms against the government? *Heller* does not say, and the Insurrectionists have no good answer, either.

The *Heller* decision suggests that under the Constitution, the government is not entitled to maintain a monopoly on the legitimate use of violence. At best, this is a half-baked idea. At worst, it poses a threat to the foundation of our democracy. At the core of the *Heller* decision lies the kind of reasoning that was employed to justify the South's decision to secede from the Union and provoke the Civil War. In effect, the entire Civil War was a test of the Union's ability to exercise the most fundamental role of any government, vindicating the principle that democratic institutions cannot be overruled by violent dissenters, particularly when the dissenters seek to challenge the state's monopoly on the legitimate use of violence. Eminent political scientist Ezra Suleiman explains that when a government loses its monopoly on force, it ceases to be a state, and "its form of organization becomes indistinguishable from other types of organization." Similarly, where there is no state capable of enforcing the political and civil rights of its citizens, there can be no democracy.[7] A state must be able to enforce its judicial or administrative rulings: if it is outgunned by individuals or factions, it is not functioning as a democratic state (in fact, it is not functioning as a state at all) and is reverting to a pregovernmental society where might makes right and political equality is at best an abstract ideal. The *Heller* decision never grapples with the idea that a state must be able to enforce its will in the face of violent dissent or lose its claim to sovereignty.

The concept of a monopoly on legitimate force may sound inconsistent with the political traditions of a country steeped in stories of our own revolution, but it is the fundamental organizing principle of any political entity, including democratic states in general and the United States in particular. At the Virginia ratifying convention, James Madison, responding to Patrick Henry's complaint that the new Constitution gave too much power over the militia to Congress, stated, "There never was a government without force. What is the meaning of government? An institution to make people do their duty. A government leaving it to a man to do his duty, or not, as he pleases, would be a new species of government, or rather no government at all."[8]

Madison prefigured Max Weber's famous definition, which states, "A compulsory political association with continuous organization . . . will be called a 'state' if and in so far as its administrative staff success-fully upholds a claim to the monopoly of the legitimate use of physical force in the enforcement of its order." Weber identified a number of other features of a modern state that qualify its prerogative to a monop-oly on force, noting that a state must possess "an administrative and le-gal order subject to change by legislation" and that "the use of force is regarded as legitimate only so far as it is either permitted by the state or prescribed by it."[9]

Weber's Insurrectionist critics often skip over these limitations. Re-searcher Harry Redner explains that

> Weber is careful, however, to qualify and nuance this crude realism, for although the expropriation of the means of violence is necessary for the formation of the state, he clearly does not regard it as sufficient. Unlike some contemporary authors . . . Weber does not propound a militaristic theory of state formation; this is underlined by his linking the idea of a monopoly of the means of violence with the concept of legitimacy.[10]

Herbert Wulf adds that "the specific characteristic of the state, accord-ing to Weber, is that it can successfully claim the legitimate physical vi-olence in a given territory and that it is the only organization that is lawfully allowed to use force. The importance of legitimacy in exercis-ing the monopoly of force needs to be recognized and can be based on three principles: on the authority of traditional rules, on charismatic au-thority and on the legality of agreed rules. In the modern state of today the political leadership is accountable for exercising legitimate physical violence and it is based on good governance."[11] As another scholar ob-serves, "The use of force is not the sole and not even the normal means for the modern state 'to realize its orders'; it is only the ultima ratio if all other means are not effective. The crucial point for Weber was the fact that the state cannot be defined by its 'ends' because there are al-most no ends that states did not try to realize in the course of history."[12]

Robert A. Dahl summarizes, "The state, remember, is a unique association whose government possesses an extraordinary capacity for obtaining compliance with its rules by (among other means) force, coercion, and violence."[13] The monopoly of force is a crucial concept for defining a functional and healthy political state, democratic or otherwise. If the United States were to lose or give up its monopoly of force, it would cease to be a viable political entity, and our relatively comfortable lives would descend into chaos.

In defending their interpretation of the Second Amendment, Insurrectionist legal scholars assert that Weber's assessment of the minimum conditions needed for a viable state simply do not apply to the United States. This argument for American exceptionalism posits that what makes our country great is our refusal to surrender the option—and the capability—to challenge political decisions with armed violence. Sanford Levinson, who created a firestorm as the first credible legal academic to embrace an individual-rights view of the Second Amendment, also finds that the Weberian definition of statehood does not translate to America: "It is a profoundly statist definition, the product of a specifically German tradition of the (strong) state rather than of a strikingly different American political tradition that is fundamentally mistrustful of state power and vigilant about maintaining ultimate power, including the power of arms, in the populace."[14] Instead, Levinson claims, Americans have adopted a more republican version of statehood in which "ordinary citizens participate in the process of law enforcement and defense of liberty rather than rely on professionalized peacekeepers, whether we call them standing armies or police."[15] David Williams claims that a reading of the Second Amendment that does not recognize its revolutionary potential is based on the Weberian "myth" and is thus inaccurate.[16]

Levinson seems to forget that the most important contributions to freedom in the United States stemmed directly from the ability to expand and mobilize both a federal bureaucracy and a standing army in the defense of democratic institutions and values. From General Washington to General Grant to General Patton, professional military forces have defended liberty and freedom in this country and in the case of World War II across the entire planet. The republican model in the Articles of Confederation barely worked prior to 1787 and was substantially modified in the Constitution—and later by the Reconstruction amendments—in favor of a stronger central government with both the legal right and the practical capability to exercise power in the defense of individual rights. America has become a great economic nation because our armed forces are professionalized and can safeguard free commerce as well as political liberties.

As for the critique offered by Williams, the Weberian model is not a normative assessment of what makes a state morally praiseworthy or blameworthy but rather a description of what defines statehood—that is, the conditions that allow for the exercise of sovereignty. Weber did not create the model; he only observed that one element of a successful state is that it controls the legitimate use of violence. No one can deny that almost a century after Weber's observation, weak states have difficulty maintaining democratic institutions. Weber's insights are especially applicable to democracies such as the United States, where democratic mechanisms offer abundant opportunities to express dissenting views and work for political change through peaceful means, along with strong legal protections for minority rights. In other words, in the United States, the monopoly on force is unquestionably legitimate because it is accountable to the people. A state is not a democracy if the democratic process is undermined by armed factions that reject the application of the law to their actions as an illegitimate exercise of power. A putative right to challenge perceived tyranny with the use of private violence is untenable in our democratic system and is by definition extraconstitutional.

The U.S. Constitution is open to amendment, but it is not a suicide pact, and it does not contain an invitation for dissenters to use force as an alternative means of challenging the results of the democratic processes it established. This is a principle that all functioning democracies must maintain. Eminent jurist Roscoe Pound wrote that a "legal right of the citizen to wage war on the government is something that cannot be admitted [because it] would defeat the whole Bill of Rights."[17]

The proposition that a state must maintain a monopoly on force actually predates Weber and is founded in the concept of sovereignty. Basic international law requires that the state be "the sole executive and legislative authority" in its territory.[18] As longtime gun-debate observer Robert Spitzer, expressing astonishment that Williams fails to appreciate the need for a state monopoly on force, wrote, "Not only does this notion sit at the epicenter of the modern nation state, it spans the writings of Hobbes and Locke . . . and traces back to Aristotle and even before."[19]

The origins of our legal system make this abundantly clear as well. As chapter 4 describes, Blackstone's "fifth auxiliary right" was not unlimited; the right consisted

> of having arms for [the subject's] defense, suitable to their condition and degree, and such as are allowed by law. . . . and is indeed a public allowance, under due restrictions, of the natural right of resistance and self-preservation, when the sanctions of society and laws are found insufficient to restrain the violence of oppression.[20]

Moreover, Blackstone expressly disavowed an Insurrectionist interpretation of this right. As Blackstone explained, a right of revolution would be

> a doctrine productive of anarchy, and (in consequence) equally that to civil liberty as tyranny itself. For civil liberty, rightly understood, consists in protecting the rights of individuals by the united force of society: society cannot be maintained, and of course can exert no protection, without obedience to some sovereign power: and obedience is an empty name, if every individual has a right to decide how far he himself shall obey.[21]

John Goldberg explains that under Blackstone's understanding of sovereignty under the unwritten English constitution, "it was impossible for a body of law actually to confer on citizens a legal right to revolt, for any such conferral would be a dissolution of government that would render the law no longer a law. . . . Any such change would be 'at once an entire dissolution of the bands of government; and the people would be reduced to a state of anarchy, with liberty to constitute to themselves a new legislative power.' "[22] In other words, taking up arms to challenge the government is always extraconstitutional, and no country where private citizens retain the power to do so is a state. This view is entirely consistent with Weber. Moreover, as discussed in chapter 4, the founders believed that the residual natural law rights to withdraw support from a government belonged to the states, not to individuals. The Constitution is an attempt permanently to bond together the states and individuals. Attempts to dissolve that compact, except through valid legal process, must be met with enough force to protect the compact.

It is true, as Daniel Polsby and Don B. Kates Jr. remind us, that force can be and has been abused by dictators (who of course under the Weberian view lack legitimacy), but creating less powerful states or arming everyone in an attempt to prevent dictatorship is a formula for disaster. These ideas have been tried, and they have failed miserably. Of course, Polsby and Kates insist that the opposite is true, adopting tortured interpretations of history in an effort to demonstrate that a state monopoly on force leads to tyranny. Their most irresponsible and logically untenable claim is perhaps their attempt to blame Weber for the civil war in the Balkans:

> Josip Broz Tito, who ruled that part of the world for thirty five years until his death in 1980, was an enthusiastic practitioner of Max Weber's idea of the state. . . . When old Yugoslavia came unstuck in the late 1980s, its armies and equipment—the most formidable in the region—devolved to the former nation's ethnic constituents. Because the Yugoslavian army had been mostly Serbian, the Serbians inherited enough munitions to face down the United States.[23]

By its own terms, this interpretation directly undercuts their primary thesis, which is that arming private individuals is the best way to protect liberty. In a society run on the every-man-for-himself idea, there is no guarantee that civilians will be equally armed; there will always be inequality in this regard, either in the types of armaments or in the number of partisans. The real problem is that Yugoslavia, which was moving toward democracy, devolved into an ethnicity-based system of competing republics as the central government lost its monopoly on force. Ethnic rivalries subsequently exploded into a brutal civil war that ultimately was ended by means of a massive foreign intervention that reestablished the monopoly of legitimate force and stopped the killing. Mary Kaldor, who observed the war in the Balkans firsthand and is now a professor and director of the Centre for the Study of Global Governance at the London School of Economics and Political Science, observes,

> What happened in Yugoslavia was the disintegration of the state both at a federal level and, in the case of Croatia and Bosnia-Herzegovina, at a republican level. If we define the state in the Weberian sense as the organization which "successfully upholds the monopoly of legitimate organized violence," then it is possible to trace, first, the collapse of legitimacy and, second, the collapse of the monopoly of organized violence.[24]

Even if Polsby and Kates had correctly described the nature of the Balkan conflict, their argument about the potential for a state with a monopoly on the use of force to exercise its power to carry out genocide is a straw man. The monopoly on the legitimate use of force is necessary but not sufficient for a viable state, much less for a state that consistently protects the rights of minorities and maintains the formal and informal institutions of democratic accountability. Attempts to challenge the state's monopoly by arming civilians with enough firepower to counter the government, however, simply complicate the task of building these institutions. To take just one recent example, consider the problems faced by the United States in attempting to stabilize Afghanistan. As one scholar notes, "Afghanistan has been characterized since the beginning of the 1990s as a country in a 'Hobbesian state of nature' which paved the way for the infamous Taliban regime; this country represents one of the cases of a total disintegration of the state and where therefore the monopoly of legitimate violence, that might have existed before, has broken down completely."[25]

Political scientists have documented the consequences when a government loses its monopoly on the use of force. "The erosion of states and the failure of domestic politics, leading to endemic state weakness and collapse are conceived by a great number of social scientists as the central cause for war, armed violence and conflict. State collapses, give rise to and sustain conflicts, prolong wars and complicate or prevent peace-building. The Democratic Republic of Congo and Somalia are used as the classic examples. The most appropriate measure, according to this analysis, is to rectify these deficits by establishing state authority, particularly the state monopoly of force."[26] Hannes Wimmer adds that "the 'failure of the state' is accompanied by the loss of control over and fragmentation of the instruments of physical coercion or a privatisation of violence by so-called warlords which leads by necessity to indiscriminate killings of large numbers of the civilian population, the destruction of property and infrastructure."[27]

The project of building a successful state is a difficult business, and the best prescription to avoid domestic conflict is to establish and continually reinforce democratic institutions and values, much as we have tried to do for more than two hundred years in the United States. Once the salutary benefits of a monopoly on force are lost, putting the genie back in the bottle becomes difficult, as our misadventures in the Middle East make abundantly clear. Even conservative columnist George Will links the initial failure in Iraq directly to Weber's analysis:

> Almost three years after the invasion, it is still not certain whether, or in what sense, Iraq is a nation. And after two elections and a referendum on its constitution, Iraq barely has a government. A defining attribute of a government is that it has a monopoly on the legitimate exercise of violence. That attribute is incompatible with the existence of private militias of the sort that maraud in Iraq.[28]

Similarly, Wulf concluded in 2004 that "the present situation in Iraq illustrates that even the most powerful military nation of the world runs into difficulties in trying to re-establish the monopoly of violence."[29]

This does not mean that totalitarian dictators who hold the monopoly on force are a good thing. They lack legitimacy, which Weber took care to emphasize as essential. In a democracy, however, the monopoly on force is legitimate because it is accountable to the people in direct and indirect ways, and that monopoly must be preserved in defense of these democratic—rather than violent—mechanisms of accountability. In fact, a consolidated democracy is clearly the best protection against internal dictatorship, and the creation and maintenance of liberal democracies "prevent government by cruel and vicious autocrats."[30] Countries with liberal democracies do not go to war with each other.[31] In addition, globalization and the rise of stronger international organizations make it increasingly difficult for states to abuse their monopoly on the use of legitimate force.[32] Threats to the monopoly on force currently held by the U.S. government are appropriately labeled "crime or terrorism."[33] The United States has spent the past five years trying to stop foreign terrorists from undercutting its monopoly on force. It is bad public policy and misguided political theory to advocate recognition of a "right" that undercuts that monopoly. This does not mean that we should ignore or excuse abusive exercises of state-sanctioned coercive power; rather, it suggests that we should zealously protect our core democratic institutions from the Insurrectionists who are attempting to pull them apart.

Unfortunately, even the political Left seems to see the federal government as an ever-growing Leviathan. The presidency of George W. Bush was characterized by extremely aggressive assertions of executive authority outside any system of democratic checks and balances, alarming civil libertarians. Warrantless wiretapping, "extraordinary" extrajudicial renditions of terrorism suspects to countries that are known to use torture, and the indefinite detention of suspects at Guantánamo Bay in an effort to deny these prisoners access to the U.S. courts all seem to lend credence to the Insurrectionist claim that the threat of overreaching by a democratic government—our own government, in fact—is a clear and present danger.

These threats to democratic accountability and individual rights are grave, but the only realistic answer to overreaching by the executive branch is to undertake the difficult and often mundane work of politics, where the only bombardment comes in the form of radio, television, and direct-mail advertising campaigns and opposing sides square off with dueling press releases and white papers instead of pistols at twenty paces. Does anyone seriously believe that the abuses of the Bush administration can or should be resisted with armed force? The Left in the United States and Western Europe dabbled in the use of political violence to challenge official policy in the 1960s and 1970s, but the groups that used bombings, kidnappings, and armed robberies as political tools succeeded only in feeding a backlash that progressives have yet to fully overcome even today. Meanwhile, the massive amount of armaments in private hands in the United States has allowed domestic antigovernment organizations to garner considerable force. For example, "The Patriot anti-government movement, barely noticed before the bombing of a federal building in Oklahoma City in 1995, represents the greatest threat of 'domestic terrorism' to the United States, because of its paramilitary nature accumulating huge amounts of arms and because of their belief in the necessity and even desirability of war as a means of realizing national or racial destiny."[34]

We are not suggesting that the United States ban the private possession of firearms, but our country should take seriously the threat that the government could lose the monopoly on force. Domestic terrorists do not need to be strong enough to topple our government to wreak havoc by assassinating government officials or forcing the government to choose between risking serious bloodshed and ignoring flagrant violations of the civil rights laws or other legal norms. This is not an unreasonable fear when most states still allow the sale of .50-caliber sniper rifles and high-capacity assault rifles without criminal background checks.

The need to maintain a monopoly of force does not mean that the government must disarm every citizen or prohibit armed self-defense. The government must, however, prevent the accumulation of arms for insurrectionary purposes or of arms especially suited for war. The monopoly on force simply means that a government must have enough strength to enforce its own laws.[35] Spitzer points out that nothing about the government's legitimate use of force "precludes justifiable personal use of force, such as in the case of self-defense, or the questioning of government authority."[36] There has always been a strong presumption in the common law and in every U.S. state that reasonable self-defense represents a justified use of force. Moreover, private security firms are generally authorized by the state to augment individual self-defense.

Weber anticipated these developments and noted that the state might well choose to delegate the use of force—for example, by permitting parents to discipline their children or by authorizing military commanders to enforce discipline among their troops.[37] Weber's concern is with a challenge to the authority of the state. It is a claim not about public health but rather about civic health. States that lose the ability to carry out and enforce decisions made through democratic processes are no longer states, much less democracies. That is unhealthy wherever it occurs. Eugene Volokh, a prolific advocate of a broad right for individuals to own and use firearms, agrees that the debate over the monopoly on force has nothing to do with whether private ownership of firearms for self-defense against crime should be permitted or encouraged: he sees Weber's position on the monopoly on force as "of no relevance to the question of private gun possession for self-defense."[38] We agree.

The plaintiffs in the *Heller* case argued that their concerns centered on establishing a right to gun possession for personal defense against common criminals, yet the Supreme Court—and to an even greater degree, the U.S. Court of Appeals for the District of Columbia Circuit—went well beyond that issue, finding that the Second Amendment protects guns for personal protection as well as for taking on the government, should it become tyrannical. As we have shown, these are fundamentally different questions that cannot be lumped together. The uncritical and undifferentiated endorsement of a right to the private ownership of firearms has cleared the path for Insurrectionist ideologues to build on the *Heller* decision to establish a dangerously wrongheaded theory of the Second Amendment as the law of the land.

CHAPTER TEN

INSURRECTIONISM AND INDIVIDUAL RIGHTS

For both moral and practical reasons, no democratic government can or should operate under principles of purely majoritarian institutions. Democracies must protect the civil rights of individuals and minority groups in addition to the political rights of all citizens to express their will in elections decided by majority rule. Political theorists, legal scholars, and jurists have long recognized that the majority, acting through the government, cannot tread in certain areas. Government is formed in recognition of the fact that in the state of nature, the strongest party always wins, but the strongest party does not always have a legitimate moral claim to make decisions that harm weaker parties. Moreover, no individual or group can count on remaining the strongest party indefinitely.[1] Individuals give up a degree of autonomy in exchange for equal protection of fundamental rights as well as an equal say on matters to be decided by a majority vote.

For example, a system that allowed members of the winning political party to appropriate the property of members of the losing party would be morally illegitimate because it would deny the members of the losing party the equal protection of their property rights. Even more importantly, no such system could be sustained. Members of the losing party would have no incentive to cooperate with a system that failed to protect their interests against the tyranny of the majority.

In recognition of this problem, democracies take steps to protect the interests of the minority against majority rule.[2] In the United States, this balance is achieved partly by establishing countermajoritarian institutions such as an independent judiciary and partly by placing some issues beyond the reach of ordinary lawmaking (i.e., by including specific substantive and procedural safeguards for individual rights in the Constitution). No ordinary law passed by Congress can abrogate these rights, and they cannot be altered except by a special process reserved for such weighty decisions.[3] For example, under the U.S. Constitution, supermajorities of the Congress and/or the states would be required to exempt flag burning from the First Amendment. Similarly, the Eighth Amendment's restrictions on cruel and unusual punishment and the Sixth Amendment's right to a jury trial are protections for the rights of criminal defendants that cannot be overturned by ordinary statutes enacted by popularly elected legislators. These mechanisms complement democratic institutions by defining the boundaries beyond which majority rule becomes a form of tyranny.

Naturally, the Insurrectionists claim they are dedicated to protecting individual rights in precisely the spirit we have just described. Former National Rifle Association (NRA) president Sandy Froman characterizes the NRA's mission as the defense of individual rights, "with a special focus on protecting the Second Amendment right to keep and bear arms."[4] It is true that the Second Amendment does offer protection against the majority, working through the federal government, to prevent state governments from maintaining militias composed of citizen-soldiers.[5] The Insurrectionists, however, have taken this countermajoritarian shield and wielded it like a sword, attempting to cut out other rights and protections that might limit the unfettered access to any firearm at any time in any place.

Property Rights and Guns at Work

Nowhere have the Insurrectionists shown more disregard for the rights of others than in their attempts to usurp private property rights. Despite the respect conservatives usually profess for property rights (at least when it serves their interests), the NRA and its allies have undertaken a shockingly intrusive campaign to establish a legal "right" to bring guns onto other people's land and into their places of business.

Liberals encountering the term *property rights* often associate this cluster of rights with segregationists barring African Americans from service at lunch counters in the 1960s, with conservatives railing against wetlands protection, or with timber companies confronting defenders of a rare frog's habitat. There can be no doubt that property rights have often been invoked in service of reactionary political goals. However, property rights hold an important place in the protection of individual liberty, and they were considered so essential by our founders that they protected property rights explicitly in the Fifth Amendment: "No person shall . . . be deprived of life, liberty, or property, without due process of law; nor shall private property be taken for public use, without just compensation."

The U.S. Supreme Court has held that a property owner's right to exclude others is fundamental. Justice Sandra Day O'Connor, in a 1987 opinion joined by liberal stalwart justices William Brennan, Thurgood Marshall, and Harry Blackmun, among others, called the right to exclude "one of the most essential sticks in the bundle of rights that are commonly characterized as property."[6] The court has also said that government interference with the right to exclude is more likely to trigger the Fifth Amendment's just compensation requirement than almost any other kind of limit on property rights.[7] A resolution adopted by the American Bar Association's House of Delegates concluded that "property rights, especially real property rights, 'have always been fundamental to and part of the preservation of liberty and personal freedom in the United States.'"[8]

When three employees of the Ogden, Utah, call center operated by America Online (AOL) brought five guns onto property leased by the company, thereby violating its no-weapons policy, AOL defended its "right to exclude" and fired the employees. Thus began an epic battle against the Insurrectionists, with the NRA in the lead, over the future of this important individual right. The confrontation developed when AOL employees Luke Hansen, Jason Melling, and Paul Carson met in the parking lot of the facility where they worked on September 14, 2000, and prepared to go to a local gun range for some recreation.

Melling and Carlson transferred two rifles and two handguns, all unloaded, to Hansen's truck. Hansen was carrying a loaded .40 Sturm, Ruger pistol in a fanny pack. AOL had a strict no-weapons policy that applied to the entire premises. Unfortunately for the three men, their actions were caught on a security camera. Terminated for violating the policy, they sued AOL for wrongful discharge, arguing that Utah's law permitting citizens to carry concealed weapons, considered one of the most permissive in the nation, prevented AOL from enforcing its workplace rules.

High-profile shootings in schools and workplaces, such as the 1999 Columbine massacre and a 1993 rampage at a San Francisco law firm, led many public- and private-sector employers to adopt or revise rules governing guns at work. These policies generally prohibit the possession and use of firearms by employees (and in some cases adopt measures to detect or prevent the introduction of guns into the workplace) in an effort to minimize the chances of workplace violence and limit liability exposure.

Employers have a common law duty—and an obligation under various state and federal workplace safety statutes—to maintain a safe and secure workplace,[9] and they may be held responsible for failing to take measures to deny access to gun-wielding attackers if the risk of danger is foreseeable.[10] Recognizing the importance of AOL's right to control its own property, business organizations in Utah, including the Ogden-Weber and Salt Lake City Chambers of Commerce, the Utah Restaurant Association, and the Utah Manufacturers Association, supported the company in a friend-of-the-court brief.[11]

The Utah Supreme Court ultimately upheld AOL's actions, concluding that the legislature "purposefully declined to give the right to keep and bear arms absolute preeminence over the right to regulate one's own private property."[12] The court acknowledged that the case presented a novel question but concluded that "the mature at-will employment law in the state of Utah rejects the idea that, in the face of a freely entered-into agreement to the contrary, an employee has the right to carry a firearm on his employer's premises."[13] The court also noted that employees were well aware of the firearms prohibition, that AOL had displayed the policy in the lobby of the call center, and that the call center workers were at-will employees who could be terminated with or without cause.[14]

Insurrectionist gadfly Larry Pratt called for a boycott of AOL, proclaiming, "By patronizing AOL you are aiding and abetting the enemy."[15] The former employees' lawyer, well-known Utah gun rights advocate Mitch Vilos, complained to a reporter from the *Deseret Morning News* that AOL and its East Coast values could not fathom Western common-sense gun laws and described the company as "a little bit hypocritical and elitist": "It shouldn't be tolerated by free people. Put that in your paper. . . . And tell them Pancho Villa sent you."[16]

At the time the AOL suit was litigated, the NRA and many state-based gun rights activists had already spent several years pressing legislators to liberalize laws governing the carrying of concealed weapons. These legislative efforts were based on a central (but ultimately false) premise of the gun rights movement: that a heavily armed civilian population helps to reduce crime because criminals will be reluctant to assault or rob victims likely to be carrying guns.[17] In many states, gun enthusiasts succeeded in convincing legislatures to adopt statutes permitting the carrying of concealed weapons, but they saw efforts to limit the places where guns could be carried as blunting the impact of the new laws. They sought, for example, to invalidate municipal ordinances barring guns from parks, government buildings, and other public property. In the case of workplace gun policies, gun rights groups argue that prohibitions against bringing guns to work, even when the firearms remain in locked automobiles, impose an important practical limitation on the ability to carry a gun. They point out that most workers are unlikely to have an alternative place to store a firearm while at work, and they assert that employees who feel threatened by carjackers or other violent criminals on the way to and from work should be entitled to carry firearms to defend themselves.[18]

In this context, it was perhaps inevitable that gun rights groups would make the issue of workplace limits on firearm possession the centerpiece of a new lobbying campaign. By the time Weyerhaeuser Company fired a group of its Oklahoma employees when guns were discovered in their vehicles during a 2002 drug search, the NRA was ready to act. It persuaded the Oklahoma Legislature to enact a series of amendments to the state's firearms laws that purport to bar employers from punishing workers who keep firearms in their vehicles while on the job.[19]

Whirlpool Corporation responded to the passage of the workplace-firearms amendments by filing a civil rights action in the U.S. District Court for the Northern District of Oklahoma, naming the governor and attorney general as defendants.[20] The complaint alleged that the statutory changes violated the company's property rights guaranteed by the Fifth and Fourteenth Amendments and sought relief pursuant to 42 U.S.C. §1983. Whirlpool contended, among other things, that the new provisions of the law prevented the company from exercising its fundamental right to exclude from its property persons of its choosing (i.e., people in possession of guns).[21]

Whirlpool owns property and operates a manufacturing facility in Tulsa, Oklahoma. Since 1996, Whirlpool has had a written policy prohibiting the possession of firearms anywhere on its property, including in personal vehicles.[22] The crux of Whirlpool's claim was that the company "possesses a fundamental property right to deny access to, or exclude persons with firearms from, its property. The right to exclude others, like the right to physically occupy real property, are fundamental and natural rights of owners of private property. Indeed, traditionally one of the most fundamental property rights is the owner's right to deny access and exclude others from entering the owner's property."[23] Almost a dozen companies joined the case as plaintiffs, but the NRA pressured some of these companies—including the original lead plaintiff, Whirlpool—to withdraw.[24] The new lead plaintiff, ConocoPhillips, contended that the firearms amendments represented a clear-cut violation of the company's property rights by allowing the public an unfettered right to bring firearms onto an employer's premises. These amendments, the argument goes, created a public right of access onto private land over the express objection of the landowner and therefore amounted to an unconstitutional taking of property.[25]

Conoco has good reason to be concerned about firearms in the workplace. Its Ponca City, Oklahoma, refinery "has a crude oil processing capacity of 194 [thousand barrels per day]. Both foreign and domestic crudes are delivered by pipeline from the Gulf of Mexico, Canada

and local production. The Ponca City refinery is a high-conversion facility that produces a full range of products, including gasoline, diesel,
jet fuel, [liquefied petroleum gas] and anode grade petroleum coke."[26]
The dangers posed by refineries, both from explosions and from release
of chemicals such as the deadly hydrofluoric gas used in the production
process, are a well-documented and serious public-health risk.[27] The
discharge of a firearm either intentionally or accidentally in this environment could have catastrophic results.

Unconcerned about the possibility that a wayward gunshot might
set loose a cloud of hydrofluoric acid that could cause severe burns and
death, the NRA has advanced a novel line of reasoning in the *Conoco*
case. The NRA suggests that Oklahoma "has a compelling interest in
promoting public safety by reducing violent crime" and asserts that
"there is ample evidence that laws promoting the carrying of firearms
outside the home, by law-abiding, adult Oklahomans, promote public
safety. Further, the State has a compelling interest in encouraging hunting as a source of revenue and a wildlife management tool,"[28] and this
interest is served by requiring employers to allow workers to keep guns
in their cars. To support its public-safety claims, the NRA cites research
purporting to show that "guns in the hands of law-abiding citizens
equal less overall violent crime in society."[29] While acknowledging that
this research "has been the subject of heated academic debate," it says,
"it ultimately is not for the parties or this Court to determine who has
the better empirical argument," because "it is not this Court's place to
second-guess the Legislature's judgment on such a fact-bound issue of
public policy."[30]

Conoco says that while the question of

whether more Oklahomans carrying more guns outside the home leads
to increased public safety is a viable theory, it remains unexplained how
infringing on fundamental property rights advances that goal. The NRA
steadfastly ignores the critical aspect of this inquiry: the fundamental
rights of private property owners to curtail or exclude activities, including otherwise lawful activities, on their private land. Private property
owners are free to make the decision as to whether they and visitors to
their property are safer with or without firearms on the property. It sim-

ply does not matter whether private property owners are correct in reaching a conclusion regarding safety and firearms on their property, or if the greater weight of law review articles support such a conclusion. The NRA fails to address the critical issue of private property rights, and its purported conclusions ring hollow.[31]

In November 2004, the court entered a temporary restraining order in *Conoco v. Henry* barring enforcement of the workplace firearms amendments, and in October 2007, the restraining orders were made permanent.[32] After the temporary order was issued, however, the NRA took its crusade to undermine property rights to the streets. In 2005, NRA chief Wayne LaPierre called for a boycott of ConocoPhillips. Unveiling a billboard in Idabel, Oklahoma, that read "ConocoPhillips is no friend of the Second Amendment,"[33] LaPierre framed the boycott in the usual terms of gun rights versus the enemies of liberty: "ConocoPhillips went to federal court to attack your freedom. Now freedom is going to fire back." He added that "Idabel, Oklahoma, is a new Concord Bridge. Our forefathers didn't run from the Redcoats in 1775 and we're not going to run from the corporations in 2005."[34] Froman got in on the action: "The right to carry saves lives. That's beyond debate. Your constitutional rights don't end where (corporate) parking lots begin. Let's teach them that the Second Amendment is non-negotiable."[35] Apparently the "lesson" did not work. ConocoPhillips's corporate profits as of 2008 are robust, and its policy against firearms at its facilities remains in place.[36]

Many on the Insurrectionist blog sites adopted the NRA's line and tried to characterize the ConocoPhillips policy as equivalent to Nazism. Commenter "Mulder" on the site Free Republic spewed, "It's about korporate Amerika, that doesn't give a damn about their employees, and would rather see them robbed, raped, and left for dead, than have a gun in their *private* automobile. It's also about a bunch of HR busybodies who brought in dogs (likely *German* shepards [sic]) to sniff around the private vehicles of their employees. If nothing else, this alone is creepy and un-American."[37] Some gun rights advocates, however, opposed the NRA on this issue, as did many conservative commentators—and with good reason. Using the government to force property owners to admit people toting guns to their places of business or homes is an affront to basic conceptions of privacy as well as private property. Under the NRA's stunted theory of property rights, a homeowner would be unable to bar a delivery person with a gun from the front porch or ask a gun-toting party guest to leave the house.

While the NRA often characterizes itself as a guardian of basic freedoms, its zealous advocacy on behalf of expansive theories of gun rights seems to have blinded it to competing claims involving other rights. As Jacob Sullum, an editor of *Reason*, a leading libertarian publication, and vocal gun control critic, wrote in commenting on the Conoco litigation, "The NRA's single-minded determination to defend its own understanding of the right to keep and bear arms can lead it to chip away at other pillars of a free society." Sullum observed that LaPierre's call for a boycott on Second Amendment grounds makes "no sense, since the Second Amendment is a restraint on government. The Second Amendment does not mean a private employer has to welcome guns in its parking lot, any more than the First Amendment means I have a right to give speeches in your living room."[38] Understanding that the NRA's willingness to restrict individual property rights threatens other individual rights, Sheldon Richman, senior fellow at the Future of Freedom Foundation, writes, "If the NRA wants to urge its members to boycott ConocoPhillips in order to pressure the company into reversing its policy, it should be free to do so. But the NRA goes further: It supports the law that limits employers' freedom to set the rules on their own property. The danger of such a move lies in the fact that an attack on one right is an attack on all rights. The rights of gun owners will not be secure if the rights of other kinds of owners are insecure. It is ownership per se that needs a consistent defense."[39]

The American Bar Association has termed the Oklahoma statute and other similar enactments "forced-entry laws" and found that they "violate the traditional rights to exclude others from one's private property, as well as the liberty to decide how, whether and when to do so." The association quotes Professor Thomas W. Merrill: "The right to exclude others is more than just 'one of the essential' constituents of property—it is the sine qua non. Give someone the right to exclude others from a valued resource, i.e. a resource that is scarce relative to the hu-

man demand for it, and you give them property. Deny someone the exclusion right and they do not have property."⁴⁰ The bar association ultimately was so shocked by the NRA's "guns at work" campaign that its
House of Delegates adopted a resolution supporting "the traditional
property rights of private employers and other private property owners
to exclude from the workplace and other private property, persons in
possession of firearms or other weapons and oppos[ing] federal, state,
territorial and local legislation that abrogates those rights."⁴¹

Undeterred, the NRA has taken its legislative crusade to additional
states, although it has met opposition from business interests otherwise
closely aligned with conservative political causes. As the Florida Legislature considered an NRA-backed "guns in parking lots bill," the
Florida Chamber of Commerce sounded the alarm:

> Businesses and their employees have been deciding this issue for them-
> selves for hundreds of years and now, shockingly, the rifle association
> wants government to decide for us. The rifle association's national cam-
> paign is a direct assault on the employer-employee relationship. Indi-
> vidual businesses and their employees should be allowed to decide what
> is best for their home and their workplace—just like they do now. The
> "Guns At Work" legislation creates a new right that does not exist and
> wrongly strips private property rights from millions of Floridians, cre-
> ates unnecessary government intrusion into basic property rights af-
> forded by the Constitution and is a big-government solution in search of
> a problem.⁴²

After a multiyear battle, the NRA finally got the Florida Legislature
to enact a "guns at work" bill in 2008 that prevents employers from prohibiting employees and customers from having firearms in their cars on
their employers' property.⁴³ Many of Florida's tourist-oriented businesses, including the state's biggest employer, Walt Disney World Corporation, and the Florida Retail Federation, opposed the law.⁴⁴ The
Chamber of Commerce and the Retail Federation immediately challenged the measure in federal court. The NRA intervened as defendant
to support the state. At a hearing on a plaintiff's motion for a prelimi-
nary injunction, Judge Robert Hinkle went so far as to call the law "stu-

pid."[45] Unfortunately, the Florida and Oklahoma statutes represent only the initial stages of what the NRA has promised will be a multi-year effort to force property owners to allow guns on their premises.

No matter how the courts ultimately resolve this controversy, the NRA is clearly willing to cast aside its professed commitment to the protection of individual rights when they come into conflict with its wildly grandiose vision of the freedom to own and use guns at any time and in any place, whether public or private. In the battle over guns at work, the NRA and the Insurrectionists have been exposed as utterly unprincipled in their approach to individual liberties. The Insurrectionists apparently are happy to use the government to intrude on other people's rights as long as unfettered access to guns at all times and all places is preserved, even if those places happen to be other people's private property. Hypocrisy is not really the organization's worst sin, though. The willingness to subvert the rights of others in the name of protecting "freedom" is fundamentally inconsistent with democratic values because it is based on the assumption that the rights of some people—gun owners—are entitled to more respect than the rights of others. This contempt for the political and legal equality of those who do not share their views on the benefits of bringing guns into the workplace speaks volumes about the Insurrectionists' selective view of the importance of individual freedom.

The Right of Redress and Immunity for the Firearm Industry

"Movement conservatives" have devoted a great deal of energy in recent years to denigrating judges they don't like as "judicial activists," notwithstanding evidence that "conservative" judges are actually more inclined than their "liberal" colleagues to countermand the politically accountable branches of government by striking down acts of Congress, which is arguably the best nonideological measure of judicial activism.[46] Under the guise of remedying judicial activism and "runaway juries," Insurrectionists have enthusiastically supported right-wing ideologues' and businesses' efforts to attack the legitimacy of the judicial system. Insurrectionists recently convinced Congress to pass a law that attempted to immunize the gun industry from civil liability. At the same time, Insurrectionists have sought to shield would-be vigilantes from criminal prosecution by working to pass "shoot-first" statutes. These laws, already adopted in Florida and a handful of other states, have allowed vigilantes to decide, without benefit of jury trials, lawyers, or the presumption of innocence, who is guilty and deserves punishment. Shoot-first laws entitle anyone who witnesses what he or she believes to be a violent crime in progress to use deadly force to stop it. Never mind calling the police, and never mind the consequences if the putative do-gooder turns out to be mistaken or accidently shoots the wrong person—these laws confer immunity from criminal prosecution for the use of force in an effort to stop a violent crime, even if a judge or jury would view the use of force as unreasonable or even reckless.

Both the immunity law and the push to enact shoot-first statutes prevent criminal and civil defendants from being evaluated (or, in the Insurrectionist view, from being second-guessed) by a jury of their peers. And both have resulted in grievous harm to the judiciary's power to vindicate individual rights, a development that does serious damage to the rule of law. The possibility that some innocent people are likely to be killed or that some guilty people will suffer injury far out of proportion to the gravity of their crimes seems not to concern the "nation's oldest civil rights organization." In fact, the NRA, which so often emphasizes the trust it places in regular folks to use firearms responsibly, apparently does not trust these same people to exercise common sense when they serve on juries. The major gun rights groups are quick to complain that the rights to a jury trial contained in the Fifth and Sixth Amendments, unlike the right to bear arms in the Second Amendment, are antiquated relics ill suited to the needs of a modern society. In his book-length polemic, *Guns, Freedom, and Terrorism*, LaPierre decries the inequity of the jury system, complaining that "alone among Western democracies, the United States still provides for juries in civil cases."[47] The NRA, normally quick to pose as the defender of the values and judgment of ordinary Americans, drops its populist pose when it comes to access to the courts and the right to a jury trial.

As the Constitution was being framed, the rights of litigants were hotly debated. All eleven state constitutions ratified prior to 1787 contained protections for the right to a jury trial in criminal and civil cases, as did the royal charters still in effect in Rhode Island and Connecticut. As originally proposed, the U.S. Constitution protected the right to a jury trial in the new federal courts for criminal defendants but did not specify how civil trials were to be conducted. The Antifederalists, fearing the "potentially anti-democratic role" that the federal judiciary might play, insisted that the jury be safeguarded in civil cases as well. This demand was met in the Bill of Rights, which of course includes the Seventh Amendment protection for the right to trial by jury to resolve legal claims where the amount in controversy exceeds twenty dollars and the Sixth Amendment right to a jury in criminal cases.[48]

Paul Carrington, a Duke University law professor, invokes noted political scientist Francis Lieber to make the point that juries are essential to the political system:

[Lieber] observed that it makes the judge "a popular magistrate looked up to with confidence and favor." And that it "makes the administration of justice a matter of the people" and thereby "awakens confidence" in the law. By giving the citizen "a constant and renewed share in one of the highest public affairs," he noted, it "binds the citizen with increased public spirit to the government of his commonwealth." Thus, he thought, it is a great institution for the development of the "love of the law" that Montesquieu and others had identified as the essential spirit of a republic. Tocqueville had expressed the same thought in describing the civil jury as a "gratuitous public school, ever open" that elevates the political good sense of jurors.[49]

In late 2005, the major gun rights groups delivered a gift to their friends in the firearms industry: they convinced Congress and the president to extinguish the rights of victims of gun violence to sue gun makers and sellers for negligent and even reckless conduct that allows criminals to obtain firearms. The Protection of Lawful Commerce in Arms Act (PLCAA, or the Immunity Act)[50] was an attempt to strip innocent victims of their ability to obtain relief in the courts for the traditional torts of negligence and nuisance, causes of action recognized by the common law for hundreds of years. This bill sought to prevent the courts from adjudicating cases alleging negligence or recklessness in the distribution and sales practices of firearms makers and sellers.

The NRA claims that the Immunity Act simply protects lawful businesses from being overwhelmed by frivolous lawsuits. Apart from the complete absence of evidence that litigation expenses posed any serious threat to the financial viability of any gun maker, the tort system has never been simply about whether a particular defendant or group of defendants has broken the law. The law of torts is a civil justice system, offering citizens the opportunity to air grievances against each other. It serves purposes different from those of the criminal justice system, where the government prosecutes wrongdoers with penalties including loss of freedom through incarceration. A gun dealer who is unable to account for hundreds of firearms missing from his or her inventory may not be in violation of any criminal statute, but the failure to keep track of firearms sold may constitute evidence of negligence that has the foreseeable consequence of allowing guns to fall into the hands of criminals. When the missing guns are later recovered by police investigating violent crimes, as was the case of the rifle used in the D.C. sniper killings, a jury might reasonably conclude that the dealer whose store originally stocked the gun failed to exercise due care when the gun is among many others reported "missing" from the store.

Likewise, firearms manufacturers that continue to supply gun dealers who are under indictment may not be violating any statutory requirement, but the decision to keep selling assault weapons to such dealers may well be negligent. As we noted in chapter 7, compared to other democracies the United States has only weak statutory restrictions on the ownership and sale of guns. The civil justice system provided a way for victims to exercise their rights and hold negligent sellers and marketers accountable for their irresponsible behavior. Moreover, in total there were never more than a few dozen lawsuits that challenged gun sellers' distribution practices, and a number of these cases were thrown out on jurisdictional grounds. Apparently this was too much pressure for the firearms industry, which needed legal protection afforded no other industry to put its actions beyond the reach of the courts unless and until they were caught committing a crime.

One of the sponsors of the immunity legislation, U.S. Representative Cliff Stearns (R-Florida), claimed that his proposal would immediately stop "predatory" lawsuits such as, among others, *Ileto v. Glock* and *Hernandez v. Kahr Arms*.[51] Tom DeLay (R-Texas), House majority leader at the time, expressed unintentionally ironic support for the bill by arguing that it protected "our constitutional freedoms in an honest and legitimate fashion."[52] And the NRA's LaPierre added, "This is an historic victory for the NRA. Freedom, truth and justice prevailed."[53] LaPierre and his allies in Congress did not explain how denying litigants with otherwise meritorious claims access to the legal system serves the causes of freedom, truth, and justice.

To illustrate the kinds of claims targeted by the new immunity law, we turn to the case of *Ileto v. Glock*. The *Ileto* lawsuit arose from events that took place on August 10, 1999, when Buford Furrow, a white supremacist with seven guns in his possession, entered the North Valley Jewish Community Center in Los Angeles, California, where he shot and injured three children, one teenager, and one adult. After fleeing, Furrow came upon Joseph Ileto, who was delivering mail, and shot and killed him. At the time of the shootings, Furrow was prohibited by federal law from possessing, purchasing, or using any firearm because he had been committed to a psychiatric hospital in 1998, indicted for a felony the same year, and convicted of second-degree assault in 1999.[54]

The plaintiffs, represented by, among others, the Educational Fund to Stop Gun Violence, an organization that is the current employer of one author and a former employer of the other, filed suit against the known manufacturers, distributors, and sellers of the weapons possessed by Furrow. The plaintiffs alleged that the defendants were negligent because their deliberate and reckless marketing strategies caused their firearms to be distributed and obtained by Furrow and that they intentionally produced more firearms than the legitimate market demands with the intent of marketing their firearms to illegal purchasers who buy guns on the secondary market without background checks.[55] Although the trial court dismissed the action, the U.S. Court of Appeals for the Ninth Circuit reversed that decision and reinstated the lawsuit against Glock, its distributor RSR, and China North Industries, the companies that marketed the two weapons that Furrow actually discharged during his rampage. The Ninth Circuit noted in its November

20, 2003, decision that under the facts alleged in the complaint, "it is reasonably foreseeable that this negligent behavior and distribution strategy will result in guns getting into the hands of people like Furrow."[56] Defendant China North petitioned the U.S. Supreme Court for a writ of certiorari, asking the Court to review the Ninth Circuit's decision to reinstate the case. On January 10, 2005, the Supreme Court denied without comment China North's petition. A month later, the case was remanded back to the federal district court.

As the litigation was proceeding, the NRA and its allies in the firearms industry worked vigorously to persuade Congress to adopt the immunity bill. President George W. Bush signed it while the discovery process in the case was under way. Two weeks after the Immunity Act was signed into law, Glock and RSR sought dismissal of the suit based on the immunity conferred by the new law.[57] More than six years after Furrow committed his crimes and more than five years after the case had been filed, the district court dismissed the case against Glock and RSR.[58] (The court did not dismiss China North as a defendant because, as a foreign manufacturer without a federal firearms license, it is not covered by the immunity statute.)[59] As of this writing, *Ileto* is back on appeal in the Ninth Circuit.

The case of *Hernandez v. Kahr Arms* also shows the kinds of claims that gun rights groups and the firearms industry wanted to eradicate with the immunity statute. The *Hernandez* litigation stemmed from a 1999 incident in which an innocent bystander, Danny Guzman, was shot and killed by a criminal wielding a 9 mm Kahr Arms handgun outside a Worcester, Massachusetts, nightclub. The gun used to kill Guzman was later found by a four-year-old who lived nearby. The handgun had been stolen from the Kahr Arms factory by Mark Cronin, a company employee, before it had even been imprinted with a serial number. Cronin had stolen several other guns from the company and traded them for drugs and money. Cronin had a long, sordid past that included alcohol and drug abuse and a criminal record for assault and battery.

A law enforcement investigation of Kahr Arms revealed that another employee with a criminal history, Scott Anderson, was also stealing guns from the company. Kahr Arms did not conduct criminal background checks on employees to weed out job applicants such as Cronin and Anderson, and it failed to undertake rudimentary security precautions at its plant. It performed no employee drug screening, and employed no metal detectors, security cameras, or security guards. The company had no inventory control system. The investigation showed that weapons were missing from the plant and that as many as sixteen shipments to customers had never arrived at their destinations. The results of the company's disregard for basic safety procedures were devastating: convicted criminals working out of its factory supplied drug dealers and other criminals with firearms free of background checks, paperwork, and even serial numbers, making the guns effectively untraceable when recovered from crime scenes.

In 2002, Guzman's heirs filed suit against Kahr Arms (as well as other individuals involved in the distribution scheme), alleging that the company was negligent and had created a public nuisance. In 2003, a state court denied the company's motion to dismiss the claims. As the case was proceeding to discovery, the Immunity Act was passed, and Kahr Arms immediately invoked the new law in an attempt to get the case dismissed. At the time of this writing, a decision is still pending. Again, seven years after the shooting that sparked the litigation and more than four years after the suit was filed, the plaintiffs may be forced out of court after investing time, energy, and emotion in the case. Worse still, they may find themselves with no remedy even if they can establish with certainty that Kahr Arms acted irresponsibly.[60]

Ileto and *Hernandez* are among a series of cases, starting in the mid-1990s, that attempted to show that manufacturers and distributors of firearms were negligent and had created a public nuisance by the manner in which they distributed their products. The firearms industry complains that these lawsuits seek to hold them accountable for the actions of criminals over whom they have no control, but the claims raised in *Ileto* and *Hernandez* are based on specific actions—and failures to act—that a reasonable jury might well conclude were responsible for the killings of innocent Americans. *Ileto* and similar cases challenge the marketing practices and lack of care that the defendants took in their businesses. The allegations in these cases are grounded in well-established principles of civil liability, not some novel legal theory that attempts to hold law-abiding businesses accountable for the actions of others outside their control. The standards of care allegedly violated by the defendants in suits such as *Ileto* and *Hernandez* are clearly established in state law. For example, in one of these cases, brought by the National Association for the Advancement of Colored People (NAACP), Judge Jack Weinstein found that

> the NAACP has demonstrated the great harm done to the New York public by the use and threat of use of illegally available handguns in urban communities. It also has shown that the diversion of large numbers of handguns into the secondary illegal market, and subsequently into dangerous criminal activities, could be substantially reduced through policies voluntarily adopted by manufacturers and distributors of handguns without additional legislation.[61]

While Weinstein ultimately dismissed the suit on the grounds that the NAACP was not entitled to bring the action, his and other court rulings have clearly shown that firearms manufacturers were going to have to change the way they did business or face liability in suits such as *Ileto* and *Hernandez* where the plaintiffs were individuals asking for damages to compensate them for the severe harm caused to them by shoddy distribution practices, as opposed to municipalities or organizations seeking sweeping judicial intervention in the way the firearms industry operates.

The ability to seek damages for injuries caused by fellow citizens is a right that dates back hundreds of years and was a staple of English common law. John Locke incorporated the right of redress into his social contract theory. According to John Goldberg, "Locke maintained that an individual's delegation of governing power to the state does not include a renunciation of his right to obtain redress from one who has wrongfully injured him. Instead, the individual consents only to channel the exercise of that right through the law, and, in return, the government is placed under an obligation to provide such law." Locke recognized that the state must provide an avenue to vindicate the right to redress because that right, like the right to self-defense, did not disappear after sovereignty was established. In Goldberg's words, "Locke's social contract theory claims that victims of wrongs possess a natural right to reparations from wrongdoers, and that government, as custodian of individuals' rights, owes it to them to provide a law of reparations." Moreover, Goldberg explains, William Blackstone also identified "the right to apply to the courts of justice for redress of injuries" as the third of the five subordinate rights guaranteed by the unwritten English constitution. Blackstone saw an "affirmative duty on the part of the King to provide law and courts. At least for those wrongs 'committed in the mutual intercourse between subject and subject,' he 'is officially bound to [provide] redress in the ordinary forms of law.' "[62]

The Insurrectionists are fond of citing Blackstone's "fifth auxiliary right," the right of individuals to bear arms for self-defense, as the basis for the Second Amendment. According to Blackstone, as we discussed earlier, the five auxiliary rights protect the three primary rights of life, liberty, and property. But Blackstone saw the auxiliary rights not as absolute individual rights that could be invoked by individual citizens without qualification but rather as rights subject to precise definition and limitation by the government or they would revert to the individual. For example, just as Saul Cornell argues that the Second Amendment protects the individual right to participate in well-regulated militias organized by the state governments, the right to redress requires that the state provide an avenue to vindicate this right—that is, a court of competent jurisdiction. Goldberg notes that "the rights to access common law courts, petition, and bear arms are presented on the same plane as the right to be governed by King-in-Parliament [the first auxiliary right]. Each is a 'structural' right that Englishmen possess so that they can enjoy their primary rights."[63]

Early American law recognized the principle that the government must provide a right to redress. As discussed previously, the Sixth and Seventh Amendments not only recognized the need for a strong court system capable of protecting individual rights but also acknowledged that these rights should be understood to include findings of fact by juries made up of community members. Professor Carl Bogus shows that antimajoritarian protections were important to colonial Americans. The trick for them, as it remains for us today, was to find the right balance between majority rule and protection for individual rights. Courts played an indispensable role in striking the right balance. In *Why Lawsuits Are Good for America*, Bogus writes,

> It is impossible to overstate how important it was to the development of American government and law that the colonies were established by dissidents attempting to escape pressures to conform to religious, political, and social orthodoxy. This gave them an ambivalence toward authority, including majoritarian authority. On the one hand, many colonialists were members of sects that had been disdained or mistreated by the dominant culture and its government and therefore had reason to find ways to limit government's role. But at the same time survival in an often hostile, new world required colonialists to create an effective social order. Weak government was not an option. They needed effective governments that worked the majority's will while respecting—indeed, even protecting—minority rights.[64]

Without courts, juries, and the availability of legal remedies enforced by the courts, individual rights cannot be protected. This means not that every plaintiff is entitled to prevail but that the legal system, through its common law heritage, has been designed to weigh the interests of the parties and that even wealthy and powerful defendants should not be able to avoid the judgment of the community.

According to many historians, this idea was enshrined in American jurisprudence by Justice John Marshall's famous Supreme Court opinion in *Marbury v. Madison* (1803). In *Marbury*, Marshall quoted Blackstone to prove the point: "It is a general and indisputable rule that where there is a legal right, there is also a legal remedy by suit or action at law whenever that right is invaded. . . . [F]or it is a settled and invariable principle in the laws of England that every right, when withheld, must have a remedy, and every injury its proper redress."[65] Historian Tracy Thomas reflects that in a democracy, the ability to seek remedies for wrongs in a court of law is "central to the concept of ordered liberty because [the remedies] define abstract rights by giving them meaning and effect in the real world."[66] Goldberg finds that the right to redress embodied as American tort law is an important democratic pillar:

Tort law involves a literal empowerment of victims—it confers on them standing to demand a response to their mistreatment. In this sense it affirms their status as persons who are entitled not to be mistreated by others. It also affirms that a victim is a person who is entitled to make demands on government. A tort claimant can insist that government provide her with the opportunity to pursue a claim of redress for the purpose of vindicating basic interests even if government officials are not inclined to do so. . . . As such, tort law contributes to political legitimacy. As a forum that is in principle available to anyone who has been victimized in a certain way, tort law demonstrates to citizens that the government has a certain level of concern for their lives, liberties, and prospects.[67]

Of course, over the past thirty years, the states have enacted a variety of "tort reform" initiatives (e.g., caps on damage awards in medical malpractice cases), and the federal government has also done so (e.g., limiting liability for vaccine and small-aircraft manufacturers). Some of these restrictions even have been tested in court and found to be constitutional. In a law review article comparing the Immunity Act to other areas of tort reform, Patricia Foster argues persuasively that the right to due process established by the U.S. Constitution includes at least a limited right to judicial relief for injuries caused by another and that the "right to sue and defend in the courts is the alternative of force. In an organized society it is the right conservative of all other rights, and lies at the foundation of orderly government."[68] In its case law, the Supreme Court has not fully endorsed a due process right to redress but has held that any effort to limit access to the courts must be scrutinized to determine that it provides "a reasonable just substitute for the common law or state tort law remedies it replaces."[69]

The Immunity Act is unique in that it provides no substitute for the common law and state tort law remedies it purports to extinguish. As Albany law professor Timothy Lytton notes,

PLCAA is not the first federal law to grant a particular industry immunity from tort liability, and other industry immunity laws have survived constitutional challenges. Examples include the National Childhood

Vaccine Injury Act of 1986, granting vaccine manufacturers immunity from tort liability, and the Air Transportation Safety and System Stabilization Act of 2001, granting the airline industry immunity from tort liability following the 9/11 terrorist attacks. But PLCAA is different. In the cases of vaccine manufacturer and airline industry immunity, Congress replaced tort liability with alternative compensation schemes. By contrast, PLCAA simply prohibits certain kinds of tort claims against the gun industry without providing plaintiffs any alternative means of pursuing their claims.[70]

Gun companies have used the Immunity Act to sweep away pending litigation and to prevent any new cases from going forward. The plaintiffs in these cases have asserted a number of constitutional challenges based on the notion that completely and retroactively eliminating a cause of action violates the due process and takings clauses of the Fifth Amendment as well as the ex post facto clause of Article I, Section 9 and the right to equal protection of the law.[71] A number of law review articles argue both for and against the constitutionality of the law,[72] and the few courts that have thus far examined the issue have issued conflicting opinions.[73] These matters will continue to be litigated in both federal and state courts of appeals for at least the next several years. As the plaintiffs in these suits include both individuals and municipalities, it is conceivable that the constitutional provisions in question could apply differently to each class of plaintiffs. One of the first courts to consider these issues identified the damage that the Immunity Act inflicted on the Constitution and the rule of law. In its lawsuit, the city of Gary, Indiana, alleges that certain firearms manufacturers engaged in, among other things, the negligent distribution of guns to criminals and high-risk gun dealers and that the manufacturers failed to take reasonable steps to control the distribution of their handguns. After the Immunity Act was passed, defendant manufacturers asked for dismissal, even though the case had been pending for six years. The trial court found that to dismiss the case would violate the city's constitutional rights:

> Under the PLCAA gun manufacturers would not have any responsibility for foreseeable harm caused by negligence in producing and distrib-

uting weapons and those harmed, past, present, and future would be wholly without a remedy in state and federal court. Under the Fifth Amendment, the City had a substantial, protectable interest in its tort claim. Inherent in the Due Process Clause, is a "separate and distinct right to seek judicial relief for some wrong." *Christopher v. Harbury,* 536 U.S. 403 (2002). It is acknowledged that Congress may regulate remedies or even limit state court remedies. Due Process is violated when Congress abolishes an existing remedy and provides no alternative. To deprive the City of its right in interest deprives the City of a vested cause of action without just compensation; thereby, the PLCAA is violative of the Due Process Clause and, therefore, unconstitutional.

Further, our Supreme Court has long recognized laws that are applied retroactively and/or laws that serve as a deprivation of existing rights are particularly unsuited to a democracy such as ours. . . . Our founding fathers were very aware of the pit-falls of retroactive legislation and have safe guarded the Republic with various provisions of the Constitution, including the *Ex-Post Facto* clause, the Fifth Amendment's Takings Clause, prohibitions on Bills of Attainder and our Due Process Clause. . . .

In the case at bar, the retroactive legislation may not be a means of retribution against unpopular groups or individuals; however, it is clearly an act which was passed in response to pressure from the gun industry. Further, it is clear that the PLCAA destroys the City's cause of action and valid state court remedies. These vested rights may not be destroyed by legislative fiat without violating our Constitution.[74]

The Immunity Act has pushed the envelope of "tort reform" to an unprecedented level that would leave innocent victims in the cold. Moreover, if this is appropriate for the firearm industry, why not the pharmaceutical industry or the auto industry? Ultimately, as Lytton writes, "The implications of PLCAA are likely to extend far beyond gun litigation. If the act succeeds in ending litigation against the gun industry, it may serve as a precedent for future efforts by other industries seeking statutory immunity from liability. If the act fails to protect the industry, it may reveal constitutional limits on using statutory immunity as a defense tactic in tort litigation."[75]

Whether the Immunity Act violates the constitutional rights of people such as Joseph Ileto and Danny Guzman will ultimately be decided by the courts. The authors believe that the Constitution requires and justice demands that one industry not be exempted from the government's age-old role, passed on from our common law tradition, of providing a forum for redress for a wrong. Democracy demands that rich and poor, strong and weak, be accountable equally for their actions. Open access to the adjudicatory process that courts provide is the best way we know not to guarantee a particular outcome but to provide an opportunity to be heard and grievances to be aired in a nonviolent manner. Colonialists viewed fair and impartial courts as an essential check on abusive power and a key ingredient to individual liberty, and they remain so to this day. While Wayne LaPierre may believe that stripping individuals of the fundamental right to redress is a victory for "freedom, truth and justice," the rest of us should see it for what it is: an unvarnished assault on individual rights.

Due Process and "Shoot First" Laws

Legislation recently passed in Florida and now being advanced in other states with the backing of the Insurrectionists fundamentally alters the law of self-defense by giving unprecedented rights and legal immunities to the shooter. Hailed by the Insurrectionists as a needed remedy to stop criminals, the enhanced rights of the shooter come at the expense of the rights of the person shot. This may be all well and good if the person is indeed a criminal, but the law is so broad that innocent people are being injured and left with no recourse. At the same time, shooters with criminal intent have a new defense to use to avoid criminal responsibility. The Insurrectionists refer to the Florida statute and similar measures as "stand your ground" provisions, while the gun control community has taken to calling them "shoot-first" laws, as in, "Shoot first, ask questions later."

Laws and statutes dictating appropriate responses to criminal danger have been around since biblical times. The Hebrew Bible describes a duty to retreat from violence if possible. However, there were exceptions to the rule, such as when one's home was burglarized at night.

There was never any glory in taking another life, even if the killing were not criminal in intent. Under Jewish law, even the justifiable or accidental taking of another life was viewed with shame, and the Bible mentions special cities reserved for these "manslayers."[76]

In his famous treatise on the common law, Blackstone makes the point that while in the home, the dweller has special rights: "And the law of England has so particular and tender a regard to the immunity of a man's house, that it stiles it his castle, and will never suffer it to be violated with impunity."[77] However, if courts are functioning and a government is in existence, the

> right of natural defense does not imply a right of attacking: for, instead of attacking one another for injuries past or impending, men need only have recourse to the proper tribunals of justice. They cannot therefore legally exercise this right of preventive defense, but in sudden and violent cases; when certain and immediate suffering would be the consequence of waiting for the assistance of the law. Wherefore, to excuse homicide by the plea of self-defense, it must appear that the slayer had no other possible means of escaping from his assailant. . . . [T]he law requires, that the person, who kills another in his own defense, should have retreated as far as he conveniently or safely can, to avoid the violence of the assault, before he turns upon his assailant; and that, not fictitiously, or in order to watch his opportunity, but from a real tenderness of shedding his brother's blood. And though it may be cowardice, in time of war between two independent nations, to flee from an enemy; yet between two fellow subjects the law countenances no such point of honour: because the king and his courts are the *vindices injuriarum* [the avengers of wrongs], and will give to the party wronged all the satisfaction he deserves.[78]

Blackstone's commentary reflects the fundamental truth that people are fallible (especially in stressful situations such as armed confrontations) and that a neutral third party such as a judge or a jury is in a better position to arrive at a just decision about whether and how to punish a criminal than a victim is likely to occupy in the heat of the moment. Vigilante justice was disfavored because the accused had rights, too—most fundamentally, that he or she should not be punished until proven guilty according to the law.

The policy against legitimizing vigilantism forms a fundamental part of the American legal system, but over time, the concept of a duty to retreat fell out of fashion in some states. As an Ohio court opined in 1876, "A true man, who is without fault, is not obliged to fly from an assailant, who by violence or surprise maliciously seeks to take his life or to do him enormous bodily harm."[79] In the words of one commentator, "State law reflects the division between the 'true man' privilege of non-retreat and the 'honorable man' duty of retreat to avoid deadly confrontation."[80] At the urging of the NRA, Florida changed its law in 2005 to eliminate the duty to retreat, but the new statute included some additional wrinkles that have never been incorporated into U.S. law. First, the right to use deadly force was permitted even where no crime involving the threat of death or grave bodily injury was involved, including such crimes as "unlawful throwing [and] any other felony which involves the use or threat of physical force or violence against any individual."[81] Second, the right to use deadly force to stop a violent crime was not subject to scrutiny by prosecutors or courts, making it virtually impossible to challenge self-defense claims in criminal trials and wrongful death suits.[82]

As a consequence, Florida's gun owners have received the privilege of deciding for themselves when deadly force is necessary. A would-be vigilante can use deadly force whenever he or she has a good-faith belief that a felony may be occurring. If the shooter is wrong and an innocent person is injured or killed, the victim has no recourse. Prosecutors are not entitled to put to a jury the question of whether the force used was reasonably necessary, and the courts are required to dismiss any civil suit filed by the victim of the shooting. This means that deadly force is now allowed even where simply walking away from a confrontation could have stopped the crime. Deadly force can be an appropriate and proportionate response to the threat of a violent attack, but when vigilantes have free rein to decide when killing a suspected criminal is justified, the dangers to public safety and to the principle of due process are not trivial.

Defending his assertion that Blackstone's *Commentaries* lend support to an individual right to raise arms against the government, Nelson Lund says, "The relevance of Blackstone may therefore lie more in his prominence as an expositor of the implications of the natural right of self-defense than in his role as an authority on English law."[83] Blackstone, however, would never have supported the new Florida law. Blackstone wrote that

> legal obedience and conformity is infinitely more desirable, than that wild and savage liberty which is sacrificed to obtain it. For no man, that considers a moment, would wish to retain the absolute and uncontrolled power of doing whatever he pleases; the consequences of which is, that every other man would also have the same power; and then there would be no security to individuals in any of the enjoyments of life. Political therefore, or civil, liberty, which is that of a member of society, is no other than natural liberty so far restrained by human laws (and no farther) as is necessary and expedient for the general advantage of the publick.[84]

The new Florida law has disrupted the age-old understanding, recognized by Blackstone, that courts should decide and mete out punishment—and determine who has a legitimate claim to self-defense and who does not—unless there is no practical alternative.

When the Texas legislature passed a similar bill in 2007, the NRA issued a press release in support of the effort: " 'I want to thank the Texas Legislature for working together to pass this vital legislation and take further steps in protecting the people of this great state,' said Chris W. Cox, NRA's chief lobbyist. 'Law-abiding citizens now have the choice to defend themselves and their families in the face of attack knowing their decision will not be second-guessed by the State of Texas.' "[85] Since when should anyone be able to shoot another person to death and *not* be "second guessed"? Gun owners talk frequently about the awesome responsibility of carrying and using a weapon,[86] but shoot-first laws relieve the shooter of the responsibility for making a bad decision, even if someone dies as a result. Protections for individual rights such as the right to trial by jury or the presumption of innocence are discarded as inconsistent with the way "real men" react when confronted by a criminal.

The shoot-first laws, in their few years of existence, have already allowed criminals to escape responsibility for egregious wrongdoing. Despite Insurrectionists' protests that these laws are a simple codification of the doctrine that no one should be forced to retreat in the face of aggression, the law has been asserted as a defense in a series of grievous slayings. In 2006, the *Orlando Sentinel* reported on at least thirteen shooting incidents in Central Florida where the law had been invoked, resulting in the death of six people and the injury of four more.[87] Only one of the ten people shot was armed. In South Florida, the law has sparked outrage as two thugs, Damon "Red Rock" Darling and Leroy "Yellow Man" Larose, invoked the protection of the law after participating in a gunfight that resulted in the death of a nine-year-old as she played on her front porch.[88] The president of the Florida Prosecuting Attorneys Association called the law "unnecessary" and said that it has given hotheads "another defense" against criminal charges. In addition, the law has created confusion among police as law enforcement agencies try to discern their responsibilities in investigating claims of self-defense.[89]

In states that followed Florida, the law is causing confusion and benefiting dangerous criminals. For example, in Kentucky, another early convert to the "stand your ground" law, James Adam Clem used the provision to escape a murder sentence for the killing of Keith Newberg. Clem had let Newberg into his apartment so that Clem could repay a drug debt. Prosecutors believe that Clem then assaulted and killed Newberg by beating him to death with a bronze lamp. Clem originally was charged with murder, but after the Kentucky shoot-first law was passed, he asserted the "stand your ground" defense. Prosecutors were then forced to accept a plea to second-degree manslaughter, and instead of spending the rest of his life in jail for murder, Clem almost immediately became eligible for parole. Commonwealth's attorney Ray Larson explained that the new law gave Clem a real chance of acquittal and that he had accepted the plea deal because some jail time was better than none. Fayette County circuit judge Sheila Isaac said, "I'm not quite sure that the drafters [of the shoot-first law] had even a marginal knowledge of criminal law or Kentucky law."[90]

The state's foremost authority on criminal law, University of Ken-

tucky law professor Robert Lawson, called the measure "the worst legislation I have ever seen in 40 years." As the Texas law neared passage,
one prosecutor railed against the bill: "'There will be a presumption
that [the vigilantes'] actions were reasonable, and 99.99 percent of the
people that's going to apply to are going to be murderers, capital mur-
ders, shootings at the bar, aggravated robberies and that sort of thing,'
said Randall Sims, a district attorney whose jurisdiction includes Ama-
rillo. 'They can't give me one example of someone who's been wrongly
convicted under the current self-defense laws. . . . They're trying to fix
a series of laws in Texas that aren't broken.'"[91] Law enforcement in
many states has organized in opposition to "shoot-first" laws, and legislators are starting to reconsider their rash votes to strip innocent victims of their rights.[92]

To get these poorly conceived laws enacted, the Insurrectionists are
willing to use advocacy tactics that most people should find repulsive in
a democracy. For example, legislators considering gun legislation often
receive threatening letters or phone calls from gun rights activists, and
gun rights groups recently have organized grassroots lobbying events
where they bring their firearms to legislative hearings or other govern-
ment-sponsored meetings. At a recent "lobby day" in the Virginia statehouse complex, members of the Virginia Citizens Defense League wore
their sidearms during legislative committee hearings (after being waved
through metal detectors at the door even as others carrying keys, cell
phones, and loose change were forced to empty their pockets and submit to searches).[93] And at a pro-gun rally outside the Pennsylvania
Statehouse, demonstrators, some of them armed, protested the introduction of a bill to register firearms by unfurling a banner that said that
the sponsor, State Representative Angel Cruz, should be "hung from the
tree of liberty for his acts of treason against the Constitution."[94]

In July 2008, *Mother Jones* magazine disclosed that an NRA mole
had for years been embedded in the gun control movement.[95] Under the
name "Mary McFate," Mary Lou Sapone had pretended to be a dedicated volunteer at several gun control organizations but in fact had been
working for a firm that specialized in corporate espionage and was being
paid by the NRA. On more than one occasion, the mole had plied the
authors for information, and she even appropriated documents for her

NRA spymasters. This type of behavior does not set a tone for civil discourse and mutual respect among legislators and advocates representing different sides of public-policy controversies. It signifies a deliberate effort to intimidate policymakers and to bully opponents. Moreover, it represents exactly the kind of tactic that the Insurrectionists are worried that the government will use. Private groups cannot throw their opponents in jail, but their efforts to bully and intimidate anyone who disagrees with them are nonetheless an odious affront to reasoned political discourse. The NRA may want to rethink it self-characterization as the "nation's oldest civil rights organization," especially since its behavior has more in common with J. Edgar Hoover than Martin Luther King Jr.

The gun rights movement's approach mirrors the mind-set of the leaders of the "conservative movement." Just as President George W. Bush adopted the formulation "You are either with us or against us" to express the idea that anyone opposed to his conception of how to fight terrorism is by definition unpatriotic, the NRA portrays opponents as anti-American statists bent on chipping away at individual freedoms. Instead of a debate about how to prevent kids from being killed by guns, the debate is now about freedom. Who among us opposes freedom? When Charlton Heston declared that he would give up his guns only when they were pried out of his "cold, dead hands," he wasn't preparing to shoot it out with the government. But he was saying something almost equally radical: that as a gun owner he occupied a special status and that his views should carry more weight than those of other citizens. When gun owners assert that they are ready to use their firearms to vindicate their political views, they are really saying that they are unwilling to abide by the American political tradition that the people without guns can tell people with guns what to do.

CHAPTER ELEVEN

EFFECTIVE DEMOCRATIC INSTITUTIONS

Both political and civil rights are integral to a well-functioning democracy. Some of these rights protect individuals from state action. The First Amendment, for example, protects people's ability to post partisan political slogans on their balconies, while other rights protect individuals by requiring state action, such as the Thirteenth Amendment, which abolished slavery. In either case, a state cannot survive long in democratic form if it lacks the internal strength to provide avenues of redress in the former case or law enforcement support in the latter. The First Amendment is little more than a platitude unless the government provides courts where people can have their grievances adjudicated and, most important, turned into judgments that can be upheld by law enforcement and a competent bureaucracy of marshals and clerks. The Thirteenth Amendment is nothing more than words on paper unless the federal government is willing to commit its resources, including the Justice Department and the Federal Bureau of Investigation (FBI), to give the amendment force.

For democracy to thrive, it is not enough to incorporate political and civil rights into laws. Democracy requires a state that is willing and able to enforce these laws. We can return to the example of African Americans after Reconstruction and before the civil rights movement. On paper, African Americans had political rights, but the government refused to enforce them. Only when the political, judicial, and administrative institutions of the federal government were strengthened were the rights of African Americans vindicated.

It is no accident that the states that have the most consolidated democracies and that provide the most freedom are also the states that have strong institutions and efficient bureaucracies. These institutions must include fair, frequent, and open elections; courts that are willing to apply the voting laws and act impartially in the resolution of disputes; and administrative organs, including an effective bureaucracy, that can carry out the laws passed by political decision makers and enforce the judgments of the courts.[1] "If and when many citizens fail to understand that democracy requires certain fundamental rights" Robert A. Dahl writes, "or fail to support the political, administrative, and judicial institutions that protect those rights, then their democracy is in danger."[2]

In light of the important role that public support for government institutions plays in the strength of our democratic system, it is unfortunate that both major political parties have made attacks on government standard elements of political campaigns. When he was president, Ronald Reagan went so far as to claim that government is not part of the solution but is in fact "the problem."[3] Even former president Bill Clinton gained political points by declaring that "the era of big Government is over."[4] However, as we will discuss, when a bevy of antitax activists, right-wing intellectuals, and the gun lobby, among others, echo that theme, they are not trying to score political points but rather are attempting to weaken the bureaucratic institutions that give the state its effectiveness. This is a dangerous prescription for democratic health.

As Ezra Suleiman argues in *Dismantling Democratic States*, "Democratic societies are based on legitimacy, which is largely based on effectiveness." He continues, "At the very least a consolidated democracy requires a state capable of carrying out its main functions (protection of citizens, collection of taxes, delivery of services) in an orderly, predictable, and legal manner."[5] We like to think of the United States as the strongest and most advanced democracy in the world, but even though we enjoy enormous economic and political freedom, many of our most important institutions are dangerously weak.

Nowhere has American democratic legitimacy been more challenged than in its ability to protect its citizens. Insurrectionists have made it difficult for law enforcement to carry out its most basic responsibilities. Law enforcement now faces serious legal and political hurdles in the investigation and prosecution of firearms-related crimes. At the Insurrectionists' urging, Congress has rejected the basic safeguard that would make it harder for criminals to get guns. As a result, violent criminals like the D.C. snipers and neo-Nazi Buford Furrow have had little difficulty in obtaining military-grade armaments without detection. These killers robbed entire communities of their freedom during highly publicized armed rampages.

To some people, the observation that gun violence denies its victims their freedom may sound like a rhetorical trick employed by political progressives in the service of values that may be legitimate but are simply not in the same category as civil liberties such as freedom of speech. The freedom to walk the streets without fear of violence, however, is more than just a precondition to the enjoyment of other freedoms in the sense that no person can exercise the other rights we recognize as fundamental in the absence of physical security. The community's ability to agree on effective means to protect itself and its members is fundamental to its functioning as a democracy. When government cannot provide security, it is failing at its most basic function. As Robert Spitzer points out, "The first purpose of government is to establish and maintain order, a task that cannot be divorced from the use, or threatened use, of state-sanctioned force."[6]

The members of America's founding generation well understood the link between a government's ability to safeguard its citizens and the freedom of these citizens as individuals. As Oliver Ellsworth, one of the drafters of the Constitution, an outspoken Federalist, and the third chief justice of the U.S. Supreme Court, explicitly stated, "A people cannot long retain their freedom, whose government is incapable of protecting them."[7] The Antifederalist "Brutus" maintained during the ratification debates that "the preservation of internal peace and good order, and the due administration of law and justice, ought to be the first care of every government."[8]

Government has a responsibility to protect its citizens from violence, and the Insurrectionists have spent a great deal of political capital making sure that when it comes to guns, the government will not have the tools it needs to live up to this responsibility. In fact, it is no exaggeration to say that the distribution of firearms in America is free from any meaningful regulation. No government agency has the power to remove a gun from the marketplace even if it shoots backward, and the Bureau of Alcohol, Tobacco, Firearms, and Explosives (ATF) faces legal, political, and budgetary constraints that leave it virtually powerless to crack down on corrupt firearms dealers, hold manufacturers accountable for using distribution and marketing tactics that feed illegal trafficking channels, and prosecute individuals who exploit loopholes to sell guns to criminals. The outcome is a free-for-all that leaves felons, drug addicts, and domestic abusers many ways to get guns.

If Congress had simply acquiesced in the Insurrectionist campaign to shield gun makers, dealers, and buyers from criminal and civil penalties for their misconduct, the public might eventually be expected to catch on and demand stronger laws, more aggressive enforcement, and a political commitment to curbing illegal gun sales. The Insurrectionists, though, have gone a step farther, covering their tracks by persuading legislators to shut down almost every avenue of information about the sources of guns used to commit crimes. ATF is now limited by statute from sharing certain trace data with local law enforcement, creating hurdles that impede efforts to identify and investigate corrupt gun dealers and illegal traffickers, and most trace data cannot be released to Congress or the general public.[9] Without access to this type of information, the public can no longer learn which dealers are among the 1.2 percent of federal firearms licensees who sell 57 percent of the guns traced in criminal investigations.[10]

ATF has long been a convenient whipping boy for the major gun rights groups, which have accused it of excessive zeal in enforcing the law and demonized it as a haven for "jack-booted Government thugs."[11] ATF is not, however, the only agency crippled by the Insurrectionists. The FBI, which is responsible for administering the National Criminal Instant Check system, which serves as the clearinghouse for information that is searched before a licensed dealer sells a gun, is barred from keeping gun-purchase records for longer than twenty-four hours,[12] and former attorney general John Ashcroft's policy, backed by the National Rifle Association (NRA), of prohibiting the FBI from comparing gun-sale data to terrorist watch lists was reversed only when the September 11, 2001, attacks made the practice politically untenable.

Gun rights enthusiasts often claim that private citizens need to arm themselves because the police are unable or unwilling to come to their aid when criminals attack, yet these same gun supporters work tirelessly to make sure that law enforcement will lack the tools it needs to reduce gun violence. Public safety in a free society requires security measures that are democratically accountable, but these institutions also must have the power necessary to protect us, or the antigovernment rhetoric about the ineffectiveness of the police will become a self-fulfilling prophecy.

The unregulated distribution and use of guns is not an accident but the result of a carefully conceived and executed plan. The firearms industry is a major beneficiary of this effort, but the political and legislative strategy that made it a reality was driven by the Insurrectionist aversion to any policy that might help hold individuals or companies accountable for making, selling, or using firearms in ways they know are likely to result in criminal activity. Indeed, when Smith & Wesson negotiated an agreement with the Clinton administration that would have led to the adoption of basic safeguards designed to keep guns away from criminals and detect diversion of firearms to illegal markets, the NRA retaliated by leading a boycott that bankrupted the company. When new owners brought Smith & Wesson out of its Chapter 11 reorganization, they renounced any intention to accept regulation—voluntary or otherwise—and the rest of the industry got the message.[13]

The resulting policies have shaped the industry in profoundly unhealthy ways. For example, major gun makers have knowingly exploited marketing channels expressly designed to reach customers who are supposed to be legally ineligible to own firearms.[14] When violent criminals—many with lengthy records of felony convictions, open arrest warrants, or histories of abuse or mental illness—take advantage of these channels to obtain guns, freedoms we once took for granted, like an evening stroll or leaving our windows open, become a thing of the past. The Insurrectionist response—that every adult citizen should carry a gun for self-protection—is no way to reclaim our freedom. A society where everyone needs to carry a gun is not merely dangerous but is no longer free. True freedom exists not in the power to shoot anyone who wrongs us but in the opportunity to go about our daily lives without the need to maintain constant vigilance in the event of an armed confrontation.

The vast amount of private armaments that seep into the civilian population occasionally results in a mass killing. But probably more devastating to our country is the illegal trafficking of firearms that robs whole communities of their safety. The Insurrectionists' answer is to privatize responsibility for security with policies such as liberal concealed-carry laws. In this view, each person is responsible for his or her own protection. In many ways, this is a return to the state of nature, where might makes right and your neighbor's concerns are not your problem. As Suleiman points out, "When citizens assume that all that matters is 'personal' responsibility, the result may be private militias, gated communities, private security forces, and so on. Developing a sense of responsibility for oneself is one thing; developing it to the exclusion of all else is a danger to the society in which we live."[15] The Insurrectionists want us to devolve into a premodern, anarchic state where the individual is the only thing that matters. That vision is inconsistent with our history and with democracy itself.

Much debate has examined the public health consequences of gun violence in America, and the evidence is clear that the untrammeled access to guns that has been the hallmark of American firearms policy—and to which the Insurrectionists cling so fanatically—poses a serious threat to public health.[16] But readers should by now sense a profound risk that the authors believe ought to trouble us even more: that the misbegotten tangle of Insurrectionist fears, resentments, crudities, and misapprehensions could endanger America's civic health.

CONCLUSION

Just a few years ago, the prospect that the Insurrectionist idea might win the respect or even the endorsement of the highest court in the United States seemed remote. When we began work on this book, we wanted to draw attention to the growing currency of Insurrectionist ideology in politics and popular conceptions of the role of guns in American society, but we did not expect it to be taken seriously as a theory of constitutional interpretation outside of a small circle of right-wing academics and propagandists. The decision in *District of Columbia v. Heller*, however, along with the D.C. Circuit opinion on which it built, demonstrates how successfully the Insurrectionist rationale for gun ownership has penetrated the mainstream of legal discourse. Briefs on both sides of the *Heller* case and newspaper opinion pieces cited the Insurrectionist fixation, only a decade earlier considered laughable. While the *Heller* majority did not wholeheartedly embrace the Insurrectionist idea as a governing principle, it certainly created plenty of room for future litigation aimed at elaborating a theory of gun rights grounded in a putative right to challenge the U.S. government with violence.

We cannot be certain whether Justice Antonin Scalia and other members of the *Heller* majority understood fully the implications of lodging a Second Amendment freedom to bear arms within a natural, individual "right" to fight government tyranny. We hope that our readers see the audacity of that claim and the danger to our democratic values and institutions if our fellow citizens accept it. If elite and popular opinion are prepared to acquiesce in the idea that self-proclaimed freedom fighters have the right to stockpile arms in preparation for a showdown with the government, to organize violent resistance to any government they decide is tyrannical, to order an armed march on the Capitol, or to give the "Fire" command, then the consensus concerning the limits of the legitimate means of political dissent on which our system depends is in doubt. As James Madison made clear to Patrick Henry and George Mason during the Virginia ratifying debates, a government powerless to uphold the rule of law is a "new species of government."[1] That is as true now as it was then. States that cannot enforce democratically enacted laws are not states. They are certainly not democracies.

We have made three claims in this book. First, a well-organized and energetic political force has been set into motion in service of the Insurrectionary fantasy that unfettered access to firearms is the touchstone of American freedom. Some of the leaders of this faction, including Wayne LaPierre, cynically wave the Insurrectionist banner to stoke their organizational engines and lend support to favored politicians. Most of the characters we have labeled as Insurrectionists, though, truly believe that guns are "the tools of political dissent."[2] Taken together, the individuals and groups working to popularize the Insurrectionist idea are a potent political and social force that cannot be ignored.

Second, the revisionist history that Insurrectionists have employed in support of their views relies on counterfactual assertions and untenable leaps of logic. The historical record of the events they routinely cite—the founding of our republic, the aftermath of the U.S. Civil War, and the Nazi takeover and destruction of Germany—fail to demonstrate that laws regulating the private ownership of firearms are inherently evil or even dangerous. Instead, these events, when properly understood, illustrate why freedom is best protected by strong and effective states that are committed to the protection of individual rights and democratic methods for making decisions.

Third, by attempting to harness the constitution in general and the Second Amendment in particular to their ideological preference for weak government, the Insurrectionists undermine support for precisely the institutions and values that provide the most effective safeguards for freedom, including the right of individuals to seek redress in the courts and the duty of law enforcement to protect public safety. Moreover, the sentiments expressed by Insurrectionist ideologues are fundamentally hostile to pluralism and tolerance, values that play an essential role in reconciling the demands of competing perspectives without violence in a diverse democracy such as the United States.

These three claims combine to make what we hope is a persuasive case that Insurrectionists' ideas and actions weaken the core of what makes this nation great. If we believed that the highest gun-death rate of any mature democracy were really the price of freedom, as some Insurrectionists have suggested, we have no doubt that the price would be worth paying. The problem is that the Insurrectionist idea has left us with the worst of both worlds—a society where firearm violence is all too prevalent even as democratic safeguards are under attack.

The debate about gun control in this country is not simply a question of public health statistics. It is essentially about how we choose to see ourselves as citizens. Are we like Timothy McVeigh, who saw gun ownership as part and parcel of antigovernment ideology? Or do we decouple gun ownership from the demands of democracy? Freedom is threatened by efforts to recruit armed citizens to counterbalance democratic government. The work of politics—knocking on doors, attending debates, showing up to vote, and teaching our children the importance of critical thinking and participation in civic life—lacks the glandular appeal of bellicose talk about voting from the rooftops with a sniper rifle. The tasks involved in meaningful engagement with the democratic process sometimes seem mundane, but they are the essence of full participation in our system of government. By hijacking the rhetoric of our democratic legacy, by endlessly circulating such slogans as "Vote Freedom First," and by referring to the Second Amendment as "America's First Freedom," the Insurrectionists have achieved a head start in this debate. It is past time to turn the tables.

The Insurrectionist idea should be vigorously challenged by citizens in the court of public opinion and now, after *Heller*, in courts of law as well. Here is what we believe needs to be done.

1. *Share a critical vision*

By inculcating in gun owners a paranoid and obsessively antigovernment ideology, the Insurrectionists have romanticized and legitimized hostility toward lawful government authority and instruments of cooperation (e.g., international treaties and environmental regulation) and pluralism (e.g., by deriding peaceful efforts toward racial and ethnic integration). In promoting the absurd, untenable conceit that no person can or should rely on anyone else, the Insurrectionist worldview shapes corrosive attitudes about government, mutual obligation, and community.

Gun control advocates—and political progressives more generally—have failed to appreciate the danger posed by this ideological perspective and the grassroots network supporting it. Without an organized and sustained effort to show how the NRA and other gun groups have become instruments of a broader reactionary movement, these forces will continue manipulating gun owners into joining a coalition of libertarians, right-wing populists, and religious "conservatives" who want to undermine support for public education, progressive taxation, civil rights, and regulation of business.

Left unchecked, Insurrectionism would threaten the shared values and institutions that comprise our democratic system by undercutting support for a strong and effective government capable of protecting individual rights (including equal protection of the laws and the freedom to walk the streets in safety as well as private property rights and freedom of speech). The animating spirit of Insurrectionism seeks to enlist well-meaning Americans who have failed to think critically about the obligations of democratic citizenship in a coalition bent on overthrowing the moderate, gradualist, conservative, and liberal traditions.

2. *Occupy the common ground*

The animating spirit behind this book, on the other hand, contains a vastly different strategic vision, elucidated as follows: Most gun owners are not Insurrectionists, although a steady diet of Insurrectionist propaganda has led many gun owners to believe that organizations such as the NRA represent their interests. In fact, most gun owners keep guns for self-protection or recreation, not to prepare for violent confrontation with the government. This fact suggests an opportunity to isolate the Insurrectionists. Self-defenders and sporting gun owners are in league with the Insurrectionists because they believe that their interests are best served by working together. Progressives must demonstrate respect for the values of recreational gun owners and self-defenders. In fact, ideological moderation is more consistent with the values that gun owners see as most important—patriotism, community, and respect for their way of life—and that deserve no one's hostility.

Progressives and moderates should start by getting behind ideas that serve goals shared with gun owners. For example, environmentalists should lobby actively and openly for protection of hunting habitat and point out how gun rights groups such as the NRA have pushed for logging and road building in our national forests, activities that have a devastating impact on hunters. For years, gun control advocates have maintained that they have no problem with the use of firearms for hunting or other shooting sports, and we need to back up these claims by sticking up for hunting as a wholesome, legitimate recreational activity.

Common ground with gun owners who see firearms as vital to their ability to defend themselves against criminals is important as well. Most people buy guns because they believe they will be safer with a firearm. These people are not the enemy, and they are not advocating a war on the government—they are simply trying to gain a measure of security and control over their lives. As parents, the authors would never bring guns into our homes. We have made this decision based on a considerable volume of research on crime and public health pointing to the conclusion that the risks of keeping a gun in the home far outweigh the benefits. We do not, however, vilify those who have come to a different conclusion. The best way to reduce the number of law-abiding members of our communities who choose to arm themselves as a hedge against violent crime is to make our communities safe. Cities across the country are employing some thoughtful crime-prevention strategies. Progressives need to make a commitment to support these efforts and help them succeed.

3. *Illuminate the relationship among guns, patriotism, and civic health*

Gun control advocates generally rely heavily on public health arguments based on contested factual claims and statistical analyses. Even the best data, however, cannot account for the role of values in the debate over firearms. Most gun control advocates simply do not believe that values have anything to do with gun policy. To put it another way, gun control advocates assume that if they win the argument about the public health consequences of gun violence, they will win the broader debate about how to regulate firearms. This line of thinking fails to account for our opponents' claims about the importance of guns to our cultural and political values. Gun control advocates have spent the past three decades trying to persuade the public that guns are dangerous, while gun rights groups have been arguing that guns are essential to our freedom. Throughout this book, the authors have maintained that the power and durability of democracy and freedom depend essentially upon public accountability and personal responsibility, not upon citizens' access to guns. We have insisted that no patriot worthy of the name will neglect the civic health of our society. The debate over guns in America should be framed not in terms of public health and as a problem of inner cities but as an essential part of America's civic health and the challenges we all face as citizens. The main questions must be, What are the demands of citizenship? Do we believe political equality and pluralism are integral to our system of government, or do we want to encourage the belief that dissenters are entitled to "vote from the rooftops" when they lose an election? Do we want to live in a society where Americans can walk safely down the street without concealed firearms, or do we accept the claim that anyone who fails to arm themselves has failed to take responsibility for their personal safety?

By framing this conflict in terms of how we see ourselves as citizens, we shift the basis of our argument from statistics to values. Insurrectionists have been driving the discussion about guns in America. They cling to a vision of the relationship between individuals and the state that borders on anarchism, and they shrug off the values of equality, tol-

erance, and the rule of law. Calling them to account for their recklessness and exposing their dreadfully impoverished conception of American democracy and civic participation are the duties of true patriots. We
hope that this book will inspire Americans to confront in their communities the conundrums and contradictions, the ideological rigidity and
shallow perspectives, of the Insurrectionist idea.

NOTES

Introduction

1. "Meacham Park Meeting Discusses Race," *STLtoday.com*, February 8, 2008.
2. *District of Columbia et al. v. Heller*, 128 S. Ct. 2783, 2802 (2008).
3. Lake Research Partners, Missouri statewide survey conducted for the American Hunters and Shooters Association, August 2006. In possession of the authors.
4. Lund, "Past and Future."
5. See Cottrol and Diamond, "Second Amendment."
6. See Polsby and Kates, "Of Holocausts."
7. Viereck, *Conservatism Revisited*, 144.
8. Viereck, *Conservatism Revisited*, 155.

Chapter 1

1. See http://www.nraila.org/Issues/FAQ/?s=27.
2. Lake Research Partners, Missouri statewide survey conducted for the American Hunters and Shooters Association, August 2006. In possession of the authors.
3. Kopel, "Trust the People" (emphasis added).
4. Lund, "Past and Future," 31.
5. Lund, "Past and Future," 46, 70–73.
6. Bridgewater, "Armed Revolution."
7. LaPierre, *Guns, Crime, and Freedom*, 7.
8. John Ashcroft, chair, Constitution, Federalism, and Property Rights Subcommittee of the Senate Judiciary Committee, statement, September 23, 1998. Available at http://www.senate.gov/nrpc/releases/1999/gc012501.htm.
9. For an overview of the patriot movement and its intersection with gun

rights groups, see *Shooting for Respectability*, 10; Dees with Corcoran, *Gathering Storm*.

10. See http://www.fec.gov/DisclosureSearch/mapApp.do.

11. See http://www.ronpaullibrary.org/document.php?id=16.

12. See http://www.pbs.org/newshour/vote2008/blog/2008/03/huckabee_con cedes_gop_race_aft.html.

13. See video of Huckabee speaking at a house party in New Hampshire at http://www.youtube.com/watch?v=53BE93_0gJc.

14. Of course, some gun rights enthusiasts assert that handguns alone are insufficient for home defense. We know of at least one firearms instructor who says he and his wife keep loaded handguns on the nightstands next to their bed "so we can fight our way to the combat shotgun we keep in the closet" in the event an intruder breaks in and attacks during the night. We have not, however, ever met anyone who claims that a semiautomatic assault rifle is necessary to adequately protect their homes.

15. See Miller, Hemenway, and Azrael, "State-Level Homicide Rates."

16. Lund, "Past and Future."

17. See Cottrol and Diamond, "Second Amendment."

18. See Polsby and Kates, "Of Holocausts."

19. LaPierre, *Global War*, 127.

20. Kopel, Firearms Law and the Second Amendment Symposium.

21. Shaun Kranish, founder of the Web site ICarry.org, question to David Kopel and Joyce Lee Malcolm, Firearms Law and the Second Amendment Symposium, George Mason University School of Law, Arlington, Virginia, October 7, 2006.

22. Kopel and Little, "Communitarians," 553.

23. Wayne LaPierre, "The Second Amendment As a Freedom Issue," speech at Commonwealth Club, San Francisco, March 11, 2004.

24. Charlton Heston, "Opening Remarks to Members," NRA Annual Meeting, Charlotte, North Carolina, May 20, 2000, http://www.nra.org/Speech.aspx?id=6044&fid=5.

25. Report of the Executive Vice President, Minutes of the Annual Meeting of Members, National Rifle Association of America, April 14, 2007. In possession of the authors.

26. "NRA Endows Chair at George Mason U. Law School," *Chronicle of Higher Education*, March 14, 2003.

27. Forte and Spalding, *Heritage Guide*.

28. See http://www.i2i.org.

29. See http://www.castlerockfoundation.org/recipients.html; http://www.southeasternlegal.org/default.aspx?page=15.

30. Kayne Robinson, "President's Column," *America's First Freedom: The Official Journal of the NRA*, February 2005, 10.

31. LaPierre, *Essential Second Amendment Guide*, vii.

32. LaPierre, "Standing Guard," 13.

33. *Freedom in Peril*, 3.

34. "Freedom Index," *America's First Freedom: The Official Journal of the National Rifle Association*, January 2007, 22.

35. *Freedom in Peril*, 9.

36. *Freedom in Peril*, 14.

37. Michel and Herbeck, *American Terrorist*, 339.

38. See http://www.mercgroup.com/services.html.

Chapter 2

1. DeWeese, "Why We Need 'The Freedom in Education Act.'"

2. Kopel, "Are They Schools?"

3. Zelman, "Taxes and Gun Rights—What Gun Owners Must Know," April 3, 2006. http://jpfo.org/pdf/cs200604.pdf.

4. Zelman and Wolfe, "Can The Second Amendment And Social Security Coexist?"

5. See LaPierre, *Global War*.

6. Video no longer available, but also quoted at http://www.washington spectator.com/articles/20060715united nations_2.cfm.

7. Blaine Harden, "NRA Pressured to Resist Bush Energy Policies," *Washington Post*, January 27, 2007.

8. *Freedom in Peril*, 23.

9. *Freedom in Peril*, 23.

10. According to Sampson, Morenoff, and Raudenbush, "Social Anatomy," 229, evidence shows that first-generation immigrants are among the least violent of criminal groups.

11. Jennifer Freeman, "Open Borders Threaten Gun Rights," n.d. http://www .libertybelles.org/articles/openborders.htm.

12. Second Amendment Foundation, "Zogby Poll Shows Americans Favor Border Control over Gun Control," September 12, 2005, http://www.saf.org/ viewpr-new.asp?id=159.

13. In his new study on Jefferson's view of the militia, historian David Konig makes it clear that Jefferson was no Insurrectionist and fully understood that the right to revolt was not enshrined in the Constitution. See Konig, "Thomas Jefferson's Armed Citizenry."

Chapter 3

1. NRA, IRS Form 990 (2004); NRA Foundation, IRS Form 990 (2004).

2. Feldman, *Ricochet*, 45–47.

3. Feldman, *Ricochet*, 123, 126.

4. See discussion of letter in Sam Verhovek, "An Angry Bush Ends His Ties to Rifle Group," *New York Times*, May 11, 1995.

5. See http://www.fec.gov/finance/disclosure/srssea.shtml.

6. "Creigh Deeds Answers Your Questions," February 21, 2006, http://www.raisingkaine.com/showDiary.do?diaryId=1709.

7. See http://www.nrapvf.org/ (see 2006 Texas 14 and Florida 21; subscription required). In possession of the authors.

8. Cassidy, "Ringleader," 46.

9. *Freedom in Peril*, 3.

10. Susan Schmidt and James V. Grimaldi, "Nonprofit Groups Funneled Money for Abramoff," *Washington Post*, June 25, 2006.

11. Reid, "Paladin Press."

12. "Ted's World," *Denver Westword*, July 27, 1994.

13. "Ted Nugent to Fellow NRAers: Get Hardcore," Associated Press, April 17, 2005.

14. Elizabeth Goodman, "Ted Nugent Threatens to Kill Barack Obama and Hillary Clinton during Vicious Onstage Rant," *Rolling Stone*, August 24, 2007.

15. U.S. Department of Justice, Respondent's Memorandum of Law in Support of Motion for Summary Judgment at 3, filed in *RSM, Inc. (d/b/a Valley Gun) v. Herbert*, No. 1:05-cv-00847.

16. *RSM, Inc. v. Herbert*, No. 1:05-cv-00847, Slip Op. at 4 (D. Md., February 23, 2006).

17. Americans for Gun Safety Foundation, "Selling Crime," 14.

18. *RSM, Inc. v. Herbert*, Slip Op. No. 06-0396 (4th Cir. 2006), 13.

19. "'Rogue Gun Dealer' Avoids Prison," *The Examiner*, Jan. 15, 2008.

20. Feldman, *Ricochet*, 268.

21. 18 U.S.C. § 925 (d).

22. Diaz, *Making a Killing*, 89.

23. Feldman, *Ricochet*, 260.

24. Feldman, *Ricochet*, 269–70.

25. See the JPFO's "Boot the BATFE" campaign, http://www.jpfo.org/filegen-a-m/bootbatfe.htm.

26. Bob Herbert, "In America; The Company They Keep," *New York Times*, February 16, 1996.

27. Steve Bailey, "A.K.A. gunnut," *Boston Globe*, August 10, 2007.

28. Second Amendment Foundation, "SAF Celebrates Patriot's Day, the Root of the Second Amendment," April 19, 2006, http://www.saf.org/viewpr-new.asp?id=179.

29. Jews for the Preservation of Firearms Ownership, "Jews and 'Gun Control': Fear of Freedom or Freedom from Fear?" n.d., http://www.jpfo.org/filegen-a-m/fear.htm.

30. Pratt, "Supreme Court Has Declared," 8.

31. Pratt, "South African Gun Owners," 6–7. For a refutation of Pratt's claim about the mountains of data showing the protective values of guns, see Miller, Hemenway, and Azrael, "State-Level Homicide Rates."

32. Zeskind, "Armed and Dangerous."

33. Zeskind, "Armed and Dangerous." For a detailed discussion of the relationship between the gun rights movement and the militia movement, see *Shooting for Respectability*, 10; Dees with Corcoran, *Gathering Storm*, 49–52.

34. Joshua Horwitz, Larry Pratt, and Joe Scarborough, conversation, March 8, 2005, on-air segment available at http://www.gunowners.org/svtb.htm.

35. Zeskind, "Armed and Dangerous."

36. U.S. Department of the Treasury, *Following the Gun*, xi.

37. Bouchard, Testimony, 34.

38. Carl J. Truscott, director of ATF, to F. James Sensenbrenner Jr., chair, House Committee on the Judiciary, November 11, 2005. In possession of the authors.

39. Michel and Herbeck, *American Terrorist*, 148, 166, 46, 142.

40. Michel and Herbeck, *American Terrorist*, 150, 269.

41. Jefferson's views about Insurrection are complicated, but "never did he describe it as a right." His famous statement regarding Shays's Rebellion—"a little rebellion now and then is a good thing"—was not an effort to justify the rebels' actions but rather to caution against a harsh repression of a political phenomenon that was natural and necessary (Konig, "Thomas Jefferson's Armed Citizenry," 263–64).

42. See Kenneth Ofgang, "Ninth Circuit Revives Suit Against Gun Makers in Valley Shootings," *Los Angeles Metropolitan News-Enterprise*, November 23, 2003; Anti-Defamation League, "Aryan Nations, Church of Jesus Christ Christian," n.d., http://www.adl.org/learn/ext_us/Aryan_Nations.asp?xpicked=3& item=11; "Daily Briefing," *Seattle Times*, May 17, 2000; "The Hate Filled Descent of Buford Furrow," *Seattle Post-Intelligencer*, September 17, 1999.

43. See www.stormfront.org, with the motto, "White Pride, World Wide," where LastReb2 (with a picture of a Confederate flag) wrote on November 9, 2006, the day after the election, "Yeap, the Democrats worry more about destroying the 2nd amendment than destroying Bin Laden and his band of terrorists. I predict that America will look like Bagdad by next year" (http://www .stormfront.org/forum/showthread.php/buy-your-guns-and-ammo-340261 .html?t=340261&highlight=gun).

44. Article and comments found at www.keepandbeararms.com/news/nl. Comment dated February 6, 2007.

45. Article and comments found at www.keepandbeararms.com/news/nl. Comment dated February 7, 2007.

46. Bob Moser, "The Abbeville Horror: A 'Patriot' Shootout Kills Two

Officers, Shatters the Peace of an Old South Town and Raises Questions about an Extremist Past—and Present," spring 2004, http://www.splcenter.org/intel/intelreport/article.jsp?pid=668.

47. See Humphrey Taylor, "Two in Five Americans Live in Gun-Owning Households," Harris Poll 25, May 30, 2001, http://www.harrisinteractive.com/harris_poll/index.asp?PID=234.

48. Lake, Snell, Perry Nationwide Survey of 1,000 registered voters for the Educational Fund to Stop Gun Violence, May 15–21, 2001. See archived press release at www.commondreams.org/news2001/0612-05.htm.

49. Testimony at Virginia Senate Courts of Justice Committee, January 16, 2006. Personal observation.

50. Shaun Kranish, founder of the Web site ICarry.org, question to David Kopel and Joyce Lee Malcolm, Firearms Law and the Second Amendment Symposium, George Mason University School of Law, Arlington, Virginia, October 7, 2006.

51. Margot Sanger-Katz, "Browns get five years in tax case," Concord (New Hampshire) Monitor, April 25, 2007.

52. Scott Brooks, "As trial goes on, he hunkers down," New Hampshire Union Leader, January 18, 2007.

53. Russell Goldman, "New Hampshire Couple Vows to Fight Feds to the Death," ABC News, June 18, 2007. http://abcnews.go.com/US/Story?id=3290003.

54. Fox News interview, June 26, 2007. http://www.youtube.com/watch?v=D2rVCI9-tSI.

55. Margot Sanger-Katz, "Feds keep close eye on Browns." Concord (New Hampshire) Monitor, September 17, 2007.

56. Carol DeMare, "Radical Politics Tied to Charges," Albany (New York) Times-Union, September 14, 2007.

57. See Margot Sanger-Katz, "When time came, Ed Brown folded," Concord (New Hampshire) Monitor, October 19, 2007.

58. Margot Sanger-Katz, "2 Judges out of Brown cases," Concord (New Hampshire) Monitor, October 18, 2007.

59. Shaun Kranish, Ed Brown under Siege, October 18, 2007. No longer available on the internet.

60. "Militia Leader Put Government on Notice Years Ago: Fincher Arrested in November on Charges of Illegal Weapons Charges," Northwest Arkansas Morning News, January 6, 2007; reader comments at http://www.nwaonline.net/articles/2007/01/07/news/010707fzfincher.txt.

61. Comment has been removed but a copy is in possession of the authors.

62. "Fincher Found Guilty of Having Illegal Weapons: Militia Leader Faces Prison Time for Machine Guns," Northwest Arkansas Morning News, January 12, 2007; reader comments at http://www.nwaonline.net/articles/2007/01/13/news/011307fzfincher.txt.

63. See nospeedbumps.com, April 23, 2006. http://nospeedbumps.com/?p=161#comment-22247.

64. Form submission to csgv@csgv.org, December 8, 2006, in possession of the authors.

65. Packing.org is now defunct, but copies of these comments are in possession of the authors.

66. Copies of these comments are in possession of the authors.

67. *U.S. v. Miller*, 307 U.S. 174,178 (1939).

68. Tribe, *American Constitutional Law*, 902.

69. Laurence H. Tribe, "Sanity and the Second Amendment," *Wall Street Journal*, March 5, 2008.

70. As we describe in chapter 4, based on the great change that occurred in the country between the revolution in 1776 and the drafting of the Constitution in 1787, we find the insurrectionary Second Amendment not plausible.

71. Levinson, "Embarrassing Second Amendment," 650; Van Alstyne, "Essay," 1249.

72. Van Alstyne, "Essay," 1243, 1244 (emphasis in the original).

73. Bogus, "History and Politics," 14.

74. Amar, "Bill of Rights," 1163, 1163 n. 151.

75. McIntosh, "Revolutionary Second Amendment," 674–75.

76. Laurence H. Tribe, "Sanity and the Second Amendment," *Wall Street Journal*, March 5, 2008.

77. Amar, "Enduring and Empowering," 107.

78. Bogus, "History and Politics," 21.

79. *District of Columbia et al. v. Heller*, 128 S. Ct. 2783 (2008).

80. *District of Columbia et al. v. Heller*, 128 S. Ct. at 2821.

81. *District of Columbia et al. v. Heller*, 128 S. Ct. at 2802.

82. Sanford Levinson, "D.C. v. Heller: A Dismaying Performance by the Supreme Court," Huffington Post, June 26, 2008, http://www.huffingtonpost .com/sanford-levinson/dc-v-heller-a-dismaying-p_b_109472.html. Levinson did make it clear that no matter the poor quality of the opinion, "as a partisan Democrat, I confess to being relieved that the dissenters did not prevail, for the upholding of the D.C. ordinance would, in effect, have served as a massive in-kind campaign contribution to John McCain."

83. Zumbo, "Assault Rifles for Hunters?"

84. *Outdoor Life* message board, February 20, 2007. Forum is no longer active, but copies of comments are in possession of the authors.

85. See http://armsandthelaw.com/archives/2007/02/Zumbo_controver.php.

86. "NRA Publications Suspends Ties to Jim Zumbo," February 22, 2007, http://www.nraila.org/News/Read/InTheNews.aspx?ID=8952.

87. Pat Wray, "How Could This Happen?" *Corvallis (Oregon) Gazette-Times*, February 24, 2007.

88. "TimJenkin," comment, February 25, 2007, http://www.keepandbear

arms.com/news/nl/read_comments.asp?nl=57846020375895&tmpD=2%2F26
%2F2007.

89. Brian Foster, comment on Wray, "How Could This Happen?" February
26, 2007, http://www.gazettetimes.com/articles/2007/02/27/sports/venture/
1ven01_wray.txt.

90. "Quoteman," comment, February 26, 2007, http://www.keepandbear
arms.com/news/nl/read_comments.asp?nl=57846020375895&tmpD=2%2F26
%2F2007.

91. See http://www.thefiringline.com/HCI/molon_labe.htm.

92. Academics have offered a number of compelling academic responses to
the insurrectionist view of the Second Amendment (e.g., Cornell, *Well-Regulated Militia*) but few responses have come from political leaders or in the popular press.

Chapter 4

1. At the NRA's 2000 Annual Meeting, association president Charlton Heston said in his opening remarks, "The smoke in the air of our Concord Bridges
and Pearl Harbors is always smelled first by the farmers, who come from their
simple homes to find the fire, and fight" (http://www.nra.org/Speech.aspx?
id=6044&fid=5).

2. Galvin, *Minute Men*, xiii, 2.

3. Much of the later Antifederalist rhetoric in opposing the Constitution and
supporting the call for a universal militia during the debate over the first militia
act was a fear of a "select" militia, a rich irony considering the most effective
militia in the colonies, that of Massachusetts, was based on a select militia concept.

4. Galvin, *Minute Men*, 11.

5. Galvin, *Minute Men*, 36, 65–66.

6. Shy, *People Numerous*, 103, 126. See also Galvin, *Minute Men*, 55.

7. Galvin, *Minute Men*, 133.

8. Galvin, *Minute Men*, 245.

9. Shy, *People Numerous*, 243.

10. George Washington, letter to the President of Congress, in *Writings*,
1:223.

11. Shy, *People Numerous*, 37.

12. Cornell, *Well-Regulated Militia*, 12–13.

13. Cornell, *Well-Regulated Militia*, 27.

14. Shy, *People Numerous*, 37.

15. Cornell, *Well-Regulated Militia*, 15–16.

16. Cornell, *Well-Regulated Militia*, 14.

17. Blackstone, *Commentaries*, book 1, chapter 1.

18. Goldberg, "Constitutional Status," 550–51, 625.

19. Wood, *Creation*, 130.

20. Wood, *Creation*, 131.

21. Wood, *Creation*, 40.

22. Chernow, *Alexander Hamilton*, 434.

23. Bridgewater, "Armed Revolution."

24. Polsby and Kates, "Of Holocausts," 1258.

25. Wood, *Creation*, 23, 25.

26. Edling, *Revolution*, 79; Wood, *Creation*, 356.

27. Edling, *Revolution*, 77–78.

28. Shy, *People Numerous*, 128.

29. Edling, *Revolution*, 80.

30. Wood, *Creation*, 415.

31. Shy, *People Numerous*, 128.

32. Randall, *George Washington*, 351, 375–76.

33. Shy, *People Numerous*, 131.

34. George Washington, "Farewell Orders to the Armies of the United States," November 2, 1783, in *Writings*, 27:226.

35. James Tilton to Gunning Bedford, December 25, 1783, in Washington, *Writings*, 27:285.

36. Edling, *Revolution*, 73.

37. Edling, *Revolution*, 82.

38. Edling, *Revolution*, 100.

39. Shy, *People Numerous*, 132.

40. Wood, *Creation*, 407.

41. Wood, *Creation*, 404, 406.

42. Wood, *Creation*, 319, 322, 324.

43. Wood, *Creation*, 327.

44. Cornell, *Well-Regulated Militia*, 30, 37; Wood, *Creation*, 433; Edling, *Revolution*, 156.

45. Cornell, *Well-Regulated Militia*, 34–35.

46. Randall, *George Washington*, 433. See also Lettieri, *Connecticut's Young Man*, 65–66.

47. Shy, *People Numerous*, 25.

48. Wood, *Creation*, 430, 432.

49. Wood, *Creation*, 432.

50. Edling, *Revolution*, 100.

51. Edling, *Revolution*, 11–12, 45; Cornell, *Well-Regulated Militia*, 40.

52. Wills, *Necessary Evil*, 212–14.

53. Edling, *Revolution*, 105–6; Cornell, *Well-Regulated Militia*, 42.

54. Madison, *Notes*, 483.

55. Madison, *Notes*, 514–15; Cornell, *Well-Regulated Militia*, 42.

56. Cornell, *Well-Regulated Militia*, 62.

57. Proceedings of the Virginia Convention, as compiled in 3 Elliot 423, June 14, 1788.

58. Proceedings of the Virginia Convention, as compiled in 3 Elliot 424, June 14, 1788.

59. See Justice John Paul Stevens's dissent in *Heller* at 128 S. Ct. at 2822. But see also how often staunch gun rights advocates such as Mike Huckabee use the phrase "The Second Amendment is not about duck hunting": "And a freedom conservative is a person who understands that the purpose of the Second Amendment is not about duck hunting and deer hunting, though I love both of them and am a lifetime member of Ducks Unlimited and I'm not a latecomer to the NRA. I was the first governor in America to have a concealed carry permit, so don't mess with me. But I'm always amused, if not amazed, when some political candidate tries to tell me that the purpose of the Second Amendment is largely about hunting. My friend, the purpose of the Second Amendment is to preserve our very freedom. And our founding fathers understood it clearly" (Mike Huckabee, Conservative Political Action Conference, Washington, D.C., March 2, 2007, http://www.conservative.org/pressroom/2007/speech_huckabee.asp).

60. Cornell, *Well-Regulated Militia*, 50–51.

61. Cornell, *Other Founders*, 31.

62. Brief of amici curiae, Jack N. Rakove, Saul Cornell, David T. Konig, William J. Novack, Lois Schwoerer et al., *District of Columbia v. Heller*, U.S. Supreme Court No. 07-290 (2008). http://www.abanet.org/publiced/preview/briefs/pdfs/07-08/07-290_PetitionerAmCuRakove.pdf.

63. Finkelman, "Well Regulated Militia," 144–45.

64. Finkelman, "Well Regulated Militia," 132.

65. Finkelman, "Well Regulated Militia," 133.

66. Wills, *Necessary Evil*, 121.

67. Cornell, "St. George Tucker," 1123, 1128.

68. Cornell, "Originalism Right."

69. Cornell, *Well-Regulated Militia*, 75.

70. Cornell, *Other Founders*, 54, 60–61.

71. Brutus, No. 7, January 3, 1788, in Storing, *Complete Anti-Federalist*, 2.9.83–87.

72. Cornell, *Other Founders*, 92–93.

73. Cornell, *Other Founders*, 110–13.

74. Cornell, *Other Founders*, 115.

75. Cornell, *Other Founders*, 117.

76. Cornell, "Don't Know Much," 679.

77. Konig, "Thomas Jefferson's Armed Citizenry," 266–67.

78. Thomas Jefferson to C. W. F. Dumas, September 10, 1787, quoted in Konig, "Thomas Jefferson's Armed Citizenry," 265.

79. Konig, "Thomas Jefferson's Armed Citizenry," 259.

80. Lund, "Past and Future," 45–46, 76 n. 72.

81. Wills, *Necessary Evil*, 215–16.

82. Cornell, *Well-Regulated Militia*, 76.

83. Hamilton, Jay, and Madison, *Federalist Papers*, No. 46, p. 299 (Madison).

84. Hamilton, Jay, and Madison, *Federalist Papers*, No. 46, p. 298 (Madison).

85. Hamilton, Jay, and Madison, *Federalist Papers*, No. 28, p. 182 (Hamilton).

86. Rossiter in Hamilton, Jay, and Madison, *Federalist Papers*, xvi.

87. Wood, *Creation*, 614.

88. Elkins and McKittrick, *Age of Federalism*, 471.

89. Elkins and McKittrick, *Age of Federalism*, 463, 482, Cornell, *Other Founders*, 202, 209.

90. Elkins and McKittrick, *Age of Federalism*, 481–82.

91. Hamilton, *Works*, 6:418–24.

92. Washington, *Writings*, 33:506–7.

93. Gallatin, *Writings*, 3:5–6.

94. Findley, *History*, 300, 177.

95. Philip S. Foner, *Democratic-Republican Societies*, 147.

96. Cornell, *Well-Regulated Militia*, 85.

97. Wills, *Necessary Evil*, 141–44, 148–49.

98. Smith, *John Marshall*, 352–57, 372–73; Ellis, *American Sphinx*, 283.

99. Konig, "Thomas Jefferson's Armed Citizenry," 270.

100. Edling, *Revolution*, 137; Ellis, *American Sphinx*, 283; Cornell, *Well-Regulated Militia*, 20.

101. See http://www.monticello.org/reports/quotes/liberty.html.

Chapter 5

1. Schwartz, *From Confederation to Nation*, 132.

2. Lincoln, *Collected Works*, 4:267; Lincoln, *Collected Works: First Supplement*, 434.

3. Lincoln originally used the word *treasonable* but deleted it in favor of *revolutionary*, perhaps offering some insight into how he viewed the "nobility" of a revolution while a constitution still functions.

4. Lincoln, *Collected Works*, 4:264–65.

5. Lincoln, *Collected Works*, 4:426.

6. Lincoln, *Collected Works*, 4:432–33.

7. Cornell, *Well-Regulated Militia*, 167.

8. *Texas v. White,* 74 U.S. 700 (1868).

9. Abraham Lincoln to James C. Conkling, August 26, 1863, quoted in White, *Eloquent President,* 213 (also known as "Letter to the Springfield Rally").

10. James C. Conkling to Abraham Lincoln, September 4, 1863, quoted in White, *Eloquent President,* 217.

11. Kauffman, *American Brutus,* 46. Booth was well acquainted with firearms. He had learned to shoot as a youth at a military academy and later, during his acting career, shot himself while cleaning a gun. After learning of Lee's surrender at Appomattox, Booth "took out his frustrations at a pistol gallery on Pennsylvania Avenue" (Kauffman, *American Brutus,* 91, 110, 207).

12. Kauffman, *American Brutus,* 7, 14; Goodwin, *Team of Rivals,* 738.

13. Kauffman, *American Brutus,* 113, 142, 253.

14. Foner and Mahoney, *House Divided,* 138.

15. Eric Foner and Brown, *Forever Free,* 78–79.

16. Although conspiracy theorists have tried to link Johnson with the plot to kill Lincoln, it has never been proven, and any evidence to that effect may have been an attempt by Booth to implicate the vice president. See Kauffman, *American Brutus,* 396.

17. Eric Foner, *Reconstruction,* 247–48.

18. Polsby and Kates, "Of Holocausts," 1265.

19. Cottrol and Diamond, "Second Amendment," 354–55.

20. Kopel, "Klan's Favorite Law."

21. Eric Foner, *Reconstruction,* 203.

22. Eric Foner, *Reconstruction,* 203.

23. Eric Foner, *Reconstruction,* 204.

24. Eric Foner, *Reconstruction,* 216.

25. Eric Foner, *Reconstruction,* 231.

26. Eric Foner, *Reconstruction,* 276–78.

27. Eric Foner, *Reconstruction,* 279.

28. Hahn, *Nation under Our Feet,* 266.

29. Eric Foner, *Reconstruction,* 425–26.

30. Hahn, *Nation under Our Feet,* 286–87.

31. Hahn, *Nation under Our Feet,* 290, 292.

32. Eric Foner, *Reconstruction,* 454–55.

33. Eric Foner, *Reconstruction,* 458–59.

34. Eric Foner, *Reconstruction,* 439.

35. Eric Foner, *Reconstruction,* 436.

36. Hahn, *Nation under Our Feet,* 266.

37. Hahn, *Nation under Our Feet,* 282–83.

38. Hahn, *Nation under Our Feet,* 283.

39. Eric Foner, *Reconstruction,* 439–40, 508.

40. Amar, *America's Constitution,* 380.

41. Eric Foner, *Reconstruction,* 562–63, 559.

42. Hahn, *Nation under Our Feet,* 297–98, 301–2.

43. Hahn, *Nation under Our Feet,* 304.

44. Hahn, *Nation under Our Feet,* 305.

45. Hahn, *Nation under Our Feet,* 306–7.

46. Eric Foner, *Reconstruction,* 437.

47. Hahn, *Nation under Our Feet,* 294–95; Eric Foner, *Reconstruction,* 437.

48. Hahn, *Nation under Our Feet,* 307, 288, 296; Eric Foner, *Reconstruction,* 438.

49. Foner, "Reconstruction Amendments."

Chapter 6

1. See http://www.jpfo.org/about.htm.

2. See, e.g.,"Turkeyman," comment on Donna J. Miller, "Report Looks at Gun Shows Nationwide," *Cleveland Plain Dealer,* November 7, 2007, http://blog.cleveland.com/metro/2007/11/_the_coalition_to_stop.html#439814.

3. La Pierre, *Guns, Crime, and Freedom,* 155.

4. LaPierre, *Global War,* 125, 158.

5. Feldman, *Ricochet,* 44.

6. Kopel and Griffiths, "Hitler's Control."

7. Harcourt, "On Gun Registration," 657.

8. Cottrol, "Liberal Democrat's Lament," 60.

9. Polsby and Kates, "Of Holocausts," 1246–47.

10. Halbrook, "Nazi Firearms Law," 484, 485–87, 494.

11. Halbrook, "Nazi Firearms Law," 495, 532.

12. Halbrook, "Nazi Firearms Law," 535.

13. Harcourt, "On Gun Registration," 671 (emphasis ours), 672 (emphasis ours), 673.

14. Kershaw, *Hitler,* 74–75.

15. Kershaw, *Hitler,* 76, 75.

16. Kershaw, *Hitler,* 89.

17. Kershaw, *Hitler,* 98–99.

18. Kershaw, *Hitler,* 111.

19. Bullock, *Hitler,* 54 n. 1.

20. Kershaw, *Hitler,* 111.

21. Bullock, *Hitler,* 57–58, 63.

22. Bullock, *Hitler,* 59, 58.

23. Adolf Hitler, *Mein Kampf,* quoted in Kershaw, *Hitler,* 97.

24. Bullock, *Hitler,* 59.

25. Kershaw, *Hitler,* 112–16; Bullock, *Hitler,* 61–62.

26. See James, "Economic Reasons."

27. Bullock, *Hitler*, 161.

28. Adolf Hitler, July 18, 1930, quoted in Bullock, *Hitler*, 162.

29. Bullock, *Hitler*, 217.

30. Bullock, *Hitler*, 217, 221, 230.

31. Kershaw, *Hitler*, 317.

32. Kershaw, *Hitler*, 324, 322.

33. Bullock, *Hitler*, 184–85.

34. Kershaw, *Hitler*, 379.

35. Bullock, *Hitler*, 209–10.

36. Kershaw, *Hitler*, 420.

37. Kershaw, *Hitler*, 424.

38. Bessel, "Why Did the Weimar Republic Collapse?" 124.

39. Bessel, *Political Violence*, 16, 27, 31, 42, 48, 2.

40. Bessel, *Political Violence*, 45.

41. Fischer, *Stormtroopers*, 6.

42. Bessel, *Political Violence*, 75 (emphasis in the original), 76.

43. Kershaw, *Hitler*, 368.

44. Bessel, *Political Violence*, 79, 82–83.

45. Kershaw, *Hitler*, 439, 445.

46. Bullock, *Hitler*, 260, 261; Bessel, *Political Violence*, 112.

47. Kershaw, *Hitler*, 459; Bullock, *Hitler*, 262–63.

48. Bullock, *Hitler*, 263.

49. Bullock, *Hitler*, 266–69; Kershaw, *Hitler*, 465–68.

50. Bullock, *Hitler*, 270; Kershaw, *Hitler*, 468.

51. Kershaw, *Hitler*, 468.

52. Bullock, *Hitler*, 270.

53. Larry Derfner, "People of the Guns," *Jerusalem Post*, May 16, 2002.

54. Harcourt, "On Gun Registration," 671.

55. Information provided by University of Hawaii political science professor Rudy Rummel.

56. Rudy Rummel to Joshua Horwitz, February 3, 2007.

57. LaPierre, *Global War*, 125, 158.

58. LaPierre, *Essential Second Amendment Guide*, 23.

59. Freedom House, "Table of Independent Countries, 2007," http://www.freedomhouse.org/template.cfm?page=365&year=2007; Derek Miller et al., *Biting the Bullet*, 7; Cukier, "Firearms Regulation."

Chapter 7

1. Spitzer, "Don't Know Much," 721–22.

2. Eric Foner, *Story*, 16.

3. Dahl, *On Democracy*, 51.

4. See Freedom House, "Map of Freedom in the World, 2007," http://www.freedomhouse.org/template.cfm?page=363&year=2007.

5. Eric Foner, *Story*, xviii–xix.

6. McPherson, *Abraham Lincoln*, 62.

7. Wood, *Creation*, xv; Barlow, *Advice*, 39, 33. (Barlow also shared with most Federalists a strong civic republican understanding of the role of the armed citizen [see chapter 4].)

Chapter 8

1. Eric Foner, *Story*, 16.

2. Cornell, *Other Founders*, 20.

3. Schwartz, *From Confederation to Nation*, 188.

4. Lincoln, *Collected Works*, 2:405–6.

5. Charles Sumner, *The Equal Rights of All: The Great Guaranty and Present Necessity, For the Sake of Security, and to Maintain a Republican Government*, vol. 10 of Sumner, *Works*, 236.

6. See Max Weber, "Bureaucracy," in Weber, *From Max Weber*, 226; Dahl, *On Democracy*, 37–38.

7. Dahl, *On Democracy*, 76–77.

8. The struggle for equal political rights is far from over, and as citizens we must constantly defend the entire basket of these rights. In the United States, we talk a lot about democracy and freedom in the rest of the world, but we still have unfinished business here at home. Butterfly ballots and hanging chads catch our attention every four years, but democracy can be equally threatened by secret earmarks, bribery, corruption, and nepotism.

9. Dahl, *On Democracy*, 147.

10. Holmes, "What Russia Teaches," 33.

11. Dahl, *On Democracy*, 47.

12. *Freedom in Peril*, 1.

13. Charlton Heston, "Opening Remarks to Members," NRA Annual Meeting, Charlotte, North Carolina, May 20, 2000, http://www.nra.org/Speech.aspx?id=6044&fid=5.

14. Kopel, "Trust the People."

15. Rupnick, "Popular Front," 13.

Chapter 9

1. See http://my.barackobama.com/page/community/post/stateupdates/gG5NxL.

2. Banner, "Second Amendment," 898, 903–4.

3. *District of Columbia et al. v. Heller*, 128 S. Ct. 2783, 2807, 2815–16 (2008).

4. *District of Columbia et al. v. Heller*, at 2801–2802.

5. *District of Columbia et al.* v. *Heller,* at 2802, 2817.

6. *Presser v. Illinois,* 116 U.S. 252, 267 (1886).

7. Suleiman, *Dismantling Democratic States,* 24, 36.

8. Proceedings of the Virginia Convention, as compiled in 3 Elliot 414, June 14, 1788.

9. Weber, *Theory,* 154, 156.

10. Redner, "Beyond Marx-Weber," 638, 640.

11. Wulf, "Bumpy Road," 3.

12. Wimmer, "State's Monopoly," 1.

13. Dahl, *On Democracy,* 44.

14. Levinson, "Embarrassing Second Amendment," 650.

15. Levinson, "Embarrassing Second Amendment," 650–51.

16. Williams, *Mythic Meanings,* 5.

17. Pound, *Development,* 90–91.

18. Brownlie, *Principles,* 72.

19. Spitzer, review, 286. See also Spitzer, "Don't Know Much."

20. Blackstone, *Commentaries,* book 1, chapter 1.

21. Blackstone, *Commentaries,* book 1, chapter 7.

22. Goldberg, "Constitutional Status," 556–57.

23. Polsby and Kates, "Of Holocausts," 1273–74.

24. Kaldor, *New and Old Wars,* 37.

25. Wimmer, "State's Monopoly," 5.

26. Wulf, "Bumpy Road," 7–8.

27. Wimmer, "State's Monopoly," 9.

28. George Will, "Rhetoric of Unreality: Where Is Iraq after Nearly 3 Years of War?" *Washington Post,* March 2, 2006.

29. Wulf, "Bumpy Road," 16.

30. Dahl, *On Democracy,* 46.

31. Kaldor, *New and Old Wars,* 31. See also Doyle, "Liberalism and World Politics."

32. Leander, "Globalisation and the State Monopoly," 7, 13.

33. Leander, "Globalisation and the State Monopoly," 8.

34. Wimmer, "State's Monopoly," 14.

35. Dahl, *On Democracy,* 41.

36. Spitzer, "Don't Know Much," 723.

37. Weber, *Theory,* 154, 156.

38. Eugene Volokh, "Monopoly on the Use of Force," April 20, 2007, http://volokh.com/archives/archive_2007_04_15-2007_04_21.shtml#1177088441.

Chapter 10

1. Spitzer, "Don't Know Much," 721–22.

2. Dahl, *After the Revolution?* 17.

3. See Dahl, *On Democracy*, 125; Wood, *Creation*, 542–43.

4. Sandy Froman, "NRA: The Largest Civil-Rights Group Ever," *WorldNet-Daily*, April 12, 2007, http://www.worldnetdaily.com/news/article.asp?ARTI CLE_ID=55148.

5. The debate over the Second Amendment is about how far the protection extends. We argue that the Second Amendment protects state sovereignty by safeguarding the militia from federal inattention or usurpation, while the Insurrectionists give it a much more expansive reading.

6. *Hodel v. Irving*, 481 U.S. 704, 716 (1987).

7. *Dolan v. City of Tigard*, 512 U.S. 374, 384 (1994); *Ruckelshaus v. Monsanto Co.*, 467 U.S. 986, 1011 (1984); *Nollan v. California Coastal Comm'n*, 483 U.S. 825, 831 (1987) are cited in *Whirlpool v. Henry*, plaintiff's briefs in support of request for permanent injunction and declaratory relief, 8. [Doc. No. 93]. All documents from the Whirlpool/Conoco litigation are from Civil Docket Report for Case No. 4:04-cv-00820-TCK-PJC, originally captioned *Whirlpool v. Henry*, and numerical references are to the indexing system in the case file.

8. American Bar Association, "Special Committee," 4, quoting Callies and Breemer, "Right to Exclude."

9. See Holbrook Mohr, "Lawsuit: Lockheed Should Have Prevented Rampage," *Jackson (Mississippi) Clarion-Ledger*, March 21, 2005: "It is the employer's responsibility to provide a safe and healthful workplace for all its employees," quoting an Occupational Safety and Health Administration official who was describing the agency's view.

10. See, e.g., *Gibbs v. Shuttleking*, 162 S.W. 3d 603 (2005).

11. "Consortium Backs AOL in Guns-at-Work Suit," Associated Press, August 9, 2001.

12. *Hansen v. America Online*, 96 P3d 950, 955 2004 UT 62 (2004).

13. *Hansen v. America Online*, 96 P3d 950, 956 2004 UT 62 (2004).

14. *Hansen v. America Online*, 96 P3d 950, 951 2004 UT 62 (2004).

15. Larry Pratt, "Driving America Online Offline," *WorldNetDaily*, January 25, 2001, http://www.worldnetdaily.com/index.php?pageId=7951.

16. "Suit by 3 Ex-AOL Workers May Set Legal Precedent," *Deseret (Utah) Morning News*, January 22, 2001.

17. See Lott and Mustard, "Crime"; Lott, "Guns, Crime, and Safety." Lott and Mustard's work has received heavy criticism: see, e.g. Ayers, and Donohue, "Shooting Down," 1193; Hemenway, review.

18. In at least one state, however, gun rights advocates have argued that laws preventing holders of permits to carry concealed weapons from bringing their firearms into restaurants, bars, or other areas designated as "gun-free" will force gun owners to leave their guns in their cars, where they will be targets for thieves. See Virginia Citizens Defense League, "VCDL Update 8/14/05," http://www2.vcdl.org/cgi-bin/wspd_cgi.sh/vcdl/vadetail.html?RE CID=841121&FILTER=. It states, "We have warned the General Assembly re-

peatedly about the dangers of forcing a permit holder to leave his gun in an un-attended car."

19. See Oklahoma Stat., Title 21, §§ 1289.7a, 1290.22(B) (Supp. 2004 and 2005). See also Greg Piatt, "Legislature Approves Gun Owner Protections," press release, May 27, 2005, http://74.125.47.132/search?q=cache:TDSbIc sjiRkJ:204.126.144.2/house/news7632.html.

20. Case No. 04-cv-820-TCK-PJC.

21. Whirlpool complaint, 8 [Doc. No. 1].

22. Whirlpool complaint, 4–5 [Doc. No. 1].

23. Whirlpool complaint, 5 [Doc. No. 1].

24. See Kris Axtman and Mark Clayton, "Worker Right or Workplace Danger?" *Christian Science Monitor*, August 12, 2005.

25. Whirlpool complaint, 10 [Doc. No. 1].

26. ConocoPhillips Fact Book 2003, 38, http://www.conocophillips.co.uk/NR/rdonlyres/98FC7635-08F2-460F-BD27-614E5B68C196/0/factbook.pdf.

27. U.S. Public Interest Research Group, "Oil Refineries Pose Unnecessary Security Risk to 17 Million Americans," press release, August 4, 2005, http://www.uspirg.org/news-releases/new-energy-future/new-energy-future/oil-refineries-pose-unnecessary-security-risk-to-17-million-americans.

28. Amicus curiae brief, National Rifle Association of America, in support of defendants and in opposition to plaintiffs' motion for permanent injunctive and declaratory relief, 3 [Doc. No. 109].

29. Amicus curiae brief, National Rifle Association of America, in support of defendants and in opposition to plaintiffs' motion for permanent injunctive and declaratory relief, 12 [Doc. No. 109].

30. Amicus curiae brief, National Rifle Association of America, in support of defendants and in opposition to plaintiffs' motion for permanent injunctive and declaratory relief, 12–14 [Doc. No. 109].

31. ConocoPhillips response brief to amicus curiae brief, National Rifle Association, 3–4 [Doc. No. 122].

32. *ConocoPhillips v. Henry*, 520 F. Supp 2d. 1282, 1295 (2007) (appeal pending as of August 2008). While the court ultimately did not find an actionable invasion of ConocoPhillips's property rights and granted the injunctions based on the Oklahoma statutes' conflict with federal regulations, the court stated that "there can be no doubt that the Amendments burden Plaintiffs' right to exclude because the Amendments prohibit exclusion of what Plaintiffs perceive to be a dangerous activity on their business properties and impede Plaintiffs' ability to 'provid[e] a safe workplace'" (*ConocoPhillips* at 1310).

33. "NRA to Boycott Companies," *Tulsa World*, August 1, 2005.

34. "NRA Calling for Boycott of ConocoPhillips," Associated Press, August 1, 2005.

35. "NRA to Boycott Companies," *Tulsa World*, August 1, 2005.

36. "ConocoPhillips Reports Second-Quarter Net Income of $5.4 Billion or $3.50 Per Share," http://www.conocophillips.com/newsroom/news_releases/2008news/07-23-2008.htm.

37. "Mulder," comment, November 29, 2004, http://www.freerepublic.com/focus/f-news/1289203/posts?q=1&&page=251.

38. Sullum, "NRA vs. the Constitution."

39. Richman, "NRA Gets It Wrong." For additional conservative commentary, see Lora, "NRA vs. the Parking Lot," which says that "to undermine property rights is to aid the state in its inexorable criminal quest." The author also suggests that gun owners may want to consider joining Jews for the Preservation of Firearm Ownership rather than the NRA because of the Jewish group's "principled stand on rights in general."

40. American Bar Association, "Special Committee," 4–5; Merrill, "Property."

41. Recommendation Approved by the ABA House of Delegates, February 12, 2007. See http://www.flchamber.com/docs/Coalitions/ABARecommendation.pdf.

42. Florida Chamber of Commerce, "Guns at Work," http://www.flchamber.com/docs/Coalitions/GunsAtWorkCoalition/WWS_GunsAtWork.pdf.

43. Preservation and Protection of the Right to Keep and Bear Arms in Motor Vehicles Act of 2008, Florida Stat., § 790.251.

44. "Walt Disney World Fires Back on Guns at Work," *Orlando Sentinel*, July 3, 2008.

45. "Guns at Work Law Upheld for Now," *Miami Herald*, July 29, 2008.

46. Paul Gerwitz and Chad Golder, "So Who Are the Activists?" *New York Times*, July 6, 2005. The authors debunk not the notion of judicial activism but the conservative definition that only liberal-leaning judges are activist: Anthony Kennedy ranked second, right behind Clarence Thomas, but third was Antonin Scalia, with a 56 percent overturn rate.

47. LaPierre, *Guns, Freedom, and Terrorism*, 119.

48. Carrington, "Civil Jury," 83.

49. Carrington, "Civil Jury," 86.

50. Public Law 109-92, U.S. Statutes at Large 119 (2005): 2095, codified at U.S.C. 15 (2005), §§ 7901–3.

51. Protection of Lawful Commerce in Arms Act, S. 397, 109th Cong., 1st sess., *Congressional Record*, October 25, 2005, E2162–63.

52. Sheryl Gay Stolberg, "House Passes Bill to Protect Gun Industry from Lawsuits," *New York Times*, October 20, 2005.

53. National Rifle Association, "Historic Victory for NRA," press release, October 20, 2005. http://www.nraila.org//news/read/NewsReleases.aspx?ID=6682.

54. First Amended Complaint, *Ileto v. Glock*, No. BC234882, (Cal. Superior Ct. filed 5/23/2001).

55. *Ileto v. Glock*, 349 F.3d 1191, 1196, (9th Cir. 2003), *cert. denied*, 543 S. Ct. 4 (2005).

56. *Ileto v. Glock*, 349 F.3d 1191, 1205 (9th Cir. 2003), *cert. denied*, 543 S. Ct. 4 (2005).

57. *Ileto v. Glock*, 421 F. Supp. 2d 1274, 1284 (C.D. Cal. 2006).

58. *Ileto v. Glock*, 421 F. Supp. 2d 1274, 1304 (C.D. Cal. 2006).

59. Civil minutes order, *Ileto v. Glock*, no. 2:01 CV 01-9762 ABC (RNB) (C.D. Cal. 9/19/2006).

60. *Hernandez v. Kahr Arms*, Worcester, Mass. Superior Court, No. 021747C. See summary from the Brady Campaign to Prevent Gun Violence, http://www.gunlawsuits.org/docket/casestatus.php?RecordNo=76.

61. *NAACP v. Acusport*, 271 F. Supp. 2d 435, 451 (E.D. N.Y. 2003).

62. Goldberg, "Constitutional Status," 541, 544, 550–51.

63. Goldberg, "Constitutional Status," 551.

64. Bogus, *Why Lawsuits Are Good*, 43.

65. *Marbury v. Madison*, 5 U.S. 137, 163 (1803). See also Goldberg, "Constitutional Status," 563.

66. Thomas, "Restriction of Tort Remedies," 985.

67. Goldberg, "Constitutional Status," 607.

68. Foster, "Good Guns," 1750.

69. *Duke Power Co. v. Carolina Env. Study Group*, 438 U.S. 59 (1978).

70. Lytton, "Afterword," 339–40.

71. Lytton, "Afterword," 351–52.

72. See, e.g., Foster, "Good Guns"; Larkin, "Protection of Lawful Commerce Act."

73. See *City of New York v. Beretta*, 524 F. 3d 384 (2d Cir. 2008) (PLCAA is constitutional); *Ileto v. Glock*, 421 F. Supp. 2d 1274 (C.D.C. 2006), appeal pending (PLCAA is constitutional); *City of Gary v. Smith & Wesson*, No. 45D05-05-CT-0243 (Ind. Sup. Ct., October 23, 2006), *affirmed* 875 N.E. 3d 422 (Ind., 2008) holding that the Immunity Act is unconstitutional because the law violates due process guarantees and separation-of-powers protections.

74. *City of Gary v. Smith & Wesson*, No. 45D05-05-CT-0243 (Ind. Sup. Ct., October 23, 2006), 4–5, *affirmed* 875 N.E. 3d 422 (Ind. 2008).

75. Lytton, "Afterword," 340.

76. Exod. 22:2; Num. 35; Deut. 19.

77. Blackstone, *Commentaries*, book 4, chapter 16.

78. Blackstone, *Commentaries*, book 4, chapter 14.

79. *Erwin v. State*, 29 Ohio St. 186, 199–200 (Ohio 1876).

80. Koons, "Gunsmoke," 629.

81. Florida Stat,. Title XLVI, § 776.08.

82. Florida Stat., Title XLVI, § 776.032.

83. Lund, "Past and Future," 15.

84. Blackstone, *Commentaries*, book 1, chapter 1.

85. National Rifle Association, "Texas Legislature Votes NRA-Backed 'Castle Doctrine' into Law," press release, March 20, 2007, http://www.nraila.org/News/Read/InTheNews.aspx?ID=9108.

86. See Fulton, *Right to Carry.*

87. "Gun Law Triggers at Least 13 Shootings," *Orlando Sentinel,* June 11, 2006.

88. "Victims' Families Want Law Changes," *Miami Herald,* September 27, 2006. For an account of another event and further analysis, see Perlstein, "View to a Kill."

89. See "Shooting Cases to Test New Self-Defense Law," *Palm Beach Post,* December 13, 2006; "New Law May Aid Acreage Shooter," *Palm Beach Post,* September 19, 2006.

90. "Plea Deal Reached in Slaying: Confusion over New 'Home Intruder' Law Cited," *Lexington (Kentucky) Herald-Leader,* August 3, 2006.

91. "Bill Expanding Self-Defense Rights Zips through House," *Dallas Morning News,* March 19, 2007.

92. See "House Reverses Itself on Right to Brandish Guns," Associated Press, February 23, 2007.

93. Joshua Horwitz, personal observation, January 21, 2008.

94. "Gun-Rights Banner at Capitol Draws Outcry over Its Language," *Philadelphia Inquirer,* April 25, 2007.

95. "There's Something about Mary: Unmasking a Gun Lobby Mole," *Mother Jones,* July 30, 2008.

Chapter 11

1. Suleiman, *Dismantling Democratic States,* 7.

2. Dahl, *On Democracy,* 50.

3. Ronald Reagan, "First Inaugural Address," January 20, 1981, http://www.reaganfoundation.org/reagan/speeches/first.asp.

4. William J. Clinton, "President's Radio Address," January 27, 1996, http://www.presidency.ucsb.edu/ws/index.php?pid=53258.

5. Suleiman, *Dismantling Democratic States,* 2, 32.

6. Spitzer, "Don't Know Much," 722.

7. Oliver Ellsworth, "Landholder V," December 3, 1787, http://teachingamericanhistory.org/library/index.asp?document=1654.

8. Brutus, No. 7, January 3, 1788, in Storing, *Complete Anti-Federalist,* 2.9.83–87.

9. Science, State, Justice, Commerce, and Related Agencies Appropriations Act of 2006, Public Law 109-108, U.S. Statutes at Large 119 (2005): 2295–96.

10. U.S. Department of the Treasury, Bureau of Alcohol, Tobacco, and Firearms, *Commerce in Firearms in the United States,* 2.

11. NRA fund-raising letter to supporters, April 13, 1995. See discussion of

letter in San Verhovek, "An Angry Bush Ends his Ties to Rifle Group," *New York Times*, May 11, 1995.

12. U.S.C. Title 28, § 25.9(b)(1)(iii).

13. Fox Butterfield and Raymond Hernandez, "Gun Makers Accord on Curbs Brings Pressure from Industry," *New York Times*, March 30, 2000; Schuck, "Why Regulating Guns," 240.

14. Bradford, Gundlach, and Wilkie, "Countermarketing," 7.

15. Suleiman, *Dismantling Democratic States*, 52.

16. Hemenway, *Private Guns.*

Conclusion

1. Proceedings of the Virginia Convention, as compiled in 3 Elliot 414, June 14, 1788.

2. Kopel, "Trust the People."

BIBLIOGRAPHY

Amar, Akhil Reed. *America's Constitution: A Biography.* New York: Random House, 2005.

Amar, Akhil Reed. "The Bill of Rights as a Constitution." *Yale Law Journal* 100 (1991): 1131–1210.

Amar, Akhil Reed. "Second Thoughts." *Law and Contemporary Problems* 65 (Spring 2002): 103–11.

American Bar Association, "Special Committee on Gun Violence Report to the House of Delegates." February 2007. http://www.abanet.org/yld/midyear07/docs/107.pdf.

Americans for Gun Safety Foundation. "Selling Crime: High Crime Gun Stores Fuel Criminals." January 2004. http://www.thirdway.org/data/product/file/98/AGSF_Selling_Crime_Report.pdf.

Ayers, Ian, and John J. Donohue III. "Shooting Down the 'More Guns, Less Crime' Hypothesis." *Stanford Law Review* 55 (2003): 1193–1307.

Banner, Stuart. "The Second Amendment, So Far." Review of *The Mythic Meanings of the Second Amendment: Taming Political Violence in a Constitutional Republic,* by David C. Williams. *Harvard Law Review* 117 (2004): 898–917.

Barlow, Joel. *Advice to the Privileged Orders in the Several States of Europe.* 1792. Ithaca: Cornell University Press, 1956.

Berlin, Isaiah. *Four Essays on Liberty.* New York: Oxford University Press, 1990.

Bessel, Richard. *Political Violence and the Rise of Nazism: The Storm Troopers in Eastern Germany, 1925–1934.* New Haven: Yale University Press, 1984.

Bessel, Richard. "Why Did the Weimar Republic Collapse?" In *Weimar: Why Did German Democracy Fail?* ed. Ian Kershaw. London: Weidenfeld and Nicolson, 1990.

Blackstone, William. *Commentaries on the Laws of England.* New York: Garland, 1978.

Bogus, Carl T. "History and Politics of Second Amendment Scholarship." *Chicago Kent Law Review* 76 (2000): 3–25.

Bogus, Carl T. *Why Lawsuits Are Good for America: Disciplined Democracy, Big Business, and the Common Law.* New York: New York University Press, 2001.

Bouchard, Michael. Testimony before the House Committee on the Judiciary, Subcommittee on Crime, Terrorism, and Homeland Security. Hearing entitled "Bureau of Alcohol, Tobacco, Firearms and Explosives (BATFE): Gun Show Enforcement, Part II," February 28, 2006, 34–49.

Bradford, Kevin D., Gregory T. Gundlach, and William L. Wilkie. "Countermarketing in the Courts: The Case of Marketing Channels and Firearms Diversion." *Journal of Public Policy and Marketing* 24 (2005): 284–98.

Bridgewater, Bill. "Armed Revolution Possible and Not so Difficult." August 1994. http://www.lizmichael.com/armedrev.htm.

Brownlie, Ian. *Principles of Public International Law.* 5th ed. New York: Oxford University Press, 1998.

Bullock, Alan. *Hitler: A Study in Tyranny.* New York: Konecky and Konecky, 1962.

Callies, David L., and J. David Breemer. "The Right to Exclude Others from Private Property: A Fundamental Constitutional Right." *Washington University Journal of Law and Policy* 3 (2000): 39–59.

Carrington, Paul D. "The Civil Jury and American Democracy." *Duke Journal of Comparative and International Law* 13 (2003): 79–94.

Cassidy, John. "The Ringleader." *New Yorker*, August 1, 2005, 42–53.

Chernow, Ron. *Alexander Hamilton.* New York: Penguin, 2004.

Cornell, Saul. "Don't Know Much about History: The Current Crisis in Second Amendment Scholarship." *Northern Kentucky Law Review* 29 (2002): 657–81.

Cornell, Saul. "Originalism Right or Originalism Lite: The Curious Case of the Second Amendment. Part Three." OUPblog, November 3, 2006. http://blog .oup.com/2006/11/originalism_rig/.

Cornell, Saul. *The Other Founders: Anti-Federalism and the Dissenting Tradition in America, 1788–1828.* Chapel Hill: University of North Carolina Press, 1999.

Cornell, Saul. "St. George Tucker and the Second Amendment: Original Understandings and Modern Misunderstandings." *William and Mary Law Review* 47 (2006): 1123–56.

Cornell, Saul. *A Well-Regulated Militia: The Founding Fathers and the Origins of Gun Control in America.* New York: Oxford University Press, 2006.

Cottrol, Robert J. "A Liberal Democrat's Lament." *American Enterprise*, September–October 1999, 58–60.

Cottrol, Robert J., and Raymond T. Diamond. "The Second Amendment: Toward an Afro-Americanist Reconsideration." *Georgetown Law Journal* 80 (1991): 309–61.

Cukier, Wendy. "Firearms Regulation: Canada in the International Context." *Chronic Diseases in Canada* 19 (1998): 25–34.

Dahl, Robert A. *After the Revolution? Authority in a Good Society.* New Haven: Yale University Press, 1970.

Dahl, Robert A. *On Democracy.* New ed. New Haven: Yale University Press, 2000.

Dees, Morris, with James Corcoran. *Gathering Storm: America's Militia Threat.* New York: HarperCollins, 1996.

DeWeese, Tom. "Why We Need 'The Freedom in Education Act.'" *Newswithviews.com*, December 10, 2005.

Diaz, Tom. *Making a Killing: The Business of Guns in America.* New York: New Press, 1999.

Doyle, Michael. "Liberalism and World Politics." *American Political Science Review* 80 (1986): 1151–69.

Edling, Max. *A Revolution in Favor of the Government: Origins of the U.S. Constitution and the Making of the American State.* New York: Oxford University Press, 2003.

Elkins, Stanley, and Eric McKittrick. *The Age of Federalism: The Early American Republic, 1788–1800.* New York: Oxford University Press, 1993.

Ellis, Joseph J. *American Sphinx: The Character of Thomas Jefferson.* New York: Knopf, 1997.

Feldman, Richard. *Ricochet: Confessions of a Gun Lobbyist.* Hoboken, N.J.: Wiley, 2008.

Findley, William. *History of Insurrection in the Four Western Counties of Pennsylvania, in the Year 1794, with a Recital of the Circumstances Specially Connected Therewith, and an Historical Review of the Previous Situation of the Country.* Philadelphia: Smith, 1796.

Finkelman, Paul. "'A Well Regulated Militia': The Second Amendment in Historical Perspective." In *The Second Amendment in Law and History*, ed. Carl Bogus. New York: New Press, 2000.

Fischer, Conan. *Stormtroopers: A Social, Economic and Ideological Analysis, 1925–35.* London: Allen and Unwin, 1983.

Foner, Eric. "The Reconstruction Amendments: Official Documents as Social History." *History Now*, December 2004, http://www.historynow.org/12_2004/historian.html.

Foner, Eric. *Reconstruction: America's Unfinished Revolution, 1863–1877.* Gloucester, Mass.: Smith, 2001.

Foner, Eric. *The Story of American Freedom.* New York: Norton, 1998.

Foner, Eric, and Joshua Brown. *Forever Free: The Story of Emancipation and Reconstruction.* New York: Knopf, 2005.

Foner, Eric, and Olivia Mahoney. *A House Divided: America in the Age of Lincoln.* New York: W. W. Norton, 1990.

Foner, Philip S. *The Democratic-Republican Societies, 1790–1800: A Documentary Sourcebook of Constitutions, Declarations, Addresses, Resolutions, and Toasts.* Westport, Conn.: Greenwood, 1976.

Forte, David, and Matthew Spalding, eds. *The Heritage Guide to the Constitution.* Washington, D.C.: Heritage Foundation, 2005.

Foster, Patricia. "Good Guns (and Good Business Practices) Provide All the Protection They Need: Why Legislation to Immunize the Gun Industry from Civil Liability Is Unconstitutional." *University of Cincinnati Law Review* 72 (2004): 1739–69.

Freedom in Peril: Guarding the 2nd Amendment in the 21st Century. Fairfax, Va.: National Rifle Association, 2006.

Fulton, Joel. *The Right to Carry: An Awesome Responsibility.* Battle Creek, Mich.: Freedom Creek, 2003.

Gallatin, Albert. *The Writings of Albert Gallatin.* Ed. Henry Adams. 3 vols. Philadelphia: Lippincott, 1879.

Galvin, John R. *The Minute Men: The First Fight—Myths and Realities of the American Revolution.* 2d rev. ed. Dulles, Va.: Brassey's, 1989.

Goldberg, John. "The Constitutional Status of Tort Law: Due Process and the Right to a Law for the Redress of Wrongs." *Yale Law Journal* 115 (2005): 524–627.

Goodwin, Doris Kearns. *Team of Rivals: The Political Genius of Abraham Lincoln.* New York: Simon and Schuster, 2005.

Hahn, Steven. *A Nation under Our Feet: Black Political Struggles in the Rural South from Slavery to the Great Migration.* Cambridge: Belknap Press of Harvard University Press, 2003.

Halbrook, Stephen. "Nazi Firearms Law and the Disarming of the German Jews." *Arizona Journal of International and Comparative Law* 17 (2000): 483–535.

Hamilton, Alexander. *The Works of Alexander Hamilton.* Ed. Henry Cabot Lodge. 12 vols. New York: Putnam's, 1904.

Hamilton, Alexander, John Jay, and James Madison. *The Federalist Papers.* Ed. Clinton Rossiter. New York: Signet, 1961.

Harcourt, Bernard E. "On Gun Registration, the NRA, Adolf Hitler, and Nazi Gun Laws: Exploding the Gun Culture Wars (A Call to Historians)." *Fordham Law Review* 73 (2005): 653–80.

Haynes, George H. *Senate of the United States, Its History and Precedent.* Boston: Houghton Mifflin, 1938.

Hemenway, David. *Private Guns, Public Health.* Ann Arbor: University of Michigan Press, 2004.

Hemenway, David. Review of *More Guns, Less Crime: Understanding Crime and Gun Control Laws. New England Journal of Medicine* 339 (1998): 2029–30.

Herz, Andrew. "Gun Crazy: Constitutional False Consciousness and Dereliction of Dialogic Responsibility." *Boston University Law Review* 75 (1995): 57–153.

Heyman, Steven J. "Natural Rights and the Second Amendment." *Chicago-Kent Law Review* 76 (2000): 237–90.

Holmes, Stephen. "What Russia Teaches Us Now: How Weak States Threaten Freedom." *American Prospect*, July–August 1997, 30–39.

James, Harold. "Economic Reasons for the Collapse of the Weimar Republic." In *Weimar: Why Did German Democracy Fail?* ed. Ian Kershaw. London: Weidenfeld and Nicolson, 1990.

Kaldor, Mary. *New and Old Wars: Organized Violence in a Global Era.* 2d ed. Stanford: Stanford University Press, 2007.

Kauffman, Michael W. *American Brutus: John Wilkes Booth and the Lincoln Conspiracies.* New York: Random House, 2006.

Kershaw, Ian. *Hitler.* Vol. 1, *Hubris, 1889–1936.* New York: Norton, 1998.

Konig, David. "Thomas Jefferson's Armed Citizenry and the Republican Militia." *Albany Government Law Review* 1 (2008): 250–91.

Koons, Judith E. "Gunsmoke and Legal Mirrors: Women Surviving Intimate Battery and Deadly Legal Doctrines." *Journal of Law and Policy* 14 (2006): 617–92.

Kopel, David B. "Are They Schools or Are They Prisons?" November 8, 1995. http://www.davekopel.com/Misc/OpEds/Schools-or-Prisons.htm.

Kopel, David B. Question and Answer session during panel on "Firearms Regulation, International Law, and Human Rights," Firearms Law and the Second Amendment Symposium. George Mason University School of Law, Arlington, Virginia, October 7, 2006. Video found at http://www.nraila.org/ActionCenter/GrassRootsActivism.aspx?id=41.

Kopel, David B. "The Klan's Favorite Law: Gun Control in the Postwar South." *Reason Online*, February 15, 2005.

Kopel, David B. "Trust the People: The Case against Gun Control." Cato Institute Policy Analysis no. 109, July 11, 1988. http://www.cato.org/pubs/pas/pa109.pdf.

Kopel, David B., and Richard Griffiths. "Hitler's Control: The Lessons of Nazi History." *National Review Online*, May 22, 2003.

Kopel, David B., and Christopher C. Little. "Communitarians, Neorepublicans, and Guns: Assessing the Case for Firearms Prohibition." *Maryland Law Review* 56 (1997): 438–554.

LaPierre, Wayne. *The Essential Second Amendment Guide.* Fairfax, Va.: Boru, 2007.

LaPierre, Wayne. *The Global War on Your Guns: Inside the UN Plan to Destroy the Bill of Rights.* Nashville: Nelson, 2006.

LaPierre, Wayne. *Guns, Crime, and Freedom.* New York: Harper Perennial, 1995.

LaPierre, Wayne. *Guns, Freedom, and Terrorism.* Nashville: Nelson, 2003.

LaPierre, Wayne. "Standing Guard." *America's First Freedom: The Official Journal of the National Rifle Association,* January 2007, 8–9.

Larkin, R. Clay. "The 'Protection of Lawful Commerce Act': Immunity for the Firearms Industry Is a (Constitutional) Bulls-Eye." *Kentucky Law Journal* 95 (2006): 187–210.

Leander, Anna. *Globalisation and the State Monopoly on the Legitimate Use of Force.* Political Science Publications 7. Odense, Denmark: Syddansk Universitet, 2004.

Lettieri, Ronald John. *Connecticut's Young Man of the Revolution: Oliver Ellsworth.* Hartford: American Revolution Bicentennial Commission of Connecticut, 1978.

Levinson, Sanford. "The Embarrassing Second Amendment." *Yale Law Review* 99 (1989): 637–59.

Lincoln, Abraham. *The Collected Works of Abraham Lincoln.* Ed. Roy P. Basler. 9 vols. New Brunswick, N.J.: Rutgers University Press, 1953–55.

Lincoln, Abraham. *The Collected Works of Abraham Lincoln: First Supplement, 1832–1865.* Ed. Roy P. Basler. Westport, Conn.: Greenwood, 1974.

Lockmiller, David A. *Sir William Blackstone.* Chapel Hill: University of North Carolina Press, 1938.

Lora, Manuel. "The NRA vs. the Parking Lot." November 4, 2005. http://www .lewrockwell.com/orig6/m.lora4.html.

Lott, John. "Guns, Crime, and Safety." *Journal of Law and Economics* 44 (2001): 605–14.

Lott, John, and David Mustard. "Crime, Deterrence, and the Right to Carry Concealed Handguns." *Journal of Legal Studies* 26 (1997): 1–68.

Lovering, John. "Loose Cannons: Creating the Arms Industry of the Twenty-First Century." In *Global Insecurity,* ed. Mary Kaldor. London: Pinter, 2000.

Lund, Nelson. "Have Gun, Can't Travel: The Right to Arms under the Privileges and Immunities Clause of Article IV," *University of Missouri–Kansas City Law Review* 73 (2005): 951–67.

Lund, Nelson. "The Past and Future of the Individual's Right to Arms." *Georgia Law Review* 31 (1996): 1–76.

Lytton, Timothy D. "Afterword: Federal Gun Industry Immunity Legislation." In *Suing the Gun Industry: A Battle at the Crossroads of Gun Control and Mass Torts,* ed. Timothy D. Lytton. Ann Arbor: University of Michigan Press, 2006.

Madison, James. *Notes of Debates in the Federal Convention of 1787.* Athens: Ohio University Press, 1984.

Mahon, John K. *The American Militia: Decade of Decision, 1789–1800.* Gainesville: University of Florida Press, 1960.

McIntosh, Brent. "The Revolutionary Second Amendment." *Alabama Law Review* 51 (2000): 673–714.

McPherson, James M. *Abraham Lincoln and the Second American Revolution.* New York: Oxford University Press, 1991.

Merrill, Thomas W. "Property and the Right to Exclude." *Nebraska Law Review* 77 (1998): 730–55.

Michel, Lou, and Dan Herbeck. *American Terrorist: Timothy McVeigh and the Oklahoma City Bombing.* New York: ReganBooks, 2001.

Miller, Derek, Wendy Cukier, Helena Vázquez, and Charlotte Watson. *Biting the Bullet 16: Regulation of Civilian Possession of Small Arms and Light Weapons.* 2003. http://www.international-alert.org/pdf/BB_Briefing161.pdf.

Miller, Matthew, David Hemenway, and Deborah Azrael. "State-Level Homicide Rates in the U.S. in Relation to Survey Measures of Household Firearm Ownership, 2001–2003." *Social Science and Medicine* 64 (2007): 656–64.

Mooney, Chris. "Circuit Breaker: If You're Worried about Conservative Control of the Federal Judiciary, Watch the District of Columbia." *American Prospect*, March 2003.

Perlstein, Rick. "A View to a Kill: The NRA's New Cause Célèbre." *New Republic Online*, December 13, 2006. http://www.tnr.com.

Polsby, Daniel, and Don B. Kates Jr. "Of Holocausts and Gun Control." 75 *Washington University Law Quarterly* 75 (1997): 1237–75.

Pound, Roscoe. *The Development of Constitutional Guarantees of Liberty.* New Haven: Yale University Press, 1957.

Pratt, Larry. "South African Gun Owners at the Cross Roads." *Gun Owner*, March 24, 2006. http://gunowners.org/op0604htm.htm.

Pratt, Larry. "The Supreme Court Has Declared Itself above the Law." *Gun Owner*, August 15, 2005. http://64.129.137.61/article/6553.html.

Randall, Willard Sterne. *George Washington: A Life.* New York: Owl, 1998.

Redner, Harry. "Beyond Marx-Weber: A Diversified and International Approach to the State." *Political Studies* 38 (1990): 638–53.

Reid, Calvin. "Paladin Press Pays Millions to Settle 'Hit Man' Case." *Publishers Weekly Online*, May 31, 1999.

Richman, Sheldon. "The NRA Gets It Wrong." August 24, 2005. http://www.fff.org/comment/com0508n.asp.

Rupnick, Jacques. "Popular Front: Eastern Europe's Turn Right." *The New Republic*, February 19, 2007, 12–14.

Sampson, R. J., J. D. Morenoff, and S. Raudenbush. "Social Anatomy of Racial and Ethnic Disparities in Violence." *American Journal of Public Health* 95 (2005): 224–32.

Schuck, Peter H. "Why Regulating Guns through Litigation Won't Work." In *Suing the Gun Industry: A Battle at the Crossroads of Gun Control and Mass Torts*, ed. Timothy D. Lytton. Ann Arbor: University of Michigan Press, 2005.

Schwartz, Bernard. *From Confederation to Nation: The American Constitution, 1835–1877.* Baltimore: Johns Hopkins University Press, 1973.

Shooting for Respectability: Firearms, False Patriots, and Politics in Montana. Helena: Montana Human Rights Network, 2003. http://www.mhrn.org/publications/specialresearchreports/GunPaper.pdf.

Shy, John. *A People Numerous and Armed: Reflections on the Military Struggle for American Independence.* Rev. ed. Ann Arbor: University of Michigan Press, 1990.

Smith, Jean Edward. *John Marshall: Definer of a Nation.* New York: Holt, 1996.

Spitzer, Robert J. "Don't Know Much about History, Politics, or Theory: A Comment." *Fordham Law Review* 73 (2004): 721–30.

Spitzer, Robert J. Review of *The Mythic Meanings of the Second Amendment: Taming Political Violence in a Constitutional Republic,* by David C. Williams. *Law and Politics Book Review* 14, no. 4 (2004): 284–87.

Storing, Herbert J., ed. *The Complete Anti-Federalist.* 7 vols. Chicago: University of Chicago Press, 1981.

Suleiman, Ezra. *Dismantling Democratic States.* Princeton: Princeton University Press, 2003.

Sullum, Jacob. "The NRA vs. the Constitution: How a Misguided Defense of Gun Rights Undermines a Free Society." *Reason,* August 5, 2005. http://www.reason.com/news/show/36007.html.

Sumner, Charles. *The Works of Charles Sumner.* 12 vols. Boston: Lee and Shepard, 1876.

Thomas, Tracy A. "Restriction of Tort Remedies and the Constraints of Due Process: The Right to an Adequate Remedy." *Akron Law Review* 39 (2006): 975–1000.

Tribe, Laurence H. *American Constitutional Law.* 3d ed. New York: Foundation, 2000.

U.S. Department of the Treasury. Bureau of Alcohol, Tobacco and Firearms. *Following the Gun: Enforcing Federal Laws Against Firearms Traffickers.* Washington, D.C.: U.S. Government Printing Office, 2000.

U.S. Department of the Treasury. Bureau of Alcohol, Tobacco and Firearms. *Commerce in Firearms in the United States.* Washington, D.C.: U.S. Government Printing Office, 2000.

Van Alstyne, William. "Essay: The Second Amendment and the Personal Right to Arms." *Duke Law Journal* 43 (1994): 1236–55.

Viereck, Peter. *Conservatism Revisited.* Book 2. New York: Collier, 1962.

Washington, George. *The Writings of George Washington from the Original Manuscript Sources, 1745–1799.* Ed. John C. Fitzpatrick. 39 vols. Washington, D.C.: U.S. Government Printing Office, 1931–44.

Weber, Max. *From Max Weber: Essays in Sociology.* Ed. H. H. Gerth and C. Wright Mills. New York: Oxford University Press, 1946.

Weber, Max. *The Theory of Social and Economic Organization.* Trans. A. M. Henderson and Talcott Parsons. New York: Oxford University Press, 1947.

White, Ronald C. *The Eloquent President: A Portrait of Lincoln through His Words.* New York: Random House, 2006.

Williams, David C. *The Mythic Meanings of the Second Amendment: Taming Political Violence in a Constitutional Republic.* New Haven: Yale University Press, 2003.

Wills, Garry. *A Necessary Evil: A History of American Distrust of Government.* New York: Simon and Schuster, 1999.

Wimmer, Hannes. "The State's Monopoly on Legitimate Violence: Violence in History and in the Contemporary World Society as Challenges to the State." Paper presented at the conference on "Transformation of Statehood from a European Perspective," Austrian Academy of Sciences, Vienna, January 23–25, 2003.

Winkler, Adam. "Scrutinizing the Second Amendment." *Michigan Law Review* 105 (2007): 683–733.

Wood, Gordon S. *The Creation of the American Republic, 1776–1787.* Chapel Hill: University of North Carolina Press, 1998.

Wulf, Herbert. "The Bumpy Road to Re-Establish a Monopoly of Violence." Paper presented at the Study Group on Europe's Security Capabilities, London School of Economics, London, 2004.

Zelman, Aaron, and Claire Wolfe. "Can the Second Amendment and Social Security Coexist? Terrified Politicians Believe One or the Other Has to Go." http://www.jpfo.org/filegen-n-z/ssandguns.htm.

Zeskind, Leonard. "Armed and Dangerous." *Rolling Stone*, November 2, 1995, 54–63.

Zumbo, Jim. "Assault Rifles for Hunters?" *Hunting with Zumbo*, February 16, 2007, http://razoreye.net/mirror/zumbo/zumbo_assault_rifles.html.

INDEX

Abortion, 23, 39
Abramoff, Jack, 41
Abrams, Sanford, 42–43
Acquiring New I.D.: How to . . .
  (Paladin Press), 42
Adams, John, 114
Adams, Samuel, 92–93
Affirmative action, 7–8
Afghanistan, 172, 181
African Americans
  in American Revolution, 90–91
  in armed militias, 132–34
  in colonial America, 85
  emancipation, 124, 128
  at gun shows, 52
  lynching, 126
  political equality, 164–66
  revisionist history, 5–6, 18–19
  right to vote, 128–30
  school integration, 141–42
  segregation, 126–27, 187
  See also Racism; Slavery
Alabama Law Review, 68
Alabama Union League, 133
Alien and Sedition Acts of 1798, 114
Allbaugh, Joe, 41
Alliance of Stocking Gun Dealers,
  14–15
"all men are created equal," 159–62, 164
Amar, Akhil Reed, 65–68
American Bar Association, 187, 193–94
American Conservative Union, 41
American Revolution
  under Articles of Confederation,
    91–96
  firearms place in, 82–83

formation of a new government,
    86–91
  Insurrectionist view of, 18–19
  Insurrectionist view of history, 5–6
  role of militia, 83–86
American Rifleman, 32
Americans for Tax Reform, 41
American Shooting Sports Council
  (ASSC), 45
America Online (AOL), 187–89
America's First Freedom, 23–24
"America's First Freedom," 36, 223
Ammunition industry. *See* Firearms
  industry
Anarchy
  in absence of government, 80
  Constitution to prevent, 107
  gun ownership and, 18
  Insurrectionist goal of, 220
  Katrina disaster, 24–25, 25–26
  revolution as doctrine for, 178
Anderson, Scott, 200–201
Animal rights, 21
Antigovernment sentiments
  domestic terrorism, 183
  gun rights absolutism and, 15–16, 58
  gun show circuit, 52–55
  Insurrectionist expression of, 2
  Insurrectionist promotion of, 7–8
  legitimization and romanticism of, 224
  overthrow of U.S. government, 49, 52,
    68, 82, 107, 224
  survival of democracy in face of,
    215–20
  See also Overthrow of government;
    U.S. Government

261

ABOUT THE AUTHORS

JOSHUA HORWITZ holds a bachelor's degree from the University of Michigan and a law degree from George Washington University. He is currently a visiting scholar at the Johns Hopkins Bloomberg School of Public Health and executive director of the Coalition to Stop Gun Violence and the Educational Fund to Stop Gun Violence. He has spent two decades working on gun violence prevention issues and has managed dozens of issue campaigns at the state and federal levels.

CASEY ANDERSON began his career as a newspaper reporter and is now a lawyer in private practice in Washington, D.C. He has also served in senior staff positions with the U.S. Congress, the Coalition to Stop Gun Violence, and Americans for Gun Safety. He holds bachelor's and law degrees from Georgetown University and a master's degree in journalism from Columbia University.